MINDWARE

MINDWARE

AN INTRODUCTION
TO THE PHILOSOPHY
OF COGNITIVE SCIENCE

Andy Clark

University of Sussex

New York   Oxford
OXFORD UNIVERSITY PRESS
2001

Oxford University Press

Oxford   New York
Athens   Auckland   Bangkok   Bogotá   Buenos Aires   Calcutta
Cape Town   Chennai   Dar es Salaam   Delhi   Florence   Hong Kong   Istanbul
Karachi   Kuala Lumpur   Madrid   Melbourne   Mexico City   Mumbai
Nairobi   Paris   São Paulo   Shanghai   Singapore   Taipei   Tokyo   Toronto   Warsaw

and associated companies in
Berlin   Ibadan

Published by Oxford University Press, Inc.
198 Madison Avenue, New York, New York, 10016
http://www.oup-usa.org

Oxford is a registered trademark of Oxford University Press

Library of Congress Cataloging-in-Publication Data

Clark, Andy, 1957–
   Mindware : an introduction to the philosophy of cognitive science / Andy Clark.
      p. cm.
   Includes bibliographical references (p.) and index.
   ISBN 0-19-513856-2 (alk. paper) — ISBN 0-19-513857-0 (pbk. : alk. paper)
      1. Cognitive science. I. Title.

BF311.M5412
153–dc21   00-033569

Printing (last digit): 10 9 8 7 6 5 4 3

Printed in the United States of America
on acid-free paper.

For Pepa,
que vale más que un cortijo

CONTENTS

PREFACE
About Mindware

"Mindware" (the term) is just a convenient label for that unruly rag-bag of stuff we intuitively count as *mental*. Beliefs, hopes, fears, thoughts, reasoning, imagery, feelings—the list is long and the puzzle is deep. The puzzle is, just what is all this stuff with which we populate our minds? What are beliefs, thoughts, and reasons, and how do they take their place among the other things that make up the natural world?

Mindware (the book) is written with these three aims in (of course) mind: To *introduce* some of the research programs that are trying (successfully, I believe) to locate the place of mindfulness in nature. To do so *briefly*, by sketching the major elements of key research programs, and then prompting the reader to accessible original sources for the full flesh and fire. And, above all, to do so *challengingly*, by devoting the bulk of the treatment to short, substantive critical discussions that try to touch some deep and tender nerves and that reach out to include front-line research in both cognitive science and philosophy.

The idea, in short, is to provide just enough of a sketch of the central research programs to then initiate and pursue a wide range of critical discussions of the conceptual terrain. These discussions do not pretend to be unbiased, exhaustive, or even to cover all the ground of a standard introductory text (although the material in the two appendices goes a little way toward filling in some gaps). Instead, the goal is to highlight challenging or problematic issues in a way likely to engage the reader in active debate. Each chapter opens with a brief sketch of a research tradition or perspective, followed by short critical discussions of several key issues. Areas covered include artificial intelligence (A.I.), connectionism, neuroscience, robotics, dynamics, and artificial life, while discussion ranges across both standard philosophical territory (levels of description, types of explanation, mental causation, the nature and the status of folk psychology) and the just-visible conceptual landscape of cutting edge cognitive science (emergence, the interplay between perception, cognition, and action, the relation between life and mind, mind as an intrinsically embodied and environmentally embedded phenomena). If these terms seem alien and empty, don't worry. They are just placeholders for the discussions to come.

The text has, deliberately, a rather strong narrative structure. I am telling a story about the last three or four decades of research into the nature of mind. It is a story told from a specific perspective, that of a philosopher, actively engaged in work and conversation with cognitive scientists, and especially engaged with work in artificial neural networks, cognitive neuroscience, robotics, and embodied, situated cognition. The narrative reflects these engagements and is thus dense where many are skimpy and (at times) skimpy where others are dense. I embrace this consequence, because I hope that my peculiar combination of interests affords a useful and perhaps less frequently encountered route into many of the central topics and discussions. I hope that the text will be useful in both basic and more advanced level courses both in philosophy of mind and in the various cognitive sciences.

The project is clearly ambitious, taking the reader all the way from the first waves of artificial intelligence through to contemporary neuroscience, robotics, and the coadaptive dance of mind, culture, and technology. In pushing an introductory text to these outer limits, I am betting on one thing: that a good way to introduce people to a living discussion is to make them a part of it and not hide the dirty laundry. There is much that is unclear, much that is ill understood, and much that will, no doubt, soon prove to be mistaken. There are places where it is not yet clear what the right *questions* are, let alone the answers. But the goal is worthy—a better understanding of ourselves and of the place of human thought in the natural order. The modest hope is just to engage the new reader in an ongoing quest and to make her part of this frustrating, fascinating, multivoiced conversation.

A word of caution in closing. Philosophy of cognitive science has something of the flavor of a random walk on a rubber landscape. No one knows quite where they are going, and every step anyone takes threatens to change the whole of the surrounding scenery. There is, shall we say, flux. So if you find these topics interesting, do, do check out the current editions of the journals, and visit some web sites.[1] You'll be amazed how things change.

Andy Clark
St. Louis

---

[1]Sites change rapidly, so it is unwise to give lists. A better bet is to search using key words such as philosophy, cognitive science, and connectionism. Or ask your tutor for his or her favorite sites. Useful journals include *Minds and Machines, Cognitive Science, Behavioral and Brain Sciences* (hard), *Mind and Language* (rather philosophical), *Philosophical Psychology, Connection Science* (technical), and *Journal of Consciousness Studies.* Also mainstream philosophy journals such as *Mind, Journal of Philosophy,* and *Synthese.* The journal *Trends in Cognitive Sciences* is a particularly useful source of user-friendly review articles, albeit one in which explicitly philosophical treatments are the exception rather than the rule.

ACKNOWLEDGMENTS

This book grew out of a variety of undergraduate classes taught in both England and the United States. In England, I am indebted to students and colleagues in philosophy and in the school of Cognitive and Computing Sciences, at the University of Sussex. In the United States, I am indebted to students and colleagues in Philosophy, in the Philosophy/Neuroscience/Psychology program, and in the Hewlett freshman Mind/Brain program, all at Washington University in St. Louis. Various friends, colleagues, and mentors, both at these institutions and elsewhere, deserve very special thanks. Their views and criticisms have helped shape everything in this book (though, as is customary, they are not to be blamed for the faults and lapses). I am thinking of (in no particular order) Daniel Dennett, Paul and Pat Churchland, Margaret Boden, Brian Cantwell Smith, Tim Van Gelder, Michael Morris, Bill Bechtel, Michael Wheeler, David Chalmers, Rick Grush, Aaron Sloman, Susan Hurley, Peter Carruthers, John Haugeland, Jesse Prinz, Ron Chrisley, Brian Keeley, Chris Peacocke, and Martin Davies. I owe a special debt to friends and colleagues working in neuroscience, robotics, psychology, artificial life, cognitive anthropology, economics, and beyond, especially David Van Essen, Charles Anderson, Douglass North, Ed Hutchins, Randy Beer, Barbara Webb, Lynn Andrea Stein, Maja Mataric, Melanie Mitchell, David Cliff, Chris Thornton, Esther Thelen, Julie Rutkowski, and Linda Smith.

Most of the present text is new, but a few chapters draw on material from published articles:

Chapter 4, Section 4.2 (c), incorporates some material from "The world, the flesh and the artificial neural network"—to appear in J. Campbell and G. Oliveri (eds.), *Language, Mind and Machines* (Oxford, England: Oxford University Press).

Chapter 5, Section 5.1 and Chapter 8, Section 8.1, include material from "Where brain, body and world collide." *Daedalus*, 127(2), 257–280, 1998.

Chapter 6, Section 6.1, draws on my entry "Embodied, situated and distributed cognition." In W. Bechtel and G. Graham (eds.), *A Companion to Cognitive Science* (Oxford, England: Blackwell, 1998).

Chapter 7, Section 7.1, reproduces case studies originally presented in two papers: "The dynamical challenge." *Cognitive Science* 21(4), 451–481, 1997, and "Time and mind," *Journal of Philosophy* 95(7), 354–376, 1998.

Chapter 8 includes some material from "MagicWords: How language augments human computation." In P. Carruthers and J. Boucher (eds.), *Language and Thought* (Cambridge, England: Cambridge University Press, 1998).

Sincere thanks to the editors and publishers for permission to use this material here.

Sources of figures are credited in the legends.

Thanks to Beth Stufflebeam, Tamara Casanova, Katherine McCabe, and Kimberly Mount for invaluable help in preparing the manuscript. And to Lolo, the cat, for sitting on it during all stages of production.

Thanks also to George Graham and a bevy of anonymous referees, whose comments and suggestions have made an enormous difference to the finished product.

And finally, essentially, but so very inadequately, thanks beyond measure to my wife and colleague, Josefa Toribio, and to my parents, Christine and James Clark. As always, your love and support meant the world.

RESOURCES

Each chapter ends with specific suggestions for further reading. But it is also worth highlighting a number of basic resources and collections:

Bechtel, W., and Graham, G. (1998). *A Companion to Cognitive Science.* Oxford, England: Blackwell. (Encyclopedia-style entries on all the important topics, with a useful historical introduction by Bechtel, Abrahamsen, and Graham.)

Boden, M. (1990). *The Philosophy of Artificial Intelligence.* Oxford, England: Oxford University Press. (Seminal papers by Turing, Searle, Newell and Simon, and Marr, with some newer contributions by Dennett, Dreyfus and Dreyfus, P.M. Churchland, and others.)

Boden, M. (1996). *The Philosophy of Artificial Life.* Oxford, England: Oxford University Press. (Nice introductory essay by Langton, and a useful window on some early debates in this area.)

Haugeland, J. (1997). *Mind Design II.* Cambridge, MA: MIT Press. (Fantastic collection, including a fine introduction by Haugeland; seminal papers by Turing, Dennett, Newell and Simon, Minsky, Dreyfus, and Searle; a comprehensive introduction to connectionism in papers by Rumelhart, Smolensky, Churchland, Rosenberg, and Clark, seminal critiques by Fodor and Pylyshyn, Ramsey, Stich, and Garon; and a hint of new frontiers from Brooks and Van Gelder. Quite indispensable.)

Lycan, W. (1990). *Mind and Cognition: A Reader.* Cambridge, MA: Blackwell. (Great value—a large and well-chosen collection concentrating on the earlier debates over functionalism, instrumentalism, eliminativism, and the language of thought, with a useful section on consciousness and qualia.)

MacDonald, C., and MacDonald, G. (1995). *Connectionism: Debates on Psychological Explanation.* Oxford, England: Blackwell. (A comprehensive sampling of the debates between connectionism and classicism, with contributions by Smolensky, Fodor and Pylyshyn (and replies by each), Ramsey et al., Stich and Warfield, and many others.)

Two recent *textbooks* have contents that nicely complement the present, cognitive scientifically oriented, perspective:

Braddon-Mitchel, D., and Jackson, F. (1996). *Philosophy of Mind and Cognition.* Oxford, England: Blackwell. (Excellent introductory text covering the more traditionally philosophical territory of identity theory, functionalism, and debates about content.

Kim, J. (1996). *Philosophy of Mind.* Boulder, CO: Westview. (A truly excellent text, covering behaviorism, identity theory, machine functionalism, and debates about consciousness and content.)

INTRODUCTION
(Not) Like a Rock

Here's how January 21, 2000 panned out for three different elements of the natural order.

Element 1: A Rock

Here is a day in the life of a small, gray-white rock nestling amidst the ivy in my St. Louis backyard. It stayed put. Some things happened to it: there was rain, and it became wet and shiny; there was wind, and it was subtly eroded; my cat chased a squirrel nearby, and this made the rock sway. That's about it, really. There is no reason to believe the rock had any thoughts, or that any of this felt like anything to the rock. Stuff happened, but that was all.

Element 2: A Cat

Lolo, my cat, had a rather different kind of day. About 80% of it was spent, as usual, asleep. But there were forays into the waking, wider world. Around 7 A.M. some inner stirring led Lolo to exit the house, making straight for the catflap from the warm perch of the living room sofa. Outside, bodily functions doubtless dominated, at least at first. Later, following a brief trip back inside (unerringly routed via the catflap and the food tray), squirrels were chased and dangers avoided. Other cats were dealt with in ways appropriate to their rank, station, girth, and meanness. There was a great deal of further sleeping.

Element 3: Myself

My day was (I think) rather more like Lolo's than like the rock's. We both (Lolo and I) pursued food and warmth. But my day included, I suspect, rather more outright *contemplation*. The kind of spiraling meta-contemplation, in fact, that has sometimes gotten philosophy a bad name. Martin Amis captured the spirit well:

> I experienced thrilling self-pity. "What will that mind of your get up to next?" I said, recognizing the self-congratulation behind this thought and the self-congratulation behind that recognition, and the self-congratulation behind recognizing that recognition.
>   Steady on. (Martin Amis, *The Rachel Papers*, p. 96)

I certainly did some of that. I had thoughts, even "trains of thought" (reasonable sequences of thinkings such as "It's 1 P.M. Time to eat. What's in the fridge?" and so on). But there were also thoughts about thoughts, as I sat back and observed my own trains of thought, alert for colorful examples to import into this text.

What, then, distinguishes cat from rock, and (perhaps) person from cat? What are the mechanisms that make thought and feeling possible? And what further tricks or artifices give my own kind of mindfulness its peculiar self-aware tinge? Such questions seem to focus attention on three different types of phenomena:

1. The feelings that characterize daily experience (hunger, sadness, desire, and so on)
2. The flow of thoughts and reasons
3. The meta-flow of thoughts about thoughts (and thoughts about feelings), of reflection on reasons, and so on.

Most of the research programs covered in this text have concentrated on the middle option. They have tried to explain how my thought that it is 1 P.M. could lead to my thought about lunch, and how it could cause my subsequent lunch-seeking actions. All three types of phenomena are, however, the subject of what philosophers call "mentalistic discourse." A typical example of mentalistic discourse is the appeal to beliefs (and desires) to explain actions. The more technical phrase "propositional attitude psychology" highlights the standard shape of such explanations: such explanations pair mental attitudes (believing, hoping, fearing, etc.) with specific propositions ("that it is raining," "that the coffee is in the kitchen," "that the squirrel is up the tree," etc.) so as to explain intelligent action. Thus in a sentence such as "Pepa hopes that the wine is chilled," the that-construction introduces a proposition ("the wine is chilled") toward which the agent is supposed to exhibit some attitude (in this case, hoping). Other attitudes (such as believing, desiring, fearing, and so on) may, of course, be taken to the same proposition. Our everyday understandings of each other's behavior involve hefty doses of propositional attitude ascription: for example, I may explain Pepa's reluctance to open the wine by saying "Pepa believes that the wine is not yet chilled and desires that it remain in the fridge for a few more minutes."

Such ways of speaking (and thinking) pay huge dividends. They support a surprising degree of predictive success, and are the common currency of many of our social and practical projects. In this vein, the philosopher Jerry Fodor suggests that commonsense psychology is *ubiquitous*, almost *invisible* (because it works so well), and practically *indispensable*. For example, it enables us to make precise plans on the basis of someone's 2-month-old statement that they will arrive on flight 594 on Friday, November 20, 1999. Such plans often work out—a truly amazing fact given the number of physical variables involved. They work out (when they do) because the statement reflects an intention (to arrive that day, on that flight) that is somehow an active shaper of my behavior. I desire that I should arrive on time. You know that I so desire. And on that basis, with a little cooperation from the world at large, miracles of coordination can occur. Or as Fodor more colorfully puts it:

> If you want to know where my physical body will be next Thursday, mechanics—our best science of middle-sized objects after all, and reputed to be pretty good in its field—is *no use to you at all*. Far the best way to find out (usually in practice, the only way to find out) is: *ask me*! (Fodor, 1987, p. 6, original emphasis)

Commonsense psychology thus works, and with a vengeance. But why? Why is it that treating each other as having beliefs, hopes, intentions, and the like allows us successfully to explain, predict, and understand so much daily behavior? Beliefs, desires, and so on are, after all, invisible. We see (what we take to be) their effects. But no one has ever actually seen a belief. Such things are (currently? permanently?) unobservable. Commonsense psychology posits these unobservables, and looks to be committed to a body of law-like relations involving them. For example, we explain Fred's jumping up and down by saying that he is happy because his sister just won the Nobel Prize. Behind this explanation lurks an implicit belief in a law-like regularity, viz. "if someone desires x, and x occurs, then (all other things being equal) they feel happy." All this makes commonsense psychology look like a theory about the invisible, *but causally potent*, roots of intelligent behavior. What, then, can be making the theory true (assuming that it is)? What *is* a belief (or a hope, or a fear) such that it can cause a human being (or perhaps a cat, dog, etc.) to act in an appropriate way?

Once upon a time, perhaps, it would have been reasonable to respond to the challenge by citing a special kind of spirit-substance: the immaterial but causally empowered seat of the mental [for some critical discussion, see Churchland (1984), pp. 7–22, and Appendix I of the present text]. Our concerns, however, lie squarely with attempts that posit nothing extra—nothing beyond the properties and organization of the material brain, body, and world. The goal is a fully materialistic story in which mindware emerges as *nothing but* the playing out of ordinary physical states and processes in the familiar physical world. Insofar as the mental is in any way *special*, according to these views, it is special because it depends on some particular and unusual ways in which ordinary physical stuff can be built, arranged, and organized.

Views of this latter kind are broadly speaking *monistic*: that is to say, they posit only one basic *kind* of stuff (the material stuff) and attempt to explain the distinctive properties of mental phenomena in terms that are continuous with, or at least appropriately grounded in, our best understanding of the workings of the nonmental universe. A common, but still informative, comparison is with the once-lively (sic) debate between vitalists and nonvitalists. The vitalist held that living things were quite fundamentally different from the rest of inanimate nature, courtesy of a special extra force or ingredient (the "vital spark"), that was missing elsewhere. This is itself a kind of dualism. The demonstration of the fundamental unity of organic and inorganic chemistry (and the absence, in that fundament, of anything resembling a vital spark) was thus a victory—as far as we can tell—for a kind of monism. The animate world, it seems, is the result of *nothing but* the fancy combination of the same kinds of ingredients and forces responsible for inanimate nature. As it was with the animate, so materialists (which is to say, nearly all those working in contemporary cognitive science, the present author included) believe it must be with the mental. The mental world, it is anticipated, must prove to depend on nothing but the fancy combination and organization of ordinary physical states and processes.

Notice, then, the problem. The mental certainly *seems* special, unusual, and different. Indeed, as we saw, it *is* special, unusual, and different: thoughts give way to other thoughts and actions in a way that *respects reasons*: the thought that the forecast was sun (to adapt the famous but less upbeat example) causes me to apply sunscreen, to don a Panama hat, and to think "just another day in paradise." And there is a qualitative feel, a "something it is like" to have a certain kind of mental life: I *experience* the stabbings of pain, the stirrings of desire, the variety of tastes, colors, and sounds. It is the burden of materialism to somehow get to grips with these various special features in a way that is continuous with, or appropriately grounded in, the way we get to grips with the rest of the physical world—by some understanding of material structure, organization, and causal flow. This is a tall order, indeed. But, as Jerry Fodor is especially fond of pointing out, there is at least one good idea floating around—albeit one that targets just one of the two special properties just mentioned: reason-respecting flow.

The idea, in a supercompressed nutshell, is that the power of a thought (e.g., that the forecast is sun) to cause further thoughts and actions (to apply sunscreen, to think "another day in paradise") is fully explained by what are broadly speaking *structural* properties of the system in which the thought occurs. By a structural property I here mean simply a physical or organizational property: something whose nature is explicable *without* invoking the specific thought-content involved. An example will help. Consider the way a pocket calculator outputs the sum of two numbers given a sequence of button pushings that we interpret as inputting "2"

"+" "2." The calculator need not (and does not) understand anything about numbers for this trick to work. It is simply structured so that those button pushings will typically lead to the output "4" as surely as a river will typically find the path of least resistance down a mountain. It is just that in the former case, but not the latter, there has been a process of design such that the physical stuff became organized *so as* its physical unfoldings would reflect the arithmetical constraints governing sensible (arithmetic-respecting) transitions in number space. Natural selection and lifetime learning, to complete the (supercompressed) picture, are then imagined to have sculpted our *brains* so that certain structure-based physical unfoldings respect the constraints on sensible sequences of thoughts and sensible thought–action transitions. Recognition of the predator thus causes running, hiding, and thoughts of escape, whereas recognition of the food causes eating, vigilance, and thoughts of where to find more. Our whole reason-respecting mental life, so the story goes, is just the unfolding of what is, at bottom, a physical and structural story. Mindfulness is just matter, nicely orchestrated.

(As to that *other* distinctive property, "qualitative feel," let's just say—and see Appendix II—that it's a problem. Maybe that too is just a property of matter, nicely orchestrated. But how the orchestration *yields* the property is in this case much less clear, even in outline. So we'll be looking where the light is.)

In the next eight chapters, I shall expand and pursue that simple idea of mindware (selected aspects!) as matter, nicely orchestrated. The chase begins with a notion of mind as a kind of souped-up pocket calculator (mind as a familiar kind of computer, but built out of meat rather than silicon). It proceeds to the vision of mind as dependent on the operation of a radically different *kind* of computational device (the kind known as artificial neural networks). And it culminates in the contemporary (and contentious) research programs that highlight the complex interactions among brains, bodies, and environmental surroundings (work on robotics, artificial life, dynamics, and situated cognition).

The narrative is, let it be said, biased. It reflects my own view of what we have learned in the past 30 or 40 years of cognitive scientific research. What we have learned, I suggest, is that there are many deeply different ways to put flesh onto that broad, materialistic framework, and that some once-promising incarnations face deep and unexpected difficulties. In particular, the simple notion of the brain as a kind of symbol-crunching computer is probably too simple, and too far removed from the neural and ecological realities of complex, time-critical interaction that sculpted animal minds. The story I tell is thus a story of (a kind of) *inner symbol flight*. But it is a story of progress, refinement, and renewal, not one of abandonment and decay. The sciences of the mind are, in fact, in a state of rude health, of exuberant flux. Time, then, to start the story, to seek the origins of mind in the whirr and buzz of well-orchestrated matter.

MEAT MACHINES
Mindware as Software

1.1 Sketches

The computer scientist Marvin Minsky once described the human brain as a meat machine—no more no less. It is, to be sure, an ugly phrase. But it is also a striking image, a compact expression of both the genuine scientific excitement and the rather gung-ho materialism that tended to characterize the early years of cognitive scientific research. Mindware—our thoughts, feelings, hopes, fears, beliefs, and intellect—is cast as nothing but the operation of the biological brain, the meat machine in our head. This notion of the brain as a meat *machine* is interesting, for it immediately invites us to focus not so much on the material (the meat) as on the machine: the way the material is organized and the kinds of operation it supports. The same machine (see Box 1.1) can, after all, often be made of iron, or steel, or tungsten, or whatever. What we confront is thus both a rejection of the idea of mind as immaterial spirit-stuff and an affirmation that mind is best studied from a kind of engineering perspective that reveals the nature of the machine that all that wet, white, gray, and sticky stuff happens to build.

What exactly is meant by casting the brain as a machine, albeit one made out of meat? There exists a historical trend, to be sure, of trying to understand the workings of the brain by analogy with various currently fashionable technologies: the telegraph, the steam engine, and the telephone switchboard are all said to have had their day in the sun. But the "meat machine" phrase is intended, it should now be clear, to do more than hint at some rough analogy. For with regard to the very special class of machines known as computers, the claim is that the brain (and, by

Box 1.1

THE "SAME MACHINE"

In what sense can "the same machine" be made out of iron, or steel, or whatever? Not, obviously, in the strict sense of numerical identity. A set of steel darts and a set of tungsten ones cannot be the *very same* (numerically identical) set of darts. The relevant sense of sameness is, rather, some sense of *functional* sameness. You can make a perfectly *good* set of darts out of either material (though not, I suppose, out of jello), just as you can make a *perfectly* good corkscrew using a myriad (in this latter case quite radically) different designs and materials. In fact, what *makes* something a corkscrew is simply that it is designed as, and is capable of acting as, a cork-removing device. The notion of a brain as a meat machine is meant to embody a similar idea: that what matters about the brain is not the stuff it is made of but the way that stuff is organized so as to support thoughts and actions. The idea is that this capability depends on quite abstract properties of the physical device that could very well be duplicated in a device made, say, out of wires and silicon. Sensible versions of this idea need not claim then that *any* material will do: perhaps, for example, a certain stability over time (a tendency not to rapidly disorganize) is needed. The point is just that given that certain preconditions are met the same functionality can be pressed from multiple different materials and designs. For some famous opposition to this view, see Searle (1980, 1992).

not unproblematic extension, the mind) actually *is* some such device. It is not that the brain is somehow *like* a computer: everything is like everything else in some respect or other. It is that neural tissues, synapses, cell assemblies, and all the rest are just nature's rather wet and sticky way of building a hunk of honest-to-God computing machinery. Mindware, it is then claimed, is found "in" the brain in just the way that software is found "in" the computing system that is running it.

The attractions of such a view can hardly be overstated. It makes the mental special without making it ghostly. It makes the mental depend on the physical, but in a rather complex and (as we shall see) liberating way. And it provides a ready-made answer to a profound puzzle: how to get sensible, reason-respecting behavior out of a hunk of physical matter. To flesh out this idea of nonmysterious reason-respecting behavior, we next review some crucial developments[1] in the history (and prehistory) of artificial intelligence.

---

[1]The next few paragraphs draw on Newell and Simon's (1976) discussion of the development of the Physical Symbol Hypothesis (see Chapter 2 following), on John Haugeland's (1981a), and on Glymour, Ford, and Hayes' (1995).

One key development was the appreciation of the power and scope of formal logics. A decent historical account of this development would take us too far afield, touching perhaps on the pioneering efforts in the seventeenth century by Pascal and Leibniz, as well as on the twentieth-century contributions of Boole, Frege, Russell, Whitehead, and others. A useful historical account can be found in Glymour, Ford, and Hayes (1995). The idea that shines through the history, however, is the idea of finding and describing "laws of reason"—an idea whose clearest expression emerged first in the arena of formal logics. Formal logics are systems comprising sets of symbols, ways of joining the symbols so as to express complex propositions, and rules specifying how to legally derive new symbol complexes from old ones. The beauty of formal logics is that the steadfast application of the rules guarantees that you will never legally infer a false conclusion from true premises, even if you have no idea what, if anything, the strings of symbols actually mean. Just follow the rules and truth will be preserved. The situation is thus a little (just a little) like a person, incompetent in practical matters, who is nonetheless able to successfully build a cabinet or bookshelf by following written instructions for the manipulation of a set of preprovided pieces. Such building behavior can look as if it is rooted in a deep appreciation of the principles and laws of woodworking: but in fact, the person is just blindly making the moves allowed or dictated by the instruction set.

Formal logics show us how to preserve at least one kind of semantic (meaning-involving: see Box 1.2) property without relying on anyone's actually appreciating the meanings (if any) of the symbol strings involved. The seemingly ghostly and ephemeral world of meanings and logical implications is respected, and in a certain sense recreated, in a realm whose operating procedures do not rely on meanings at all! It is recreated as a realm of marks or "tokens," recognized by their physical ("syntactic") characteristics alone and manipulated according to rules that refer only to those physical characteristics (characteristics such as the shape of the symbol—see Box 1.2). As Newell and Simon comment:

> Logic . . . was a game played with meaningless tokens according to certain purely syntactic rules. Thus progress was first made by walking away from all that seemed relevant to meaning and human symbols. (Newell and Simon, 1976, p. 43)

Or, to put it in the more famous words of the philosopher John Haugeland:

> If you take care of the syntax, *the semantics will take care of itself.* (Haugeland, 1981a, p. 23, original emphasis)

This shift from meaning to form (from semantics to syntax if you will) also begins to suggest an attractive liberalism concerning actual physical structure. For what matters, as far as the identity of these formal systems is concerned, is not, e.g., the precise shape of the symbol for "and." The shape could be "AND" or "and" or "&" or "∧" or whatever. All that matters is that the shape is used consistently and that the rules are set up so as to specify how to treat strings of symbols joined by that shape: to allow, for example, the derivation of "A" from the string "A and

Box 1.2

Syntax and Semantics

Semantic properties are the "meaning-involving" properties of words, sentences, and internal representations. *Syntactic* properties, at least as philosophers tend to use the term, are nonsemantic properties of, e.g., written or spoken words, or of any kinds of inscriptions of meaningful items (e.g., the physical states that the pocket calculator uses to store a number in memory). Two synonymous written words ("dog" and "chien") are thus semantically identical but syntactically distinct, whereas ambiguous words ("bank" as in river or "bank" as in high street) are syntactically identical but semantically distinct. The idea of a *token* is the idea of a specific syntactic item (e.g., *this* occurrence of the word "dog"). A pocket calculator manipulates physical tokens (inner syntactic states) to which the operation of the device is sensitive. It is by being sensitive to the distinct syntactic features of the inner tokens that the calculator manages to behave in an arithmetic-respecting fashion: it is set up *precisely* so that syntax-driven operations on inner tokens standing for numbers respect meaningful arithmetical relations between the numbers. Taking care of the syntax, in Haugeland's famous phrase, thus allows the semantics to take care of itself.

B." Logics are thus first-rate examples of *formal systems* in the sense of Haugeland (1981a, 1997). They are systems whose essence lies not in the precise physical details but in the web of legal moves and transitions.

Most games, Haugeland notes, are formal systems in exactly this sense. You can play chess on a board of wood or marble, using pieces shaped like animals, movie stars, or the crew of the star ship Enterprise. You could even, Haugeland suggests, play chess using helicopters as pieces and a grid of helipads on top of tall buildings as the board. All that matters is again the web of legal moves and the physical distinguishability of the tokens.

Thinking about formal systems thus liberates us in two very powerful ways at a single stroke. Semantic relations (such as truth preservation: if "A and B" is true, "A" is true) are seen to be respected in virtue of procedures that make no intrinsic reference to meanings. And the specific physical details of any such system are seen to be unimportant, since what matters is the golden web of moves and transitions. Semantics is thus made unmysterious without making it brute physical. Who says you can't have your cake and eat it?

The next big development was the formalization (Turing, 1936) of the notion of computation itself. Turing's work, which predates the development of the digital computer, introduced the foundational notion of (what has since come to be known as) the Turing machine. This is an imaginary device consisting of an infinite tape, a simple processor (a "finite state machine"), and a read/write head. The tape acts as data store, using some fixed set of symbols. The read/write head can read a symbol off the tape, move itself one square backward or forward on the tape, and write onto the tape. The finite state machine (a kind of central processor) has enough memory to recall what symbol was just read and what state it (the finite state machine) was in. These two facts together determine the next action, which is carried out by the read/write head, and determine also the next state of the finite state machine. What Turing showed was that some such device, performing a sequence of simple computations governed by the symbols on the tape, could compute the answer to any sufficiently well-specified problem (see Box 1.3).

We thus confront a quite marvelous confluence of ideas. Turing's work clearly suggested the notion of a physical machine whose syntax-following properties would enable it to solve any well-specified problem. Set alongside the earlier work on logics and formal systems, this amounted to nothing less than

> . . . the emergence of a new level of analysis, independent of physics yet mechanistic in spirit . . . a science of structure and function divorced from material substance. (Pylyshyn, 1986, p. 68)

Thus was classical cognitive science conceived. The vision finally became flesh, however, only because of a third (and final) innovation: the actual construction of general purpose electronic computing machinery and the development of flexible, high-level programming techniques. The bedrock machinery (the digital computer) was designed by John von Neumann in the 1940s and with its advent all the pieces seemed to fall finally into place. For it was now clear that once realized in the physical medium of an electronic computer, a formal system could run *on its own*, without a human being sitting there deciding how and when to apply the rules to initiate the legal transformations. The well-programmed electronic computer, as John Haugeland nicely points out, is really just an automatic ("self-moving") formal system:

> It is like a chess set that sits there and plays chess by itself, without any intervention from the players, or an automatic formal system that writes out its own proofs and theorems without any help from the mathematician. (Haugeland, 1981a, p. 10; also Haugeland, 1997, pp. 11–12)

Of course, the machine needs a program. And programs were, in those days (but see Chapter 4), written by good old-fashioned human beings. But once the program was in place, and the power on, the machine took care of the rest. The transitions between legal syntactic states (states that also, under interpretation, *meant* something) no longer required a human operator. The physical world suddenly included clear, nonevolved, nonorganic examples of what Daniel Dennett would later dub "syntactic engines"—quasiautonomous systems whose sheer physical make-

Box 1.3

A Turing Machine

To make the idea of Turing machine computation concrete, let us borrow an example from Kim (1996, pp. 80–85). Suppose the goal is to get a Turing machine to add positive numbers. Express the numbers to be added as a sequence of the symbols "#" (marking the beginning and end of numbers) "1" and "+." So the sum 3 + 2 is encoded on the tape as shown in Figure 1.1. A neat program for adding the numbers (where "∧ A" indicates the initial location and initial state of the read/write head) is as follows:

Instruction 1: If read-write head is in machine state A and encounters a "1," it moves one square to the right, and the head stays in state A.

Instruction 2: If the head is in state A and encounters a "+," it replaces it with a "1," stays in state A, and moves one square to the right.

Instruction 3: If the head is in state A and it encounters a "#," move one square left and go into machine state B.

Instruction 4: If the head is in machine state B and encounters a "1," delete it, replace with a "#," and halt.

You should be able to see how this works. Basically, the machine starts "pointed" at the leftmost "1." It scans right seeking a "+," which it replaces with a "1." It continues scanning right until the "#" indicates the end of the sum, at which point it moves one square left, deletes a single "1," and replaces it with a "#." The tape now displays the answer to the addition problem in the same notation used to encode the question, as shown in Figure 1.2.

Similar set-ups (try to imagine how they work) can do subtraction, multiplication, and more (see Kim, 1996, pp. 83–85). But Turing's most strik-

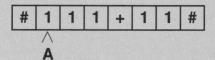

Figure 1.1 (After Kim, 1996, p. 81.)

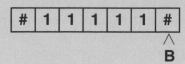

Figure 1.2 (After Kim, 1996, p. 81.)

ing achievement in this area was to show that you could then define a special kind of Turing machine (the aptly-named universal Turing machine)
able to imitate any other Turing machine. The symbols on the tape, in this
universal case, encode a description of the behavior of the other machine.
The universal Turing machine uses this description to mimic the input–
output function of any other such device and hence is itself capable of carrying out *any* sufficiently well-specified computation. (For detailed accounts
see Franklin, 1995; Haugeland, 1985; Turing, 1936, 1950.)

The Turing machine affords a fine example of a simple case in which
syntax-driven operations support a semantics-respecting (meaning-respect-
ing) process. Notice also that you could *build* a simple Turing machine out
of many different materials. It is the formal (syntactic) organization that matters for its semantic success.

up ensured (under interpretation) some kind of ongoing reason-respecting behavior. No wonder the early researchers were jubilant! Newell and Simon nicely
capture the mood:

> It is not my aim to surprise or shock you. . . . But the simplest way I can summarize
> is to say that there are now in the world machines that think, that learn and that cre-
> ate. Moreover, their ability to do these things is going to increase rapidly until—in a
> visible future—the range of problems they can handle will be co-extensive with the
> range to which the human mind has been applied. (Newell and Simon, 1958, p. 6,
> quoted in Dreyfus and Dreyfus, 1990, p. 312)

This jubilant mood deepened as advanced programming techniques[2] brought
forth impressive problem-solving displays, while the broader theoretical and philosophical implications (see Box 1.4) of these early successes could hardly have been
more striking. The once-mysterious realm of mindware (represented, admittedly,
by just two of its many denizens: truth preservation and abstract problem solving)
looked ripe for conquest and understanding. Mind was not ghostly stuff, but the
operation of a formal, computational system implemented in the meatware of the
brain.

Such is the heart of the matter. Mindware, it was claimed, is to the neural meat
machine as software is to the computer. The brain may be the standard (local,
earthly, biological) implementation—but cognition is a program-level thing. Mind

---

[2]For example, list-processing languages, as pioneered in Newell and Simon's Logic Theorist program
in 1956 and perfected in McCarthy's LISP around 1960, encouraged the use of more complex "recursive programming" strategies in which symbols point to data structures that contain symbols pointing
to further data structures and so on. They also made full use of the fact that the same electronic memory could store both program and data, a feature that allowed programs to be modified and operated
on in the same ways as data. LISP even boasted a universal function, EVAL, that made it as powerful,
modulo finite memory limitations, as a Universal Turing Machine.

Box 1.4

MACHINE FUNCTIONALISM

The leading philosophical offspring of the developments in artificial intelligence went by the name of machine functionalism, and it was offered as an answer to one of the deepest questions ever asked by humankind, viz. what is the essence (the deep nature) of the mental? What fundamental facts make it the case that some parts of the physical world have mental lives (thoughts, beliefs, feelings, and all the rest) and others do not? Substance dualists, recall, thought that the answer lay in the presence or absence of a special kind of mental *stuff*. Reacting against this idea (and against so-called philosophical behaviorism—see Appendix I). Mind–brain identity theorists, such as Smart (1959) (and again, see Appendix I), claimed that mental states *just are* processes going on in the brain. This bald identity claim, however, threatened to make the link between mental states and specific, material brain states a little too intimate. A key worry (e.g., Putnam, 1960, 1967) was that if it was really essential to being in a certain mental state that one be in a specific brain state, it would seem to follow that creatures lacking brains built just like ours (say, Martians or silicon-based robots) could not be in those very same mental states. But surely, the intuition went, creatures with very different brains from ours could, at least in principle, share, e.g., the belief that it is raining. Where, then, should we look for the commonality that could unite the robot, the Martian, and the Bostonian? The work in logic and formal systems, Turing machines, and electronic computation now suggested an answer: look not to the specific physical story (of neurons and wetware), nor to the surface behavior, but to the inner organization, that is to say, to the golden web: to the abstract, formal organization of the system. It is this organization—depicted by the machine functionalists as a web of links between possible inputs, inner computational states, and outputs (actions, speech)—that fixes the shape and contents of a mental life. The building materials do not matter: the web of transitions could be realized in flesh, silicon, or cream cheese (Putnam, 1975, p. 291). To be in such and such a mental state is simply to be a physical device, of whatever composition, that satisfies a specific formal description. Mindware, in humans, happens to run on a meat machine. But the very same mindware (as picked out by the web of legal state transitions) might run in some silicon device, or in the alien organic matter of a Martian.

is thus ghostly enough to float fairly free of the gory neuroscientific details. But it is not so ghostly as to escape the nets of more abstract (formal, computational) scientific investigation. This is an appealing story. But is it correct? Let's worry.

1.2 Discussion

(A brief note of reassurance: many of the topics treated below recur again and again in subsequent chapters. At this point, we lack much of the detailed background needed to really do them justice. But it is time to test the waters.)

A. WHY TREAT THOUGHT AS COMPUTATION?

Why treat thought as computation? The principal reason (apart from the fact that it seems to work!) is that thinkers are physical devices whose behavior patterns are reason respecting. Thinkers act in ways that are usefully understood as sensitively guided by reasons, ideas, and beliefs. Electronic computing devices show us one way in which this strange "dual profile" (of physical substance and reason-respecting behavior) can actually come about.

The notion of reason-respecting behavior, however, bears immediate amplification. A nice example of this kind of behavior is given by Zenon Pylyshyn. Pylyshyn (1986) describes the case of the pedestrian who witnesses a car crash, runs to a telephone, and punches out 911. We could, as Pylyshyn notes, try to explain this behavior by telling a purely physical story (maybe involving specific neurons, or even quantum events, whatever). But such a story, Pylyshyn argues, will not help us understand the behavior in its *reason-guided* aspects. For example, suppose we ask: what would happen if the phone was dead, or if it was a dial phone instead of a touch-tone phone, or if the accident occurred in England instead of the United States? The neural story underlying the behavioral response will differ widely if the agent dials 999 (the emergency code in England) and not 911, or must run to find a working phone. Yet common sense psychological talk makes sense of all these options at a stroke by depicting the agent as seeing a crash and *wanting to get help*. What we need, Pylyshyn powerfully suggests, is a scientific story that remains in touch with this more abstract and reason-involving characterization. And the simplest way to provide one is to imagine that the agent's brain contains states ("symbols") that represent the event *as* a car crash and that the computational state-transitions occurring inside the system (realized as physical events in the brain) then lead to new sets of states (more symbols) whose proper interpretation is, e.g., "seek help," "find a telephone," and so on. The interpretations thus glue inner states to sensible real-world behaviors. Cognizers, it is claimed, "instantiate . . . representation physically as cognitive codes and . . . their behavior is a causal consequence of operations carried out on those codes" (Pylyshyn, 1986, p. xiii).

The same argument can be found in, e.g., Fodor (1987), couched as a point about content-determined transitions in trains of thought, as when the thought "it is raining" leads to the thought "let's go indoors." This, for Fodor (but see Chapters 4 onward), is the essence of human rationality. How is such rationality mechanically possible? A good empirical hypothesis, Fodor suggests, is that there are neural symbols (inner states apt for interpretation) that mean, e.g., "it is raining" and whose physical properties lead in context to the generation of other symbols that mean "let's go indoors." If that is how the brain works then the brain is indeed a computer in exactly the sense displayed earlier. And if such were the case, then the mystery concerning reason-guided (content-determined) transitions in thought is resolved:

> If the mind is a sort of computer, we begin to see how . . . there could be non-arbitrary content-relations among causally related thoughts. (Fodor, 1987, p. 19)

Such arguments aim to show that the mind *must* be understood as a kind of computer implemented in the wetware of the brain, on pain of failing empirically to account for rational transitions among thoughts. Reason-guided action, it seems, makes good scientific sense if we imagine a neural economy organized as a syntax-driven engine that tracks the shape of semantic space (see, e.g., Fodor, 1987, pp. 19–20).

B. IS SOFTWARE AN AUTONOMOUS LEVEL IN NATURE?

The mindware/software equation is as beguiling as it is, at times, distortive. One immediate concern is that all this emphasis on algorithms, symbols, and programs tends to promote a somewhat misleading vision of *crisp level distinctions in nature.* The impact of the theoretical independence of algorithms from hardware is an artifact of the long-term neglect of issues concerning real-world action taking and the time course of computations. For an algorithm or program as such is just a sequence of steps with no inbuilt relation to real-world timing. Such timing depends crucially on the particular way in which the algorithm is implemented on a real device. Given this basic fact, the theoretical independence of algorithm from hardware is unlikely to have made much of an impact on Nature. We must expect to find biological computational strategies closely tailored to getting useful real-time results from available, slow, wetware components. In practice, it is thus unlikely that we will be able to fully appreciate the formal organization of natural systems without some quite detailed reference to the nature of the neural hardware that provides the supporting implementation. In general, attention to the nature of real biological hardware looks likely to provide both important clues about and constraints on the kinds of computational strategy used by real brains. This topic is explored in more depth in Chapters 4 through 6.

Furthermore, the claim that mindware is software is—to say the least—merely schematic. For the space of possible types of explanatory story, all broadly computational (but see Box 1.5), is very large indeed. The comments by Fodor and by

Box 1.5

WHAT IS COMPUTATION?

It is perhaps worth mentioning that the foundational notion of computation is itself still surprisingly ill understood. What do we really mean by calling some phenomenon "computational" in the first place? There is no current consensus at least (in the cognitive scientific community) concerning the answer to this question. It is mostly a case of "we know one when we see one." Nonetheless, there is a reasonable consensus concerning what I'll dub the "basic profile," which is well expressed by the following statement:

> we count something as a computer because, and only when, its inputs and outputs can be usefully and systematically interpreted as representing the ordered pairs of some function that interests us. (Churchland and Sejnowski, 1992, p. 65)

Thus consider a pocket calculator. This physical device computes, on this account, because first, there is a reliable and systematic way of interpreting various states of the device (the marks and numerals on the screen and keyboard) as representing other things (numbers). And second, because the device is set up so that under that interpretation, its physical state changes mirror semantic (meaningful) transitions in the arithmetical domain. Its physical structure thus forces it to respect mathematical constraints so that inputs such as "4 × 3" lead to outputs such as "12" and so on.

A truly robust notion of the conditions under which some actual phenomenon counts as computational would require, however, some rather more *objective* criterion for determining when an encountered (nondesigned) physical process is actually implementing a computation—some criterion that does not place our interpretive activities and interests so firmly at center stage.

The best such account I know of is due to Dave Chalmers (1996, Chapter 9). Chalmers' goal is to give an "objective criterion for implementing a computation" (p. 319). Intuitively, a physical device 'implements' an abstract, formal computational specification just in case the physical device is set up to undergo state changes that march in step with those detailed in the specification. In this sense a specific word-processing program might, for example, constitute a formal specification that can (appropriately configured) be made to run on various kinds of physical device (MACS, PCs, etc.).

Chalmers' proposal, in essence, is that a physical device implements an abstract formal description (a specification of states and state-transition relations) just in case "the causal structure of the system mirrors the formal structure of the computation" (1996, p. 317). The notion of mirroring is then cashed out in terms of a fairly fine-grained mapping of states and state changes in the physical device onto the elements and transitions present in the abstract specification. Chalmer's allows that every physical system will implement some computational description. But the appeal to fine-grained mappings is meant to ensure that you cannot interpret *every* physical system as implementing *every* computational description. So although the claim that the brain implements *some* computational description is fairly trivial, the claim that it implements a *specific* computational description is not. And it is the brain's implementation of a specific computational description that is meant to explain mental properties.

The computational profile of most familiar devices is, of course, the result of the deliberate imposition of a mapping, via some process of intelligent design. But the account is not intrinsically so restricted. Thus suppose some creature has evolved organic inner states that represent matters of adaptive importance such as the size, number, and speed of approach of predators. If that evolutionary process results in a physical system whose causal state transitions, under that interpretation, make semantic sense (e.g., if fewer than two predators detected cause a "stand and fight" inner token leading to aggressive output behavior, whereas three or more yield a "run and hide" response), then Nature has, on this account, evolved a small computer. The brain, if the conjectures scouted earlier prove correct, is just such a natural computer, incorporating inner states that represent external events (such as the presence of predators) and exploiting state-transition routines that make sensible use of the information thus encoded.

Pylyshyn do, it is true, suggest a rather specific kind of computational story (one pursued in detail in the next chapter). But the bare explanatory schema, in which semantic patterns emerge from an underlying syntactic, computational organization, covers a staggeringly wide range of cases. The range includes, for example, standard artificial intelligence (A.I.) approaches involving symbols and rules, "connectionist" approaches that mimic something of the behavior of neural assemblies (see Chapter 4), and even Heath Robinsonesque devices involving liquids, pulleys, and analog computations. Taken very liberally, the commitment to understanding mind as the operation of a syntactic engine can amount to little more than a bare assertion of physicalism—the denial of spirit-stuff.[3]

To make matters worse, a variety of different computational stories may be told about one and the same physical device. Depending on the grain of analysis

[3]Given our notion of computation (see Box 1.5), the claim is just a little stronger, since it also requires the presence of systematically interpretable inner states, i.e., internal representations.

used, a single device may be depicted as carrying out a complex parallel search or as serially transforming an input x into an output y. Clearly, what grain we choose will be determined by what questions we hope to answer. Seeing the transition as involving a nested episode of parallel search may help explain specific error profiles or why certain problems take longer to solve than others, yet treating the process as a simple unstructured transformation of x to y may be the best choice for understanding the larger scale organization of the system. There will thus be a constant interaction between our choice of explanatory targets and our choice of grain and level of computational description. In general, there seems little reason to expect a single type or level of description to do all the work we require. Explaining the relative speed at which we solve different problems, and the kinds of interference effects we experience when trying to solve several problems at once (e.g., remembering two closely similar telephone numbers), may well require explanations that involve very specific details about how inner representations are stored and structured, whereas merely accounting for, e.g., the bare facts about rational transitions between content-related thoughts may require only a coarser grained computational gloss. [It is for precisely this reason that connectionists (see Chapter 4) describe themselves as exploring the microstructure of cognition.] The explanatory aspirations of psychology and cognitive science, it seems clear, are sufficiently wide and various as to require the provision of explanations at a variety of different levels of grain and type.

In sum, the image of mindware as software gains its most fundamental appeal from the need to accommodate reason-guided transitions in a world of merely physical flux. At the most schematic level, this equation of mindware and software is useful and revealing. But we should not be misled into believing either (1) that "software" names a single, clearly understood level of neural organization or (2) that the equation of mindware and software provides any deep warrant for cognitive science to ignore facts about the biological brain.

C. MIMICKING, MODELING, AND BEHAVIOR

Computer programs, it often seems, offer only shallow and brittle simulacrums of the kind of understanding that humans (and other animals) manage to display. Are these just teething troubles, or do the repeated shortfalls indicate some fundamental problem with the computational approach itself? The worry is a good one. There are, alas, all too many ways in which a given computer program may merely mimic, but not illuminate, various aspects of our mental life. There is, for example, a symbolic A.I. program that does a very fine job of mimicking the verbal responses of a paranoid schizophrenic. The program ("PARRY," Colby, 1975; Boden, 1977, Chapter 5) uses tricks such as scanning input sentences for key words (such as "mother") and responding with canned, defensive outbursts. It is capable, at times, of fooling experienced psychoanalysts. But no one would claim that it is a useful psychological model of paranoid schizophrenia, still less that it is (when up and running on a computer) a paranoid schizophrenic itself!

Or consider a chess computer such as Deep Blue. Deep Blue, although capable of outstanding play, relies heavily on the brute-force technique of using its superfast computing resources to examine all potential outcomes for up to seven moves ahead. This strategy differs markedly from that of human grandmasters, who seem to rely much more on stored knowledge and skilled pattern recognition (see Chapter 4). Yet, viewed from a certain height, Deep Blue is not a bad simulation of human chess competence. Deep Blue and the human grandmaster are, after all, more likely to agree on a particular move (as a response to a given board state) than are the human grandmaster and the human novice! At the level of gross input–output profiles, the human grandmaster and Deep Blue are thus clearly similar (not identical, as the difference in underlying strategy—brute force versus pattern recognition—sometimes shines through). Yet once again, it is hard to avoid the impression that all that the machine is achieving is top-level mimicking: that there is something amiss with the underlying strategy that either renders it unfit as a substrate for a real intelligence, or else reveals it as a kind of intelligence very alien to our own.

This last caveat is important. For we must be careful to distinguish the question of whether such and such a program constitutes a good model of *human* intelligence from the question of whether the program (when up and running) displays some kind of *real, but perhaps nonhuman* form of intelligence and understanding. PARRY and Deep Blue, one feels, fail on both counts. Clearly, neither constitutes a faithful psychological model of the inner states that underlie human performance. And something about the basic style of these two computational solutions (canned sentences activated by key words, and brute-force look-ahead) even makes us uneasy with the (otherwise charitable) thought that they might nonetheless display real, albeit alien, kinds of intelligence and awareness.

How, though, are we to decide what kinds of computational substructure *might* be appropriate? Lacking, as we must, first-person knowledge of what (if anything) it is like to be PARRY or Deep Blue, we have only a few options. We could insist that all real thinkers must solve problems using exactly the same kinds of computational strategy as human brains (too anthropocentric, surely). We could hope, optimistically, for some future scientific understanding of the *fundamentals* of cognition that will allow us to recognize (on broad theoretical grounds) the shape of alternative, but genuine, ways in which various computational organizations might support cognition. Or we could look to the gross behavior of the systems in question, insisting, for example, on a broad and flexible range of responses to a multiplicity of environmental demands and situations. Deep Blue and PARRY would then fail to make the grade not merely because their inner organizations looked alien to us (an ethically dangerous move) but because the behavioral repertoire they support is too limited. Deep Blue cannot recognize a mate (well, only a checkmate!), nor cook an omelette. PARRY cannot decide to become a hermit or take up the harmonica, and so on.

This move to behavior is not without its own problems and dangers, as we will see in Chapter 3. But it should now be clearer why some influential theorists (especially Turing, 1950) argued that a sufficient degree of behavioral success should be allowed to settle the issue and to establish once and for all that a candidate system is a genuine thinker (albeit one whose inner workings may differ greatly from our own). Turing proposed a test (now known as the Turing Test) that involved a human interrogator trying to spot (from verbal responses) whether a hidden conversant was a human or a machine. Any system capable of fooling the interrogator in ongoing, open-ended conversation, Turing proposed, should be counted as an intelligent agent. Sustained, top-level verbal behavior, if this is right, is a sufficient test for the presence of real intelligence. The Turing Test invites consideration of a wealth of issues that we cannot dwell on here (several surface in Chapter 3). It may be, for example, that Turing's original restriction to a verbal test leaves too much scope for "tricks and cheats" and that a better test would focus more heavily on real-world activity (see Harnad, 1994).

It thus remains unclear whether we should allow that surface behaviors (however complex) are sufficient to distinguish (beyond all theoretical doubt) real thinking from mere mimicry. Practically speaking, however, it seems less morally dangerous to allow behavioral profiles to lead the way (imagine that it is discovered that you and you alone have a mutant brain that uses brute-force, Deep Blue-like strategies where others use quite different techniques: has science discovered that *you* are not a conscious, thinking, reasoning being after all?).

D. CONSCIOUSNESS, INFORMATION, AND PIZZA

"If one had to describe the deepest motivation for materialism, one might say that it is simply a terror of consciousness" (Searle, 1992, p. 55). Oh dear. If I had my way, I would give in to the terror and just not mention consciousness at all. But it is worth a word or two now (and see Appendix II) for two reasons. One is because it is all too easy to see the facts about conscious experience (the "second aspect of the problem of mindfulness" described in the Introduction) as constituting a knock-down refutation of the strongest version of the computationalist hypothesis. The other is because consideration of these issues helps to highlight important differences between informational and "merely physical" phenomena. So here goes.

How could a device made of silicon be conscious? How could it feel pain, joy, fear, pleasure, and foreboding? It certainly seems unlikely that such exotic capacities should flourish in such an unusual (silicon) setting. But a moment's reflection should convince you that it is equally amazing that such capacities should show up in, of all things, meat (for a sustained reflection on this theme, see the skit in Section 1.3). It is true, of course, that the only known cases of conscious awareness on this planet *are* cases of consciousness in carbon-based organic life forms. But this fact is rendered somewhat less impressive once we realize that all earthly life forms share a common chemical ancestry and lines of descent. In any case, the question, at least as far as the central thesis of the present chapter is concerned, is not whether our local carbon-based organic structure is crucial to all possible versions of conscious awareness (though it sounds anthropocentric in the extreme to believe that it is), but whether meeting a certain abstract computational specification is enough to *guarantee* such conscious awareness. Thus even the philosopher John Searle, who is famous for his attacks on the equation of mind-ware with software, allows that "consciousness might have been evolved in systems that are not carbon-based, but use some other sort of chemistry altogether" (Searle, 1992, p. 91). What is at issue, it is worth repeating, is not whether other kinds of stuff and substance might support conscious awareness but whether the fact that a system exhibits a certain computational profile is enough (is "sufficient") to ensure that it has thoughts, feelings, and conscious experiences. For it is crucial to the strongest version of the computationalist hypothesis that where our mental life is concerned, *the stuff doesn't matter*. That is to say, mental states depend solely on the program-level, computational profile of the system. If conscious awareness were to turn out to depend much more closely than this on the nature of the actual physical stuff out of which the system is built, then this global thesis would be either false or (depending on the details) severely compromised.

Matters are complicated by the fact that the term "conscious awareness" is something of a weasel word, covering a variety of different phenomena. Some use it to mean the high-level capacity to reflect on the contents of one's own thoughts. Others have no more in mind that the distinction between being awake and being asleep! But the relevant sense for the present discussion (see Block, 1997; Chalmers, 1996) is the one in which to be conscious is to be a subject of experience—to feel the toothache, to taste the bananas, to smell the croissant, and so on. To experience some *x* is thus to do more than just register, recognize, or respond to *x*. Electronic detectors can register the presence of semtex and other plastic explosives. But, I hope, they have no experiences of so doing. A sniffer dog, however, may be a different kettle of fish. Perhaps the dog, like us, is a subject of experience; a haven of what philosophers call "qualia"—the qualitative sensations that make life rich, interesting, or intolerable. Some theorists (notably John Searle) believe that computational accounts fall down at precisely this point, and that as far as we can tell it is the implementation, not the program, that explains the presence of such qualitative awareness. Searle's direct attack on computationalism is treated in the next chapter. For now, let us just look at two popular, but flawed, reasons for endorsing such a skeptical conclusion.

The first is the observation that "simulation is not the same as instantiation." A rainstorm, simulated in a computational medium, does not make anything actually wet. Likewise, it may seem obvious that a simulation, in a computational medium, of the brain states involved in a bout of black depression will not add one single iota (thank heaven) to the sum of real sadness in the world.

The second worry (related to, but not identical to the first) is that many feelings and emotions look to have a clear chemical or hormonal basis and hence (hence?) may be resistant to reproduction in any merely electronic medium. Sure, a silicon-based agent can play chess and stack crates, but can it get drunk, get an adrenaline high, experience the effects of ecstasy and acid, and so on?

The (genuine) intuitive appeal of these considerations notwithstanding, they by no means constitute the knock-down arguments they may at first appear. For everything here depends on what *kind* of phenomenon consciousness turns out to be. Thus suppose the skeptic argues as follows: "even if you get the overall inner computational profile just right, and the system behaves just like you and I, it will still be lacking the inner baths of chemicals, hormones, and neurotransmitters, etc. that flood our brains and bodies. Maybe without these all is darkness within—it just looks like the "agent" has feelings, emotions, etc., but really it is just [what Haugeland (1981a) terms] a "hollow shell." This possibility is vividly expressed in John Searle's example of the person who, hoping to cure a degenerative brain disease, allows parts of her brain to be gradually replaced by silicon chips. The chips preserve the input–output functions of the real brain components. One logical possibility here, Searle suggests, is that "as the silicon is progressively implanted into your dwindling brain, you find that the area of your conscious experience is shrinking, but that this shows no effect on your external behavior" (Searle, 1992, p. 66). In this scenario (which is merely one of several that Searle considers), your actions and words continue to be generated as usual. Your loved ones are glad that the operation is a success! But from the inside, you experience a growing darkness until, one day, nothing is left. There is no consciousness there. You are a zombie.

The imaginary case is problematic, to say the least. It is not even clear that we here confront a genuine logical possibility. [For detailed discussion see Chalmers (1996) and Dennett (1991a)—just look up zombies in the indexes!] Certainly the alternative scenario in which you *continue* your conscious mental life with no ill effects from the silicon surgery strikes many cognitive scientists (myself included) as the more plausible outcome. But the "shrinking consciousness" nightmare does help to focus our attention on the right question. The question is, just *what is* the role of all the hormones, chemicals, and organic matter that build normal human brains? There are two very different possibilities here and, so far, no one knows which is correct. One is that the chemicals, etc. affect our conscious experiences *only by affecting* the way information flows and is processed in the brain. If that were the case, the same kinds of modulation may be achieved in other media by other means. Simplistically, if some chemical's effect is, e.g., to speed up the processing in some areas, slow it down in others, and allow more information leakage between adjacent sites, then perhaps the same effect may be achieved in a purely electronic medium, by some series of modulations and modifications of current flow. Mind-altering "drugs," for silicon-based thinkers, may thus take the form of black-market software packages—packages that temporary induce a new pattern of flow and functionality in the old hardware.

There remains, however, a second possibility: perhaps the experienced nature of our mental life is not (or is not just) a function of the flow of information. Perhaps it is to some degree a direct effect of some still-to-be-discovered physical cause or even a kind of basic property of some types of matter (for extended discussion of these and other possibilities, see Chalmers, 1996). If this were true, then getting the information-processing profile exactly right would still fail to guarantee the presence of conscious experience.

The frog at the bottom of the beer glass is thus revealed. The bedrock, unsolved problem is whether conscious awareness is an *informational* phenomenon. Consider the difference. A lunch order is certainly an informational phenomenon. You can phone it, fax it, E-mail it—whatever the medium, it is the same lunch order. But no one ever faxes you your lunch. There is, of course, the infamous Internet Pizza Server. You specify size, consistency, and toppings and await the on-screen arrival of the feast. But as James Gleick recently commented, "By the time a heavily engineered software engine delivers the final product, you begin to suspect that they've actually forgotten the difference between a pizza and *a picture* of a pizza" (Gleick, 1995, p. 44). This, indeed, is Searle's accusation in a nutshell. Searle believes that the conscious mind, like pizza, just *ain't an informational phenomenon*. The stuff, like the topping, really counts. This could be the case, notice, even if many of the *other* central characteristics of mindware reward an understanding that is indeed more informational than physical. Fodor's focus on reason-guided state-transitions, for example, is especially well designed to focus attention away from qualitative experience and onto capacities (such as deciding to stay indoors when it is raining) that can be visibly guaranteed once a suitable formal, functional profile is fixed.

We are now eyeball to eyeball with the frog. To the extent that mind is an informational phenomenon, we may be confident that a good enough computational simulation will yield an actual instance of mindfulness. A good simulation of a calculator is an instance of a calculator. It adds, subtracts, does all the things we expect a calculator to do. Maybe it even follows the same hidden procedures as the original calculator, in which case we have what Pylyshyn (1986) terms "strong equivalence"—equivalence at the level of an underlying program. If a phenomenon is informational, strong equivalence is surely sufficient[4] to guarantee that we confront not just a model (simulation) of something, but a new exemplar (in-

---

[4]Sufficient, but probably not necessary. x is sufficient for y if when x obtains, y always follows. Being a banana is thus a sufficient condition for being a fruit. x is necessary for y if, should x fail to obtain, y cannot be the case. Being a banana is thus not a necessary condition for being a fruit—being an apple will do just as well.

stantiation) of that very thing. For noninformational phenomena, such as "being a pizza," the rules are different, and the flesh comes into its own. Is consciousness like calculation, or is it more like pizza? The jury is still out.

1.3 A Diversion

[This is extracted from a story by Terry Bisson called "Alien/Nation" first published in *Omni* (1991). Reproduced by kind permission of the author.]

"They're made out of meat."

"Meat?"

"Meat. They're made out of meat."

"Meat?"

"There's no doubt about it. We picked several from different parts of the planet, took them aboard our recon vessels, probed them all the way through. They're completely meat."

"That's impossible. What about the radio signals? The messages to the stars."

"They use the radio waves to talk, but the signals don't come from them. The signals come from machines."

"So who made the machines? That's who we want to contact."

"They made the machines. That's what I'm trying to tell you. Meat made the machines."

"That's ridiculous. How can meat make a machine? You're asking me to believe in sentient meat."

"I'm not asking you, I'm telling you. These creatures are the only sentient race in the sector and they're made out of meat."

"Maybe they're like the Orfolei. You know, a carbon-based intelligence that goes through a meat stage."

"Nope. They're born meat and they die meat. We studied them for several of their life spans, which didn't take too long. Do you have any idea of the life span of meat?"

"Spare me. Okay, maybe they're only part meat. You know, like the Weddilei. A meat head with an electron plasma brain inside."

"Nope. We thought of that, since they do have meat heads like the Weddilei. But I told you, we probed them. They're meat all the way through."

"No brain?"

"Oh, there is a brain all right. It's just that the brain is made out of meat!"

"So . . . what does the thinking?"

"You're not understanding, are you? The brain does the thinking. The meat."

"Thinking meat! You're asking me to believe in thinking meat!"

"Yes, thinking meat! Conscious meat! Loving meat. Dreaming meat. The meat is the whole deal! Are you getting the picture?"

"Omigod. You're serious then. They're made out of meat."

"Finally, Yes. They are indeed made out of meat. And they've been trying to get in touch with us for almost a hundred of their years."

"So what does the meat have in mind?"

"First it wants to talk to us. Then I imagine it wants to explore the universe, contact other sentients, swap ideas and information. The usual."

"We're supposed to talk to meat?"

"That's the idea. That's the message they're sending out by radio. Hello. Anyone out there? Anyone home? That sort of thing."

"They actually do talk, then. They use words, ideas, concepts?"

"Oh, yes. Except they do it with meat."

"I thought you just told me they used radio."

"They do, but what do you think is on the radio? Meat sounds. You know how when you slap or flap meat it makes a noise? They talk by flapping their meat at each other. They can even sing by squirting air through their meat."

"Omigod. Singing meat. This is altogether too much. So what do you advise?"

"Officially or unofficially?"

"Both."

"Officially, we are required to contact, welcome, and log in any and all sentient races or multi beings in the quadrant, without prejudice, fear, or favor. Unofficially, I advise that we erase the records and forget the whole thing."

"I was hoping you would say that."

"It seems harsh, but there is a limit. Do we really want to make contact with meat?"

"I agree one hundred percent. What's there to say?" 'Hello, meat. How's it going?' But will this work? How many planets are we dealing with here?"

"Just one. They can travel to other planets in special meat containers, but they can't live on them. And being meat, they only travel through C space. Which limits them to the speed of light and makes the possibility of their ever making contact pretty slim. Infinitesimal, in fact." "So we just pretend there's no one home in the universe."

"That's it."

"Cruel. But you said it yourself, who wants to meet meat? And the ones who have been aboard our vessels, the ones you have probed? You're sure they won't remember?"

"They'll be considered crackpots if they do. We went into their heads and smoothed out their meat so that we're just a dream to them."

"A dream to meat! How strangely appropriate, that we should be meat's dream."

"And we can mark this sector unoccupied."

"Good. Agreed, officially and unofficially. Case closed. Any others? Anyone interesting on that side of the galaxy?"

"Yes, a rather shy but sweet hydrogen core cluster intelligence in a class nine star in G445 zone. Was in contact two galactic rotations ago, wants to be friendly again."

"They always come around."

"And why not? Imagine how unbearably, how unutterably cold the universe would be if one were all alone."

1.4 Suggested Readings

For an up-to-date, and indeed somewhat sympathetic, account of the *varieties of dualism*, see D. Chalmers, *The Conscious Mind* (New York: Oxford University Press, 1996, Chapter 4).

For *general philosophical background* (identity theory, behaviorism, machine functionalism) a good place to start is Appendix I of this text and then P. M. Churchland, *Matter & Consciousness* (Cambridge, MA: MIT Press, 1984, and subsequent expanded editions). Another excellent resource is D. Braddon-Mitchell and F. Jackson, *Philosophy of Mind and Cognition* (Oxford, England: Blackwell, 1996, Chapters 1, 2, 3, 5, 6, and 7).

For the *broad notion of a computational view of mind*, try the Introductions to J. Haugeland, *Mind Design*, 1st ed. (Cambridge, MA: MIT Press, 1981) and *Mind Design II* (Cambridge, MA: MIT Press, 1997). The former ("Semantic engines: An introduction to mind design") is especially good on the syntax/semantics distinction, and the latter ("What is mind design?") adds useful discussion of recent developments.

For more on *Turing machines*, see J. Kim, "Mind as a computer," [Chapter 4 of his excellent book, *Philosophy of Mind* (Boulder, CO: Westview Press, 1996)]. Chapters 1–3 cover *dualism, behaviorism, and identity theory* and are also highly recommended. Chapter 4 focuses on the advent of *machine functionalism* and includes detailed discussion of the antireductionist themes that surface as the "structure not stuff" claim discussed in our text.

For *philosophical accounts of machine functionalism, and critiques*, see H. Putnam, "The nature of mental states." In H. Putnam (ed.), *Mind, Language & Reality: Philosophical Papers*, Vol. 2 (Cambridge, England: Cambridge University Press, 1975) (a classic and very readable account of machine functionalism) and N. Block, "Introduction: What is functionalism?" and "Troubles with functionalism." Both in his *Readings in Philosophy of Psychology*, Vol. 1 (Cambridge, MA: Harvard University Press, 1980). (Clean and critical expositions that nicely reflect the flavor of the original debates.)

J. Searle, "The critique of cognitive reason," Chapter 9 of his book, *The Rediscovery of the Mind* (Cambridge, MA: MIT Press, 1992) is a characteristically direct *critique of the basic computationalistic claims* and assumptions.

A useful, *up-to-date introduction to the empirical issues* is S. Franklin, *Artificial Minds* (Cambridge, MA: MIT Press, 1995), and an excellent general *collection of papers* may be found in J. Haugeland, *Mind Design II* (Cambridge, MA: MIT Press, 1997).

SYMBOL SYSTEMS 2

2.1 Sketches

The study of logic and computers has revealed to us that intelligence resides in physical-symbol systems. This is computer science's most basic law of qualitative structure. (Newell and Simon, 1976, p. 108)

The equation of mindware with software (Chapter 1) found clear expression and concrete computational substance in a flurry of work on *physical-symbol systems*. A physical-symbol system, as defined by Newell and Simon (1976, pp. 85–88) is a physical device that contains a set of interpretable and combinable items (symbols) and a set of processes that can operate on the items (copying, conjoining, creating, and destroying them according to instructions). To ensure that the symbols have meanings and are not just empty syntactic shells, the device must be located in a wider web of real-world items and events. Relative to this wider web, a symbolic expression will be said to pick out (or designate) an object if "given the expression, the system can either affect the object itself or behave in ways depending on the object" (Newell and Simon, 1976, p. 86). Given this specification, Newell and Simon make a bold claim:

> *The Physical Symbol System Hypothesis.* A physical symbol system has the necessary and sufficient means for general intelligent action. (Newell and Simon, 1976, p. 87)

The claim, in less formal language, is that a symbol cruncher of the kind just sketched possesses all that matters for thought and intelligence. Any such machine "of sufficient size" can (it is argued) always be programmed so as to support intelligent behavior, hence being a physical-symbol system is *sufficient* for intelligence. And nothing can be intelligent unless it is an instance of a physical-symbol system (PSS), so being a PSS is also a *necessary* condition for "general intelligent behavior." As Newell and Simon are quick to stress, we thus confront a strong *empirical* hypothesis. The notion of a PSS is meant to delimit a class of actual and potential systems and the claim is that all cases of general intelligent action will, as a matter of scientific fact, turn out to be produced by members of that class.

So just what *is* that class? The question is, unfortunately, more difficult than it at first appears. Clearly, we are being told that intelligent behavior depends on (and only on) processes that are broadly computational in the sense described in Chapter 1. That is to say, they involve inner states that can be organized so as to preserve semantic sense. Moreover, there is a commitment to the existence of inner *symbols* that are not just any old inner states capable of systematic interpretation, but that are in addition capable of participating in processes of copying, conjoining, and other familiar types of internal manipulation. It is this kind of inner economy, in which symbols exist as stable entities that are moved, copied, conjoined, and manipulated, that has *in practice* most clearly characterized work in the PSS paradigm and that differentiates it from the bare notion of mindware as software

Nonetheless, it is important to be clear about what this commitment to inner symbols actually involves. It is a commitment to the existence of a computational symbol-manipulating regime *at the level of description most appropriate to understanding the device as a cognitive (reasoning, thinking) engine.* This claim is thus fully compatible with the discovery that the brain is at bottom some other kind of device. What matters is not the computational profile at the hardware level, but the one "higher up" at the level of what is sometimes called a "virtual machine." (This is like saying: "don't worry about the form of the machine code—look at the elements and operations provided by some higher level language.") It is at this higher, virtual level that the system must provide the set of symbols and symbol-manipulating capacities associated with classical computation (copying, reading and amending symbol strings, comparing currently generated symbol strings to target sequences, and so on). In some cases these symbols will be systematically interpretable in ways that line up with our intuitive ideas about the elements of the task domain. For example, a program for reasoning about the behavior of liquids may use procedures defined over symbols for items such as "liquid," "flow," "edge," "viscous," and so on (see, e.g., Hayes 1979, 1985). Or a chess-playing program may use procedures applied to symbols for rook, king, checkmate, etc., whereas a sentence parser might use symbols for noun, verb, subject, and so on. These kinds of symbols reflect our own ideas about the task domain (chess, liquids, whatever). Systems whose computational operations are defined over this type of familiar symbolic elements may be termed *semantically transparent systems* (Clark, 1989, p. 17). The great advantage of semantically transparent systems, it should be clear, is that they make it immediately obvious *why* the physical device is able to respect specific semantic regularities. It is obvious that getting such symbols to behave ap-

Box 2.1

THE RESTAURANT SCRIPT

Schank's (1975) program could, for example, infer that someone who eats and enjoys a restaurant meal will probably have left a tip. It does so by referring to a background knowledge base encoding the "script" for a stereotypic restaurant visit. The script uses symbols for standard events and a special symbolic code for action types. In the extract below, "PTrans" stands for the change of location of an object and "Atrans" signifies the transfer of a relationship, e.g., my money becomes the waitresses' money in Scene 4. Here, then, is the script:

Script: Restaurant
Roles: customer; waitress; chef; cashier.
Reason: to get food so as to go down in hunger and up in pleasure.

Scene 1: ENTERING
    PTRANS: go into restaurant
    MBUILD: find table
    PTRANS: go to table
    MOVE: sit down
Scene 2: ORDERING
    ATRANS: receive menu
    ATTEND: look at it
    MBUILD: decide on order
    MTRANS: tell order to waitress
Scene 3: EATING
    ATRANS: receive food
    INGEST: eat food
Scene 4: EXITING
    MTRANS: ask for check
    ATRANS: give tip to waitress
    PTRANS: go to cashier
    MTRANS: give money to cashier
    PTRANS: go out of restaurant
       (Schank, 1975, p. 131, quoted in Dreyfus, 1997, pp. 167–168)

Basically, then, the program compares the details it is given in a short story to the fuller scenario laid out in the appropriate scripts, and calls on this knowledge (all accessed and deployed according to form-based syntactic matching procedures) to help answer questions that go beyond the specific details given in the story.

propriately will yield good reasoning about chess (or whatever), since many of the reason-respecting transitions are then visibly encoded in the system.

To get the flavor of the PSS hypothesis in action, consider first a program from Schank (1975). The goal of the program was story understanding: given a short text, it was meant to be able to answer some questions requiring a modicum of "common sense." To this end, Schank's program deployed so-called *scripts*, which used a symbolic event description language to encode background information about certain kinds of situations. For example, there was a script that laid out the typical sequence of actions involved in a visit to a restaurant (see Box 2.1). Now suppose you input a short story: "Jack goes into the restaurant, orders a hamburger, sits down. Later, he leaves after tipping the waiters." You can then ask: "Did Jack eat the hamburger?" and the computer, courtesy of the background information available in the script, can reply by guessing that he did.

Or consider SOAR (see Box 2.2). SOAR is a large-scale, on-going project that aims to apply the basic tenets of the PSS approach so as to implement general intelligence by computational means. It is, in many ways, the contemporary successor to the pioneering work on general problem solving (Newell, Shaw, and Simon, 1959) that helped set the agenda for the first three decades of work in artificial intelligence. SOAR is a symbol-processing architecture in which all long-term knowledge is stored using a uniform format known as a production memory. In a production memory, knowledge is encoded in the form of condition–action structures ("productions") whose contents are of the form: "If such and such is the case, then do so and so."[1] When it confronts a specific problem, SOAR accesses this general memory store until all relevant productions have been executed. This results in the transfer, into a temporary buffer or "working memory," of all the stuff that SOAR "knows" that looks like it might be relevant to the problem at hand. This body of knowledge will include a mixture of knowledge of facts, knowledge about actions that can be taken, and knowledge about what actions are desirable. A decision procedure then selects one action to perform on the basis of retrieved information concerning relative desirability ("preferences"). Naturally, SOAR is able to coordinate a sequence of such operations so as to achieve a specified goal. SOAR can work toward a distant goal by creating and attempting to resolve subgoals that reduce the distance between its current state and an overall solution. Such problem solving is conducted within so-called problem spaces populated by sets of states (representing situations) and operations (actions that can be applied to the states so as to yield further states). It is part of SOAR's job, given a goal, to select a problem space in which to pursue the goal, and to create a state that represents the ini-

---

[1]SOAR's productions differ from standard production-system structures insofar as SOAR incorporates a decision level (see text) that takes over some of the work traditionally done by the productions themselves. See Rosenbloom et al. (1992, pp. 294–295) for details.

Box 2.2

SOAR POINTS

The SOAR architecture has been used to solve problems in a wide variety of domains including computer configuration, algorithm design, medical diagnosis, and job-shop scheduling, as well as for less knowledge-intensive tasks such as playing tic-tac-toe. A simple demonstration, outlined in Rosenbloom et al. (1992, pp. 301–308), is the use of SOAR to do multicolumn subtraction. Here SOAR learns an effective procedure by searching in a subtraction problem space whose structure is provided in advance. The space contains the necessary "primitive acts" for a multicolumn "borrowing" procedure, in the form of operations such as the following:

Write-difference: If the difference between the top digit and the bottom digit of the current column is known, then write the difference as an answer to the current column.

Borrow-into: If the result of adding 10 to the top digit of the current column is known, and the digit to the left of it has a scratch mark on it, then replace the top digit with the result. (From Rosenbloom et al., 1992, p. 303, Figure 4)

The problem space contains a variety of such operators and a test procedure of the form "if each column has an answer, then succeed." SOAR then searches for a way to select and sequence these operations so as to succeed at the task. The search is constrained by productions associated with each operator that specify preferences concerning its use. SOAR is able to search the space of possible operator applications so as to discover a working procedure that makes use of the chunking maneuver to learn integrated, larger scale sequences that simplify future subtraction tasks.

A note in closing. SOAR, as a helpful referee reminds me, is at heart a universal programming system that can support pretty well *any* functional profile you like, so long as it is equipped with the right specialized sets of productions. The worries I raise in the text are thus not worries about what the bedrock programming system could *possibly* do, so much as worries about the particular configurations and strategies pursued in actual SOAR-based research (e.g., as exemplified in Rosenbloom et al., 1992). These configurations and strategies do indeed reflect the various practical commitments of the physical symbol system hypothesis as outlined earlier, and it is these commitments (rather than the bedrock programming system) that are critically examined in the text.

tial situation (the problem). An operator is then applied to that state, yielding a new state, and so on until (with luck) a solution is discovered. All these decisions (problem-space selection, state generation, operator selection) are based on the knowledge retrieved from the long-term production memory. In addition, the basic SOAR architecture exploits a single, uniform *learning mechanism*, known as "chunking," in which a successful sequence of subgoal generations can be stored away as a single unit. If SOAR later encounters a problem that looks similar to the earlier one, it can retrieve the unit and carry out the chunked sequence of moves without needing to search at each substage for the next move.

The actual practice of PSS-inspired artificial intelligence thus displays three key commitments. The first is the use of a symbolic code as a means of storing all of the system's long-term knowledge. The second is the depiction of intelligence as the ability to successfully search a symbolic problem-space. A physical symbol system "exercises its intelligence in problem-solving by search—that is, by generating and progressively modifying symbol structures until it reaches a solution structure" (Newell and Simon, 1976, p. 96). The third is that intelligence resides at, or close to, the level of deliberative thought. This is, if you like, the theoretical motivation for the development of semantically transparent systems—ones that directly encode and exploit the kinds of information that a human agent might consciously access when trying to solve a problem. Rosenbloom et al. (1992, pp. 290–291) thus describe SOAR as targeting the "cognitive band" in which contentful thoughts seem to flow in a serial sequence and in which most significant events occur in a time frame of 10 milliseconds to 10 seconds. This restriction effectively ensures that the computational story will at the same time function as a *knowledge-level*[2] story—a story that shows, rather directly, how knowledge and goals (beliefs and desires) can be encoded and processed in ways that lead to semantically sensible choices and actions. This is, of course, just the kind of story that Fodor (Chapter 1) insists we must provide so as to answer the question, "How is rationality mechanically possible?" (Fodor, 1986, p. 20).

So there it is. Intelligence resides at, or close to,[3] the level of deliberative thought. It consists in the retrieval of symbolically stored information and its use in processes of search. Such processes involve the generation, composition, and transformation of symbolic structures until the specified conditions for a solution are met. And it works, kind of. What could be wrong with that?

---

[2]For much more on the ideas of a "cognitive band" and a "knowledge level," see Newell (1990).

[3]The full story, as told in Newell (1990), recognizes four levels of cognitive activity as together constituting the "cognitive band." Only the topmost of these four levels (the "unit task" level) actually coincides with the consciously reportable steps of human problem solving. But all four levels involve operations on encoded knowledge, elementary choices, retrieval of distal information, and so on. In this respect, all four sublevels involve recognizably semantic or knowledge-involving operations.

2.2 Discussion

A. THE CHINESE ROOM

The most famous worry about symbol-crunching[4] artificial intelligence is predicated upon John Searle's (1980) "Chinese Room" thought experiment. Searle asks us to imagine a monolingual English speaker, placed in a large room, and confronted with a pile of papers covered with apparently unintelligible shapes and squiggles. The squiggles are, in fact, Chinese ideograms, but to the person in the room, they are just shapes on a page: just syntactic shells devoid of appreciable meaning. A new batch of squiggles then arrives, along with a set of instructions, in English, telling the person how to manipulate the apparently meaningless squiggles according to certain rules. The upshot of these manipulations, unbeknownst to the person in the room, is the creation of an intelligent response, in Chinese, to questions (also in Chinese) encoded in the incoming batch of papers.

The scenario, though strained and unlikely, cannot be ruled out. We saw, in Chapter 1, that any well-specified, intelligent behavior can be performed by a well-programmed computing device. What Searle has done is, in effect, to (1) replace the operating system and central processing unit of a computer (or the read-write head and finite state machine of a Turing machine) with a human agent and book of instructions, and (2) replace the real-world knowledge encoded in the computer's general memory (or the Turing machine's tape) with knowledge encoded (in Chinese) in the pile of papers. Under such circumstances, if the agent follows the rules, then (assuming, as we must, that the program is correct) the output will indeed be a sensible response in Chinese. The agent is "taking care of the syntax." And just as Haugeland (Chapter 1) said, the semantics is taking care of itself!

But says Searle, this is surely an illusion. It may seem like the overall system (the agent in the room) understands Chinese. But there is no real understanding at all. It seems to converse in Chinese, but no Chinese is actually understood! The monolingual agent is just doing syntactic matching. And the room and papers surely do not understand anything at all. Real understanding, Searle concludes, depends on more than just getting the formal operations right. Real understanding requires, Searle suggests, certain actual (though still largely unknown) physical properties, instantiated in biological brains. Stuff counts. Symbol manipulation alone is not enough.

Searle's argument has spawned a thousand attempts at rebuttal and refutation. A popular response is to insist that despite our intuitions, the room plus papers plus agent really does constitute a system that understands Chinese, has conscious experiences, and all the rest. And certainly, nothing that Searle (or anyone else)

---

[4]In fact, Searle (1992) extends his thought-experiment so as to (try to) cast doubt on connectionist approaches (see Chapter 4) also. Given my diagnosis (see the text) of the grain of truth in Searle's critique, this extension will not succeed. For a similar response, see Churchland and Churchland (1990).

says can rule that out as an empirical possibility. Appeals to intuition ("it doesn't *look* much like a system that really understands Chinese") are practically useless at the edges of scientific understanding.

It is also possible, however, that Searle is right, but for all the wrong reasons. For the Chinese room was initially envisioned as a weird and souped-up version of the story-understanding program mentioned earlier (see Box 2.1, and Schank and Abelson, 1977). As such, we were to imagine an inner computational econ-omy in which semantically transparent symbols were being manipulated, in a step-wise, serial fashion, in ways specified by a further set of symbolic instructions. In short, we were to envision a fairly coarse-grained approach in which the system's stored knowledge, as encoded in the Chinese squiggles, might include general knowledge (about what happens when, for example, someone visits a restaurant) in a chunky, language-like format such as the following:

Script: Restaurant

    Scene 1: ENTERING
        PTRANS: go into restaurant
        MBUILD: find table
        PTRANS: go to table
        MOVE: sit down
            Extracted from Schank (1975, p. 131)

(Recall that symbols such as PTRANS form part of a special event description lan-guage devised by Schank, and are defined elsewhere in the program. PTRANS, for example, signifies the transfer of physical location of an object.)

Much of the *intuitive* appeal of Searle's argument, I believe, comes not from its logical structure but from a certain discomfort with the idea that a simulation *pitched at that kind of level* could actually amount to an instantiation of under-standing, as opposed to a kind of superficial structural echo. Considered as a fully general logical argument, Searle's case is flimsy indeed. He aims to convince us that no amount of syntactic, formal organization can yield real understanding. But the only evidence [beyond the question-begging assertion that syntax is not sufficient for semantics—see, e.g., Churchland and Churchland (1990) for a nice discussion] is the reader's intuitive agreement, perhaps based on quite superficial features of the example.

Yet for all that the original thought experiment strikes a nerve. But the nerve is not (as Searle believes) the unbridgeability of the gap between syntax and se-mantics. It rather (concerns) the need for a finer grained specification of the rele-vant computational and syntactic structure. For it is plausible to suppose that if we seek to genuinely instantiate (not just roughly simulate) mental states in a com-puter, we will need to do more than just run a program that manipulates relatively high-level (semantically transparent) symbolic structures.

   To begin to fix this idea (whose full expression must however wait until Chapter 4), we may introduce a contrast between functionalism and what I once termed (Clark, 1989) *microfunctionalism.* The functionalist, you will recall (Chapter 1), identifies being in a mental state with being in an abstract functional state, where a functional state is just some pattern of inputs, outputs, and internal state transitions taken to be characteristic of being in the mental state in question. But at what level of description should the functional story be told?

   Consider a second famous thought experiment, this time due to Ned Block (1980, pp. 276–278) Block imagines that we somehow get the whole population of China to implement the functional profile of a given mental state by having them passing around letters or other formal symbols. But such an instantiation of the formal symbol-trading structure, Block fears, surely will not actually possess the target mental properties. At any rate, it will not be a thinking, feeling being in its own right. There will be no qualia, no raw feelings, no pains and pleasures for the country as a whole. The various individuals will have their own mental states, of course. But no new ones will come into being courtesy of the larger functional organization created by passing around slips of paper alone. From such considerations, Block concludes that functional identity cannot guarantee full-blooded (qualia-involving) mental identity. But once again, it all depends on our (unreliable) intuitions. Why shouldn't the Chinese room, or Block's Chinese population, actually have real, and qualitatively rich, mental states? Our discomfort, I suggest, flows not from the bedrock idea that the right formal structure could guarantee the presence of such states so much as from a nagging suspicion that the formal structures that will be implemented will prove too shallow, too much like the restaurant script structure rehearsed earlier. Now imagine instead a much finer grained formal description, a kind of "microfunctionalism" that fixes the fine detail of the internal state-transitions as, for example, a web of complex mathematical relations between simple processing units. Once we imagine such a finer grained formal specification, intuitions begin to shift. Perhaps once these microformal properties are in place, qualitative mental states will always emerge just as they do in real brains? It is somewhat harder to imagine just how these more microstructural features are to replicated by the manipulations of slips of paper, beer cans (another of Searle's favorites), or the population of China. But if these unlikely substrates *were* thus delicately organized, it does not strike me as crazy to suppose that real mental events might ensue. Or rather, it seems no *more* unlikely than the fact that they also ensue in a well-organized mush of tissue and synapses!

   We will encounter, in Chapter 4, a somewhat different kind of computational model that pitches its descriptions of the formal structure of mind at just such a fine-grained level. These "connectionist" (or "neural network") approaches trade semantic transparency (the use of formal symbols to stand directly for familiar concepts, objects, events, and properties) against fineness of grain. They posit formal descriptions pitched at a level far distant from daily talk. They do not restrict their attention to the level of Newell's "cognitive band" or to operations that (in real

brains) take over 100 milliseconds to occur. They do, however, preserve the guiding vision of attending to the (micro)syntax and letting the semantics take care of
itself.

B. EVERYDAY COPING

Here is a very different kind of criticism of the program of symbol-crunching A.I.
Symbolic A.I., it has been suggested, is congenitally unable to come to grips with
fast, fluent, everyday activity. It cannot do so because such activity is not, and could
not be, supported by any set of symbolically coded rules, facts, or propositions. Instead, our everyday skills, which amount to a kind of expert engagement with the
practical world, are said to depend on a foundation of "holistic similarity recognition" and bodily, lived experience. Such, in essence, is the criticism developed in
a sequence of works by the philosopher Hubert Dreyfus (see, e.g., Dreyfus, 1972,
1992; Dreyfus and Dreyfus, 1986) and partially inspired by the ideas of Martin Heidegger (1927:1961).

Dreyfus' central concern is with the apparently bottomless richness of the understanding that we bring to our daily lives. Recall, for example, the simple restaurant script whose structure was displayed earlier. The point of such a script is to
capture a stereotypical course of events (go into a restaurant, order food, eat it,
leave tip) so as to provide some background knowledge for use in problem-
solving behavior. But human minds seem able to respond sensibly to an apparently infinite set of potential variations on such a situation. What will the symbolic
A.I. program do if it confronts a Martian in the kitchen, or a Harley-Davidson rid-
den into the restaurant?

Classical artificial intelligence has only two real responses to this problem of
"depth of understanding." One is to add more and more (and more and more)
knowledge in the form of explicitly coded information. [Doug Lenat's CYC project described in Lenat and Feigenbaum (1992) is an example of this strategy.] The
other is to use powerful inference engines to press maximal effect from what the
system already knows (the SOAR project discussed earlier displays something of
this strategy). Both such strategies really amount to doing "more of the same," albeit with different emphases. Dreyfus' radical suggestion, by contrast, is that no
amount of symbolically couched knowledge or inference can possibly reproduce
the required "thickness" of understanding, since the thickness flows not from our
knowledge of facts or our inferential capacities but from a kind of pattern-recog-
nition ability honed by extensive bodily and real-world experience. The product of
this experience is not a set of symbolic strings squirreled away in the brain but a
kind of "knowing-how"—a knowing-how that cannot be reduced to any set, however extensive, of "knowing-thats" (see, e.g., Dreyfus, 1981, p. 198).

For example, we are asked to consider the contrast between the novice chess
player (or car driver, or whatever) and the real expert. The novice, Dreyfus suggests, relies heavily on the conscious rehearsal of explicit symbol strings—rules like

"get your queen out early." The expert, by contrast, experiences "a compelling sense of the issue and the best move." Excellent chess players, we are told, can distinguish at a glance "roughly 50,000 types of position," and can, if necessary, choose moves at a speed that effectively precludes conscious analysis of the situation. The resultant flexibility of expert competence contrasts strongly with the oft-remarked "brittleness" of classical A.I. programs that rely on symbolically coded knowledge and make wild errors when faced with new or unexpected situations. Expert know-how, Dreyfus and Dreyfus (1986, p. 28) suggest, may be more fruitfully modeled using the alternative, pattern-recognition-based technologies (see Chapter 4) of connectionism and artificial neural networks. Since such expertise pervades the bulk of our daily lives (we are all, or most of us, "experts" at making tea and coffee, avoiding traffic accidents, engaging in social interactions, cooking dinner, making sandwiches, riding bicycles, and so on), the criticism that such activity lies outside the scope of symbolic A.I. is damning indeed. Is Dreyfus right? It is hard to fault the observation that symbolic A.I. seems to yield limited and brittle systems whose common sense understanding leaves plenty to be desired. In exactly this vein, for example, a skeptical computer scientist, commenting on the SOAR project, once offered the following "friendly challenge":

> Give us "Agent-Soar" [a system capable of] operating continuously, selectively perceiving a complex unpredictable environment, noticing situations of interest. Show us how it integrates concurrent tasks and coordinates their interacting needs . . . show us how it modifies its knowledge based on experience and makes the best use of dynamic but limited resources under real-time constraints. (Hayes-Roth, 1994, p. 96)

It is only fair to note, however, that much the same challenge could be raised regarding the connectionist research program presented in Chapter 4. My own view, then, is that the "argument from fluent everyday coping" actually points to much that is wrong with *both* connectionist *and* symbol-processing artificial intelligence. This point is not lost on Dreyfus and Dreyfus (1990) who note that human beings may be even more "holistic" than neural nets, and wonder whether we need to consider a larger "unit of analysis" comprising brain, body, and cultural environment [a "whole organism geared into a whole cultural world" (p. 331)]. Such issues will return to haunt us in the closing chapters. For now, we may simply conclude that everyday coping poses extremely difficult problems for any staunchly symbolic approach and that any move away from reliance on explicit, coarse-grained symbol structures and toward fast, flexible pattern-recognition-based models is probably a step in the right direction.

C. REAL BRAINS AND THE BAG OF TRICKS

One of the guiding assumptions of classical symbol-crunching A.I. is, we saw, that the scientific study of mind and cognition may proceed without essential reference to matters of implementation. This assumption, clearly displayed in, e.g., the SOAR team's decision to focus purely on the "cognitive band," is open to serious doubt. The situation is nicely summed-up by the cognitive scientist Donald Norman:

> Soar . . . espouses the software independence approach to modeling. That is, psychological functions are assumed to be independent of hardware implementation, so it is safe to study the cognitive band without examination of the implementation methods of the neural band, without consideration of the physical body in which the organism is embedded, and without consideration of non-cognitive aspects of behavior. (Norman, 1992, p. 343)

The worries concerning the potential roles of the physical body (and the wider environment) will occupy us in later chapters. An immediate question, however, concerns the attempt to model psychological functions without reference to the details of neural implementation.

On the positive side, we can say this: it is probably true that at least some psychological states will be *multiply realizable*. That is to say, several different hardware and software organizations will be capable of supporting the same mental states. The point about multiple *hardware* realizability flows directly from the bedrock idea of mind as a formal system, and the consequent focus on structure not stuff. The point about multiple *software* realizability is trickier (and is further pursued in the next chapter). But there exist, for example, a variety of different procedures for sorting a set of numbers or letters into sequence (Quick-sort and BUBBLE-sort to name but two). Is it not similarly unlikely that there is just one algorithmic structure capable of supporting, e.g., the mental state of believing it is raining?

On the negative side, however, it is *equally* unlikely that we will discover a good model of the formal structure of human thought if we proceed in a neurophysiological vacuum. Consider, for example, the SOAR team's commitment to a single type of long-term memory (but see Box 2.2 for an important caveat). SOAR thus used relies on a uniform production memory to store all its long-term knowledge. Is this assumption legitimate? Donald Norman (among others) argues that it is not, since human memory seems to involve multiple psychologically and neurophysiologically distinct systems.[5] For example, the distinction between semantic memory (memory for facts, such as "dogs have four legs") and episodic memory (memory of specific experiences and events, such as the day the dog buried the tortoise). SOAR can, it is true, reproduce much of the surface behavior associated with each memory type (see Newell, 1990, Chapter 6). But this surface mimicry, as Norman points out, does little to counter the growing body of neuropsychological evidence in favor of the psychological realism of multiple memory systems. Much of the relevant evidence comes not from normal, daily behavior but from

---

[5]See, e.g., Tulving (1983). The debate over multiple memory types continues today. But for our purposes, it does not really matter what the final story is. The example serves merely to illustrate the potential for conflict between specific uses of SOAR and neuropsychological data.

studies of brain damage and brain abnormalities, for example, studies of amnesi-
acs whose episodic memory is much more severely impaired than their semantic
memory.[6] There is also some neuroimaging work (using scanning techniques to
plot blood flow in the brain) that suggests that different neural areas are active in
different kinds of memory tasks. Such studies all combine to suggest real and psychologically significant differences between various memory systems.

The point about multiple memory systems may be carried a step further by
considering the more general idea of multiple cognitive systems. Recent work in
so-called evolutionary psychology (see, e.g., Tooby and Cosmides, 1992) challenges
the ideas of uniformity and simplicity stressed by Rosenbloom et al. (1992, p. 293)
and enshrined in their particular configuration of SOAR. Instead of a uniform
learning procedure, single long-term memory, and a small set of inference engines,
the evolutionary psychologists depict the mind as a kind of grab-bag of quite specialized knowledge-and-action stores, developed in a piecemeal fashion (over evolutionary time) to serve specific, adaptively important ends. They thus liken the
mind to a Swiss army knife—a collection of surprisingly various specialized implements housed in a single shell. Such cognitive implements (sometimes called
"modules") might include one for thinking about spatial relations, one for tool
use, one for social understanding, and so on (see, e.g., the list in Tooby and Cosmides, 1992, p. 113). Evolutionary psychology presents a radical and as yet not
fully worked-out vision. [For a balanced assessment see Mitchell (1999).] But the
general image of human cognition as to some degree a "bag of tricks" rather than
a neat, integrated system is winning support from a variety of quarters. It is gaining ground in work in real-world robotics, since special-purpose tricks are often
the only way to generate adaptive behavior in real time (see Chapter 6). And it is
gaining ground in some neuroscientific and neuropsychological research programs.[7] In a great many quarters, the idea that intelligent activity is mediated by
the sequential, serial retrieval of symbol structures from some functionally homogeneous inner store is being abandoned in favor of a more neurologically realistic
vision of multiple representational types and processes, operating in parallel and
communicating in a wide range of different ways. Notice, then, the extreme distance that separates this image of cognition from the idea (Newell, 1990, p. 50) of
a single sequence of cognitive actions drawing on a unified knowledge store. Serial retrieval of items from a homogeneous knowledge store may work well as a
model of a few isolated fragments of human behavior (such as doing a crossword).
But, to quote Marvin Minsky:

> Imagine yourself sipping a drink at a party while moving about and talking with friends.
> How many streams of processing are involved in shaping your hand to keep the cup

[6]Squire and Zola-Morgan (1988) and Tulving (1989).

[7]See, e.g., Churchland, Ramachandran, and Sejnowski (1994). See also Ballard (1991). This work is discussed at length in Clark (1997).

level, while choosing where to place your feet? How many processes help choose the words that say what you mean while arranging those words into suitable strings . . . what about those other thoughts that clearly go on in parallel as one part of your mind keeps humming a tune while another sub-mind plans a path that escapes from this person and approaches that one. (Minsky, 1994, p. 101)

Minsky's alternative vision depicts mind as an assortment of subagencies, some of which deploy special-purpose routines and knowledge stores. The neuroscientist Michael Arbib offers a related vision of neural computation as essentially distributed with different brain regions supporting different kinds of "partial representations." Cognitive effects, Arbib suggests, arise from the complex interactions of a multitude of such concurrently active partial representations. The point, he says, is that "no single, central, logical representation of the world need link perception and action—the representation of the world is *the pattern of relationships between all its partial representations*" (Arbib, 1994, p. 29, original emphasis).

We should not, of course, mistake every criticism of a particular use of SOAR[8] for a criticism of classical, symbol-crunching A.I. per se. Perhaps one day there will be symbol-processing systems (perhaps even a version of SOAR—see Box 2.2) that take much more account of the parallel, distributed, fragmentary nature of real neural processing. Certainly there is nothing in the bedrock ideas of classical A.I. (see Chapter 1) that rules out either the use of parallel processing or of multiple, special-purpose tricks and strategies. There are even up-and-running programs that prove the point. What seems most at stake is the once-standard image of the actual nature of the symbol structures involved. For the contents of such multiple, "partial" representations are unlikely to be semantically transparent in the sense described earlier; they are unlikely to admit of easy interpretation in terms of our high-level understanding of some problem domain. Instead, we must attend to a panoply of harder to interpret, "partial," perhaps "subsymbolic" (see Chapter 4) states whose cumulative effect is to sculpt behavior in ways that respect the space of reasons and semantic sense. The spirit of this enterprise, it seems to me, is genuinely distinct from that of symbol system A.I. Instead of going straight for the jugular and directly recapitulating the space of thought and reasons using logical operations and a language-like inner code, the goal is to coax semantically sensible behavior from a seething mass of hard-to-manage parallel interactions between semantically opaque inner elements and resources.

2.3 Suggested Readings

On *classical A.I. and the physical symbol system hypothesis*, see A. Newell and H. Simon, "Computer science as empirical inquiry: Symbols and search." In J. Haugeland (ed.), *Mind Design II* (Cambridge, MA: MIT Press, 1997, pp. 81–110). (Nice original account of the Physical Symbol System Hypothesis from two of the early stars of classical artificial intelli-

[8]For replies to some of these criticisms, see Rosenbloom and Laird (1993)

gence.) For *the classical A.I. endeavor in modern dress,* see P. Rosenbloom, J. Laird, A. Newell, and R. McCarl, "A preliminary analysis of the SOAR architecture as a basis for general intelligence." In D. Kirsh (ed.), *Foundations of Artificial Intelligence* (Cambridge, MA: MIT Press, 1992, pp. 289–325).

For *important critiques of classical A.I.,* see J. Searle, "Minds, brains and programs." In J. Haugeland (ed.), *Mind Design II* (Cambridge, MA: MIT Press, 1997, pp. 183-204). (Crisp, provocative critique of classical AI using the infamous Chinese Room thought experiment.) H. Dreyfus, "Introduction" to his *What Computers Still Can't Do* (Cambridge, MA: MIT Press, 1992). (The "everyday coping" objections, and some intriguing comments on the connectionist alternative to classical A.I.) D. Dennett, "Cognitive wheels: The frame problem of AI." In M. Boden (ed.), *The Philosophy of Artificial Intelligence* (Oxford, England: Oxford University Press, 1990, pp. 147–170). (Another take on the problem of formalizing common-sense reasoning, written with Dennett's customary verve and dash.)

For *some recent retrospectives on classical A.I., its attractions and pitfalls,* see S. Franklin, *Artificial Minds* (Cambridge, MA: MIT Press, 1995, Chapters 4 and 5), and the various perspectives represented in the 11 reviews collected in Section 1 ("Symbolic models of mind") of W. Clancey, S. Smoliar, and M. Stefik (eds.), *Contemplating Minds* (Cambridge, MA: MIT Press, 1994, pp. 1–166). A *useful collection* is J. Haugeland's *Mind Design II* (Cambridge, MA: MIT Press, 1997), especially (in addition to the pieces by Searle and by Newell and Simon cited above) the introduction "What is mind design?" by J. Haugeland and the papers by Minsky ("A framework for representing knowledge") and Dreyfus ("From micro-worlds to knowledge representation: A.I. at an Impasse").

PATTERNS, CONTENTS, AND CAUSES

3.1 Sketches

The seductive allure of symbol-crunching cognitive science, for the philosopher, lay not just in its promise to explain intelligent behavior. It lay also in the promise of accounting, in a rather direct way, for the dramatic explanatory and predictive powers of daily mentalistic discourse. We have seen hints of this interest in the preceding chapters. It is now time to confront the issues head on.

Recall Fodor's suggestion (rehearsed in the Introduction) that the practice of treating one another as mental agents—as loci of beliefs, desires and so on—serves us so well because it embodies a basically true theory of our inner workings. It works because beliefs, desires, and the like are indeed real inner states with causal powers. Fodor's belief, clearly laid out in Chapter 1 of his *Psychosemantics* (1987), is that the bedrock story told by symbol-crunching artificial intelligence is largely true, and that this constitutes a scientific "vindication" (Fodor's term) of daily "folk psychological" discourse. Fodor thus holds that the image of mindware as a collection of inner symbols and computational processes defined over them actually shows *how* talk of beliefs, desires, and so on can be (generally speaking) true, useful, and predictively potent.

The vindication, properly laid out, takes the form of what Fodor calls the Representational Theory of Mind (RTM) and it goes like this:

1. Propositional attitudes pick out computational relations to internal representations.

2. Mental processes are causal processes that involve transitions between internal representations.

These two claims (Fodor, 1987, pp. 16–20) yield a swift, simple account of the surprising success of folk psychology and of the phenomenon of reason-respecting chains of thought. For the folk psychological discourse is now imagined to track real, causally potent inner states whose contents, at least in central cases, match the contents specified by the "that-clause." If I predict your going indoors because I have been told you believe it is going to rain, my prediction works (according to this story) because your brain does indeed contain an inner state that *means* "it is going to rain" and because that inner state is such as to cause both further mental states (such as your belief that it would be wise to go indoors) and actions (your actually going indoors). In Fodor's words:

> To a first approximation, to think "it's going to rain; so I'll go indoors" is to have a tokening of a mental representation that means *I'll go indoors* caused, in a certain way, by a tokening of a mental representation that means, *it's going to rain.* (Fodor, 1987, p. 17)

We have already met this kind of story in the previous chapters. The stress there was on showing how rationality could be physically ("mechanistically") possible. It is now clear that giving a simple, scientific story to explain the success of folk psychological explanation and prediction is simply the other side of the same coin. The key move, in both cases, is to assert that mental contents and inner causally potent states march closely in step. Commonsense psychology works, according to Fodor, because it really does track these causally potent inner states. There are, naturally, some caveats and wrinkles (see, e.g., Fodor, 1987, pp. 20–26; Clark, 1993, pp. 12, 13). But such is the big picture nonetheless.

But what if there are no inner states that so closely match the structures and contents of propositional attitude talk? Such is the view of a second major protagonist in the debate over folk psychology, the neurophilosopher Paul Churchland. We shall examine, in the next chapter, the shape of the alternative ("connectionist") vision of the inner realm that Churchland endorses. For the present, it will suffice to take note of his very different attitude toward commonsense psychology.

Commonsense psychology (see Box 3.1), Churchland believes, is a quasiscientific theory of the unseen causes of our behavior. But whereas Fodor thinks the theory is basically true, Churchland holds it to be superficial, distortive, and false both in spirit and in detail. Its predictive successes, Churchland argues, are shallower and less encompassing than Fodor and others believe. For example, Churchland (1981) depicts folk psychology as inadequate in that

1. it works only in a limited domain (viz. some aspects of the mental life of normal, human agents),
2. its origins and evolution give cause for concern, and
3. it does not seem to "fit in" with the rest of our scientific picture of ourselves.

COMMONSENSE PSYCHOLOGY

At the heart of commonsense psychology (also known as folk psychology, daily mentalistic discourse, etc.) lies the familiar practice of combining attitudes (types of mental states such as believing, hoping, fearing, etc.) with propositions (e.g. "it is raining") to describe the inner wellsprings of human action. Thus I might explain your use of sunscreen by saying that you believe that solar rays can be harmful and desire that you have a long and healthy life, or your going to the fridge by your desire for a beer, and your belief that there is beer in the fridge.

Commonsense psychology is sometimes said to be a *theory* because we use it to explain behavior, because "explanations presuppose laws," and because a body of laws amounts to a theory. In what way do explanations presuppose laws? The idea is that it is only because we implicitly accept law-like generalizations, such as

> If someone wants something, and gets it, then other things being equal they should be happy

that we count a claim such as "she is happy because she just got the raise she asked for" as *explaining* someone's state or behavior. If a body of such implicit laws or generalizations constitutes a theory, then commonsense psychology should, it seems, be accorded theoretical status. (For some discussion, see Clark, 1987.)

Regarding (1) Churchland cites sleep, creativity, memory, mental illness, and infant and animal thought as phenomena on which folk psychology has shed no light. Regarding (2) he notes the general unreliability of unscientific folk theories (of astronomy, physics, etc.) and the fact that the theory does not seem to have altered and progressed over the years. Regarding (3) he notes that there is no sign as yet of any systematic translation of the folk talk into hard neuroscience or physics. It is this last worry that, I think, actually bears most of the weight of Churchland's skepticism. He believes, like Fodor, that folk psychology requires a very specific kind of "scientific vindication"—one that effectively requires the discovery of inner items that share the contents and structures of the folk psychological apparatus. But whereas Fodor, influenced by the format of basic physical symbol system A.I., thinks that such inner analogues are indeed to be found, Churchland, influenced by neuroscience and alternative forms of computational models, thinks such an outcome unlikely in the extreme. Failing some such outcome, the folk apparatus, Churchland believes, is discredited. His conclusion is thus directly opposed to Fodor's.

> We . . . need an entirely new kinematics and dynamics with which to comprehend human cognitive activity. One drawn, perhaps, from computational neuroscience and connectionist A.I. Folk psychology could then be put aside in favor of this descriptively more accurate and explanatorily more powerful portrayal of the reality within. (Churchland, 1989, p. 125)

There is however, a third possibility: perhaps the (putative) lack of inner structural analogues to the folk apparatus is not so damning after all. Perhaps the folk framework does not *need* "vindication" by any such inner scientific story. Such, in barest outline, is the view of the third key player in this debate, the philosopher Daniel Dennett. He asks us, for example, to consider the following story:

> Suppose, for the sake of drama, that it turns out that the sub-personal cognitive psychology [the inner cognitive organization] of some people turns out to be dramatically different from that of others. One can imagine the newspaper headlines: "Scientists Prove Most Left-Handers Incapable of Belief" or "Startling Discovery—Diabetics Have No Desires." But this is not what we would say, no matter how the science turns out. And our reluctance would not be just conceptual conservatism, but the recognition of an obvious empirical fact. For let left and right-handers (or men and women, or any other subsets of people) be as internally different as you like, we already know that there are reliable, robust patterns in which all behaviorally normal people participate— the patterns we traditionally describe in terms of belief and desire and the other terms of folk-psychology. (Dennett, 1987, pp. 234–235)

It will be useful, at this point, to clearly distinguish between two types of question that may be raised concerning the apparent successes of commonsense psychology, viz.

1. Empirical or scientific questions such as why does commonsense mental talk work in the case of, e.g., normal, adult human agents?

2. More philosophical or conceptual questions such as what *must be the case* if such commonsense explanations are to be good, proper, true, or otherwise legitimate, for humans or for any other beings we may one day encounter?

These two broad classes of questions interrelate in various ways. But they are nonetheless quite distinct. For example, it may be that mentalistic talk works when applied to us because we are indeed physical symbol systems as defined in the previous chapter. Yet even if that were so, it would not follow that such talk is incorrectly applied to beings whose behaviors issue from some alternative kind of inner organization. This is what Dennett's fable seeks to illustrate. The *philosophical* grail, it seems, is thus an answer to a more general question, viz.

3. What determines membership of the general class of beings that may properly be described using the apparatus of daily mentalistic discourse?

Thus, for example, the general class of *gases* includes oxygen and hydrogen, and membership is determined by the property of indefinite expansion at ordinary temperatures. Not all general classes, of course, need be scientifically determined—the class of charitable acts, for example.

The literature displays two broad types of answers to the "class membership" question. One type of answer, favored by both Fodor and Churchland, asserts that membership is fixed by facts about inner cognitive organization, along perhaps with relations between such inner facts and worldly states (see Box 3.2). The other type of answer asserts that membership depends only on behavior patterns, however caused. Dennett's fable about the right- and left-handers illustrates his apparent (but see below) commitment to this second type of answer. Let us now lay out Dennett's position in more detail.

Whenever we understand, predict, or explain the behavior of some object by talking about it as believing *x*, desiring *y*, and so on, we are, in Dennett's phrase, adopting an "intentional stance." We are treating the system as if it were making intelligent choices in line with its beliefs, desires, and needs. It is noteworthy, however, that the class of systems to which we may successfully apply such a strategy is disquietingly large. We say that the car wants more petrol, the plant is seeking the light, the dishwasher believes the cycle is finished, and so on. It is somewhat unnerving, then, to hear Dennett roundly assert that

> any object . . . whose behavior is well predicted by this strategy is in the fullest sense of the word a believer. What it is to be a true believer is to be an intentional system, a system whose behavior is reliably and voluminously predictable via the intentional strategy. (Dennett, 1987, p. 15)

Part of Dennett's project here is to convince us that the *cornerstone* of the distinctive kind of behavioral success enjoyed by human agents is precisely the kind of good design displayed by a very wide variety of cases of biological systems (plants, other animals) and by some humanly created artifacts. The leading idea is that commonsense psychology operates on the assumption that the target system (the person, animal, dishwasher, or whatever) is *well designed* and that it will therefore behave in ways that make sense: it will not just act randomly, but will instead tend to do what is effective (given its needs or purposes) and tend to believe what is true and useful to it (see Dennett, 1987, pp. 49, 73). Thus imagine a creature (call it a Den) that inhabits an environment consisting of green food particles and yellow poison particles. Den has, unsurprisingly, evolved decent color vision. Den must also eat about every 4 hours to survive. We observe Den resting for several hours, then awakening, approaching a green particle, and ingesting it. Taking the intentional stance we comment that "Den wanted some food, and chose the green particles because he believed they are good to eat." The folk psychological gloss works because Den is well designed. Evolution tolerates only those of her children

Box 3.2

How Do Mental Representations
Get Their Content?

Suppose, for the sake of argument, that the story told by symbol-crunching artificial intelligence is true: there *are* inner syntactic items that are the vehicles of content and that participate in the physical processes underlying thought and reason. A question still remains, viz. in virtue of what do the inner items bear the scientific contents they do? Consider, for example, the printed word "dog." The letter forms and sequence (the syntactic features) do not fix the meaning. So what does? In the case of a word such as "dog," we may appeal to some kind of history of use: some kind of communal convention by which we (as it were) agree to use the word "dog" to signify *dogs*. In the case of (putative) inner symbols in the head, however, we seem to need a different kind of story: one that does not itself *depend* on our having thoughts with certain contents (e.g., about dogs), but instead explains how such thoughts get their contents in the first place. Another way to raise the question is this. Consider our old friend the pocket calculator. It has a physical structure that, as we might say, *tolerates* a certain interpretative practice whereby we treat it as manipulating representations of numbers. But it might also tolerate some other interpretation—maybe as calculating good moves in some alien board game. Suppose now that the calculator was a natural phenomenon, found growing on Mars. An appeal to successful interpretative practice could not decide which, if either, story was to be preferred. If we are unhappy with this kind of indeterminacy (some are not) we will need something more than facts about possible interpretations to fix the facts about content.

There are two main possibilities (and various combinations and gradations of the two):

1. Content is itself fixed by the local properties of the system (e.g., intrinsic properties of the body and brain).

2. Content varies depending on broader properties such as the history of the system and the *relations* between its inner states and states of the world.

If content is locally determined, then there must be a kind of content such that it can be shared by two physically identical beings even if the broader context in which they operate is very different. So long as the local operations are the same, they will be in states that share what Putnam and others term "narrow contents."

It seems likely, however, that there are *kinds* of content that are not captured by any such narrow facts. Kim (1996, p. 191) tells the story of two frogs, the Earth frog and the Alien frog. Each inhabits a very similar environment and each has evolved a similar strategy for detecting and acquiring food. Each has a visual capacity to detect small, black, mobile items and a sensorimotor capacity to acquire them with a tongue flick. But on earth, the food is flies whereas in the alien world it is a small, black flying reptile (a "schmy"). It seems natural, in glossing the Earth-frog's perceptual content, to say it represents *flies*, but to say of the alien frog that it represents *schmies*.

This is the idea behind so-called externalist or broad accounts of content. According to the externalist, the contents that get "glued" to inner states depend not just on the inner facts, but on the relations between the inner states and states of the external environment. What *kind* of relations might these be? Here, the literature offers a complex and bewildering array of options and considerations. Some theories opt for facts about simple *causal* relations and correlations: it is flies, not schmies, that typically cause inner tokenings in the Earth-frog. Others opt for more historical accounts—either evolutionary (Earth-frog evolution developed strategies to cope with flies not schmies) or baptismal (what was out there when the word was first coined). Still others stress more complex kinds of causal relations and counterfactual correlation. Moreover, there is substantial debate concerning the proper balance between appeals to narrow and to broad content, especially in the context of psychological and folk-psychological explanation. Thus some authors believe that appeals to both are necessary so as to capture both what is similar and what is different in the case of Earth-frogs and Alien-frogs, etc. For more on these topics, see Kim (1996, Chapter 8), Braddon-Mitchell and Jackson (1996, Chapters 11 and 12), and (for an alternative vision) Cummins (1996, Chapter 5). For baptismal, historical, and evolutionary-based accounts, see Kripke (1980), Dretske (1988), and Millikan (1984). For the original treatment of narrow and broad content, see Putnam (1975), Burge (1979, 1986), and Fodor (1987). For a much more complex causal story, see Fodor (1987, Chapter 4) and for some second thoughts on narrow content, try Fodor (1994, Chapter 2).

who seek what is good for them, and who perceive things aright. Creatures not thus endowed exhibit, in Quine's tender words,

> A pathetic but praiseworthy tendency to die before reproducing their kind. (Quine, 1969, p. 126)

The intentional stance is thus presented as a special case of what Dennett calls the "design stance" viz. a way of understanding objects by reference to what they are supposed to do. What the intentional stance adds to an ordinary design-oriented perspective is the idea that the target system is not just well designed but rational—in receipt of information and capable of directing its actions (in light of such information) in ways likely to yield successful behaviors and the satisfaction of its needs.

The close link between the intentional stance and the assumptions of good design and rational choice means, of course, that there will be occasions when the strategy fails. For design and evolution are, at the end of the day, unable to produce the perfect cognizer. The perfect cognizer would be, for example, aware of all truths, prone to no illusions or errors, and capable of instant cost-free decision making. Would that we were! Real cognizers, by contrast, are at best imperfect engines of reason and perception. Recall Den. Den may, for example, employ an optical system subject to the following illusions: when the light source is dim and at an angle of 37° to the eye, yellow looks green and vice versa. Bad news for evening meals! Bad news too for evening applications of the intentional stance, for under those specific circumstances a prediction based on the idea that the system will act optimally will fail. Den will eat the poison particles and suffer the consequences.

The intentional stance is thus a tool that we may use to make sense of the bulk of the daily behavior of well-designed, rational beings. It is a tool that will, however, fail us in the face of design flaws, hardware failures, and the like. Commonsense mentalistic discourse, shot through with the use of the intentional stance, is thus to be viewed as

> a rationalistic (i.e., rationality-assuming) calculus of interpretation and prediction—an idealizing, abstract, instrumentalistic interpretation method that has evolved because it works and that works because we have evolved. (Dennett, 1987, p. 49)

What is most contentious about Dennett's claim is the idea that being a believer (which we now treat as shorthand for being the proper object of a variety of propositional attitude ascriptions) just *is* being a creature whose behavior can usefully be understood by means of the intentional stance. For the intentional stance is just that—a stance. And, as we saw, we may take it toward anything, regardless of its provenance or construction, just so long as we find it useful to do so. This can seem to make "being a believer" into what some critics dub a *stance-dependent* feature: an agent *X* has beliefs stance—dependently just in case some other agent *Y* finds it predictively useful to treat *X as if* it had beliefs. Stance-independent features, by contrast, are possessed (or not possessed) regardless of anyone actually, or even potentially, looking at the object in a certain way. As Lynne Rudder-Baker puts it,

> although one may correctly predict that a certain glass of water will freeze at 0 degrees centigrade, the water's having the property of freezing at 0 degrees centigrade does not depend on anyone's (possible) predictive strategies. On [Dennett's] theory, on the other

hand, the feature that someone has of believing that water freezes at 0 degrees is determined by the (possible) predictive strategies of others. (Rudder-Baker, 1994, p. 334)

It is worth bearing in mind, however, that Dennett explicitly rejects the idea that "being a believer" is all "in the eye of the beholder." Instead, the claim is that the intentional stance gets a grip *because* there exist real, objective patterns in human and animal behavior that are fully observer independent. An observer who failed to see the pattern would be missing "something perfectly objective" (Dennett, 1987, p. 25). These patterns are discernible, however, only through the special lens of a mentalistic perspective, much as an objective pattern in a light display may be discernible only via a lens that highlights specific frequencies and suppresses others (see Box 3.3).

This emphasis on real patterns is important. For what Dennett most fears is the "misplaced concreteness" (1987, p. 55) of the image of beliefs (etc.) as literally written out in an inner code. Although not flatly denying the possibility of such "inner sentences," Dennett is adamant that commonsense mentalistic talk does not *require* the existence of such inner items to establish its legitimacy. Instead, the commonsense discourse is said to be "abstract" in that the mental states it attributes are not required to show up as "intervening distinguishable states of an internal behavior-causing system" (Dennett, 1987, p. 52). Belief-states and the like are thus real in just the same sense as other "abstracta" such as centers of gravity, the equator, and so on. A center of gravity, being a mathematical point, has no spatial extension. Yet we can, it seems, truly assert that the gravitational attraction between the earth and the moon is a force acting between the centers of gravity of the two bodies (see Dennett, 1987, p. 72). Dennett is suggesting that

> beliefs . . . are *like that*—[they are] *abstracta* rather than part of the "furniture of the physical world" and [are] attributed in statements that are true only if we exempt them from a certain familiar standard of literality. (Dennett, 1987, p. 72)

The particular structure and articulation of the folk framework, Dennett believes, is unlikely to be replicated in any inner arena. The genuine inner concreta to be found in the brain, he suspects, will not look anything like the beliefs we identify in the folk discourse. Instead, they will be "as yet unnamed and unimagined neural data-structures of vastly different properties" (Dennett, 1987, p. 70). But the folk talk nonetheless serves to pick out real patterns in the behavior of more-or-less rational, well-designed agents. Such folk explanations are (for Dennett) no more undermined by the lack of corresponding inner concreta than are scientific stories invoking extensionless items such as centers of gravity.

The triangle is thus complete. At the base, and in direct but purely empirical opposition, we find Fodor and Churchland. Fodor expects science to validate the folk image by identifying inner states whose contents and structures closely match the contents and structures of daily ascriptions of beliefs, desires, and so on.

Box 3.3

REAL PATTERNS

Dennett's claim is that there are real (objective) patterns in human behavior that you will miss if (for example) you adopt a resolutely nonmentalistic perspective on events. This is illustrated using a variety of devices. Here are two.

1. Dennett (1987) tells a story similar to Zenon Pylyshyn's account (see Chapter 1) of the car accident:

> Take a particular instance in which the Martians observe a stockbroker deciding to place an order for 500 shares of General Motors. They predict [via extensive physical/neural knowledge] the exact motions of his fingers as he dials the phone and the exact vibrations of his vocal chords as he intones his order. But if the Martians do not see that indefinitely many *different* patters of finger motions and vocal chord vibrations . . . could have been substituted [e.g., he sends an email instead of phoning, etc, etc.] . . . then they have failed to see a real pattern in the world they are observing. (Dennett, 1987, pp. 25–26)

Similarly, the sequences 2, 4, 6 and 8, 10, 12 are different yet exhibit a common pattern (add 2). Objective patterns "pop out" when we view the world through appropriate (in this latter case arithmetical) lenses. The intentional stance, Dennett is suggesting, is one such lens.

2. Dennett (1998) offers the example of John Conway's Game of Life. In the Life-world computer simulation, activation propagates across a displayed grid in accordance with three simple rules defined over the (maximally) eight neighbors of each square (cell) on the grid:

Rule 1: If exactly two neighbors are active, the square remains as it is (active or inactive).

Rule 2: If exactly three neighbors are active, the square becomes active.

Rule 3: Else, the square becomes inactive.

With these simple rules determining the generation and decay (birth and death) of active cells, a grid seeded with some initial activity displays a fascinating kind of behavior. Active cells form shapes that persist, interact, decay, and propagate. The resulting "grid ecology" can be described using a vocabulary geared to the emerging macroevents and patterns. A "flasher," for example, occurs when part of the grid is configured as in Figure 3.1. Applying the simple rules yields (at the next time step) Figure 3.2. Reapplying the rules returns us to the first configuration, and so it will continue ("flashing") unless it is interrupted by activity propagating from elsewhere on the grid.

Dennett's claim is that talk of "flashers' (and puffers, gliders, eaters, and other exotic flora and fauna) highlights real patterns and makes available potent generalizations and predictions (e.g., that flashers will persist unless interfered with, and so on). To *miss* the patterns is to miss something *real* and explanatorily useful, even though everything that occurs depends on the underlying three rules (the "physics") in the end.

How good is this analogy? Does the Life-world really illustrate the same point highlighted by the stockbroker example? See the discussion in Section 3.2 and suggested readings at the end of the chapter.

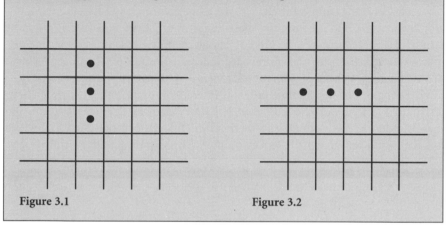

Figure 3.1   **Figure 3.2**

Churchland anticipates no such match and pronounces the folk framework misguided and chimerical: a "dead parrot" (Churchland, 1989, p. 127). At the apex, and pursuing the debate in rather different terms, sits Dennett. Like Churchland, he anticipates no close match between the folk and the scientific images. But unlike both Churchland and Fodor, he holds the goodness of the folk framework to be established independently of particular facts concerning the forms of inner processing and data storage. Roll up and place your bets.

3.2 Discussion

A. CAUSES, REASONS, AND SCATTERED CAUSES

Why believe that the folk stories need inner echoes to legitimate them? The main reason, I think, is the idea that reasons (as identified in folk explanations) must be straightforward *causes*. Any genuine realist concerning the mental, according to, e.g., Fodor, 1987, p. 12), must treat mental states as causally potent. Such states must make things happen. Any genuine vindication of folk psychology must thus show how the mental states it names have causal powers. How else, one might ask, could my belief that the beer is chilled explain my going to the fridge? Only, surely, if the belief somehow exists inside me and actually gives my legs a shove.[1] This is crudely put, but you get the idea. The validation of our commonsense claims seems to depend on the existence of inner states whose causal powers line up with their semantic interpretation, their *content*. The image of mind as a physical symbol system and the scientific validation of commonsense psychology thus look, at first blush, to go hand in hand.

Second blushes, however, can be revealing. For it is one thing to insist that my belief that it is raining must be a genuine cause and quite another to insist, as Fodor seems to do, that there be a neat, well-individuated inner item that corresponds to it.

Consider, for example, the claim that a global depression caused increased unemployment in Ohio. The phrase "global depression" here names what might be termed a scattered cause.[2] The kind of causal chain we imagine is, in such cases, rather different from the straightforward image of simple "push and shove" causation. There is, to be sure, some residual sense of "shove" implied: the sense of a force arising out of the combination and interaction of multiple, widely spatially distributed factors and acting so as to induce cases of local unemployment. But there is nothing corresponding to the kind of "billiard ball causation," in which one real world object actually strikes another. As one philosopher recently put it:

> a belief is not portrayed by folk wisdom as a mechanical part of a person. It is not that Erica's belief pushed on part C, which activated engine E and so on. (Lycan, 1991, p. 279)

It is tempting, to treat the folk framework as naming something like scattered causes. This may even be what Dennett has in mind when speaking of the folk constructs as abstracta and insisting on the goodness of a folk psychological explanation despite any lack of neat inner analogues to the states and processes invoked.

We should, however, distinguish this idea of (real but) scattered mental causation from the much more problematic idea of (what I will call) *ungrounded* causation. Scattered causation occurs when a number of physically distinct influences are usefully grouped together (as in the notion of an economic depression) and are treated as a unified force for some explanatory purpose. Ungrounded causation, by contrast, occurs when we confront a robust regularity and seek to estab-

---

[1] I here suppress a subdebate centered on the notion of emergent rule following. Dennett (1981, p. 107) gives the example of the chess-playing machine that is usefully treated as "wanting to get its queen out early" yet whose program contains no explicit line or lines of code stating any such goal. In such cases, Dennett suggests, the lack of a neat inner echo in no way undermines the play-level characterization. In response, Fodor (1987) introduces the idea of core cases. Roughly he insists that putative mental contents need inner tokens, but that psychological laws and tendencies do not—such laws and tendencies may instead be emergent out of other explicitly represented procedures or out of sheer hardware implementation (Fodor, 1987, p. 25). Dennett accepts the idea of core representation (Dennett, 1987, p. 70), but denies that the folk framework need find an echo even there.

[2] The term is based on Lycan's (1991) notion of a "scattered representation"—see Lycan (1991, p. 279).

lish it as causal with no reference to any underlying complex (however scattered and disparate) of physical influences. One way to do this is to employ a validation strategy that invokes only what Ruben (1994) calls "same-level counterfactuals." A counterfactual is just a claim of the form "If such and such had (or had not) occurred, then so and so would have followed"—for example "If she had not played a lob, she would have lost the match."

How might such counterfactuals help in the case of putative instances of mental causation? Consider (yet again) the belief that it is raining and the event of my taking the umbrella. What makes it the case that the former actually caused the latter? According to a purely counterfactual approach, the causal relevance is established by the truth of a number of claims such as "if he had not believed it was raining then (other things being equal) he would not have taken the umbrella." Such counterfactuals highlight the special relevance of the belief that it is raining to the specific action of taking the umbrella. Perhaps I also believe that my cat is enormous (I do). But the counterfactual "if Andy did not believe his cat was enormous he would not have taken the umbrella" is simply false. My beliefs about the enormity of my cat are not, it seems, relevant to my umbrella-taking behaviors.

Such counterfactual indicators can (and should) be invoked as evidence of causal relations, as in "if there was no global depression then (other things being equal) there would be less unemployment in Ohio." The counterfactuals, in such cases, are plausibly seen as *explained* by an underlying but scattered and disparate chain of real causal influences. A more radical suggestion, however, would be that patterns of counterfactuals may directly establish causal relevance, and hence that the details of the underlying physical story are strictly irrelevant to the project of establishing what causes what.

Despite its surface attractions (enough to tempt the present writer—see Clark, 1993, Chapter 10), I now doubt that the purely counterfactual, ungrounded approach can be made to work. The issues are complex and somewhat beyond the scope of this brief treatment. But two obvious problems may be cited.

First, as noted above, it is rather odd to appeal to counterfactuals to *constitute* causal facts. Instead, we should expect the causal facts to explain *why* certain counterfactuals hold. And second, the approach seems to assume the existence of beliefs, etc. in setting up the same level counterfactuals. It thus looks ill suited to figure as an argument in favor of the validity of that very framework. In the end, all that the bare counterfactuals show is what we knew already: that the folk framework enjoys some degree of predictive success. But then (as Churchland, 1989, p. 126 and elsewhere reminds us) so did alchemy, and the astronomical theory of nested crystal spheres!

The more plausible claim is that the folk discourse typically names scattered inner (and possibly inner and outer—see Chapter 8) causes. Scattered causes can have distinctive origins and reliable effects, and it is these regularities that motivate their conceptualization *as* scattered causes, i.e., as *items* (such as an economic depression). What the various counterfactuals do is to highlight these regularities so as to help justify our use of simple unitary labels (such as "the economic depression" or "the belief that it is raining") in some explanatory context (and see Box 3.4 for a related proposal).

This is not to say, of course, that the notion of scattered causation is itself unproblematic. In particular, we need to be much clearer (see Section B following) about what distinguishes a case of "genuine but scattered" causation from the case of no causation at all! But the picture of scattered causes at least maintains the link between causal claims and scientific stories concerning real physical effects. And the image fits nicely with recent work (see Chapters 4–8) on connectionism, collective effects, emergence, and dynamic systems. It is, in any event, important to be as clear as possible concerning what is being claimed when we say that beliefs are somehow real yet do not correspond to "things" in the head. Dennett invites us to treat them as abstracta. But we may wonder if the real idea (see, e.g., Dennett, 1987, pp. 71–76) isn't that they may be *scattered concreta* (scattered, perhaps, not just inside the skull, but even across the brain and the world—see Chapter 8 and comments in Dennett, 1996, pp. 134–152).

B. STANCES

Dennett's attempt to liberate commonsense psychology from full-blooded Fodorian realism while avoiding Churchland-style "eliminativism"[3] involves one easily misunderstood element, viz. the appeal to an intentional stance. The idea, as we saw, is that facts about belief, desire, and so on are only facts about the tendency of some object (e.g., a person, or a car) to succumb to a certain interpretative approach, viz. an approach that treats the object as a rational agent and ascribes to it beliefs and desires (for this reason, the position is sometimes called "ascriptivism"). What makes all this stance talk superficially uncomfortable, of course, is the staunch realist intuition that my having certain beliefs is logically independent of anyone else (actually or possibly) finding it useful to ascribe them to me at all. Conversely, it looks—from the same staunchly realist position—as if someone might find it useful to ascribe to me all kinds of beliefs that I in fact do not have, just so long as this helps them to predict my behavior (just as ideas about nested crystal spheres helped some people predict astronomical events, despite proving ultimately false).

(Mis)taken as pure ascriptivism, Dennett's position certainly confronts problems. Apart from the sheer counterintuitiveness of the proposal, it leads to all sorts of internal problems. Thus Rudder-Baker (1994, p. 336) notes that Dennett, like the rest of us, "takes beliefs to provide reasons that cause us to behave one way

---

[3]So-called because Churchland proposes to eliminate the commonsense notions from our final inventory of the real contents of the universe.

Box 3.4

CAUSAL EFFICACY AND PROGRAM EXPLANATIONS

An intriguing spin on the general idea of "picking out salient threads in the complex weave of causation" is pursued by Jackson and Pettit (1988), who depict the folk descriptions as something like placeholders for an open-ended variety of "real" causal explanations, but placeholders with a special and unique value. The authors note that we may, for example:

> Explain [a] conductor's annoyance at a concert by the fact that someone coughed. [Yet] what will have actually caused the conductor's annoyance will be the coughing of some particular person, Fred, say. (Jackson and Pettit, 1988, p. 394)

Now suppose someone was to insist that since the *real* cause of the annoyance was Fred's coughing, any explanation that cites "someone's coughing" must be false or inaccurate. This would be a mistake insofar as the latter explanation actually fulfills a special purpose: it makes it clear that the conductor would have (counterfactually) been annoyed *whoever* coughed— it just so happened that Fred was the culprit on that day. There is thus a valuable increase in generality bought by *not* citing the entity (Fred) that participated in the actual causal chain. Jackson and Pettit call explanations that thus invoke higher level placeholders "program explanations." Perhaps then, the folk explanations are good program explanations. To say that Pepa did x because she believed that y is to say that Pepa occupies one of an open-ended variety of complex inner states whose unifying feature is that they all give rise to the kinds of large-scale behavioral profile we associate with believing y. The folk state of believing y is thus not depicted as a simple cause but as a placeholder for a whole range of microstructural possibilities.

A further option is to agree with Jackson and Pettit that the folk-talk picks out whole ranges of microstructural possibilities, but to insist that in so doing it is discerning causes in exactly the usual sense. For all causal talk, it may be argued, functions by grouping together various instances into more general sets ("equivalence classes") and focusing attention on the common worldly effects of the various members. Folk psychological talk is thus on a par with, e.g., the assertion that it was the *poison* in the apple that caused the death. Should we really insist that just because the poison was, in fact, strychnine then the former explanation is not properly causal but is merely (as Jackson more recently put it) "causally relevant even if not causally efficacious" (Jackson, 1996, p. 397)? One reason for so doing is a fear of "too many causes": We don't want to allow that someone died from *both* strychnine intake *and* poisoning. Or do we? For a thorough discussion, see Jackson (1996).

rather than another" and cites Dennett (1984, Chapter 2) as evidence. But, she argues, if beliefs are to have such causal efficacy they cannot be "merely stance-dependent," but must instead be real features of the world, irrespective of anyone's possible predictive strategies. One way out would be to treat causal efficacy as itself a stance-dependent feature. But there is no sign that this is Dennett's wish and his avowed realism about ordinary physical phenomena seems to point the other way. Rudder-Baker thus accuses Dennett of widespread inconsistencies (for other examples, see Rudder-Baker, 1994) in his use of the idea of beliefs, etc. as stance-dependent features.

Further pressure on the notion of intentional states as merely stance-dependent features comes from the eliminativist camp led by Paul Churchland. Churchland and Dennett are, we saw, of one mind in doubting that the neuroscientific facts will prove compatible with the full-blown Fodorian idea of inner symbol strings that replicate the structures and contents of folk psychological mental state ascriptions. Yet Dennett holds that beliefs are as real and legitimate as centers of gravity and economic depressions—abstracta in good standing, while Churchland holds beliefs to be as unreal as alchemical essences and phlogiston—the putative concreta of misguided theories, ripe for overthrow and wholesale replacement. Given their agreement concerning what is likely to be found "in the head," Churchland is puzzled by Dennett's continued defense of folk psychology. He accuses Dennett of "arbitrary protectionism" and "ill motivated special pleading" (Churchland, 1989, p. 125). By the same token, Churchland argues, we might as well protect the false theories of alchemy, impetus, and nested crystal spheres:

> we could, of course, set about insisting that these "things" are real and genuine after all, though mere abstracta to be sure. But none of us is tempted to salvage their reality by such a tortured and transparent ploy. Why should we be tempted in the case of the propositional attitudes? (Churchland, 1989, p.126)

The best response to both Churchland and Rudder-Baker is to abandon any suggestion that human mental states are merely stance dependent. Mentalistic discourse, as Dennett repeatedly insists, picks out *real* threads in the fabric of causation. We need not, however, think that such threads must show up as neat items in an inner neural economy. Instead, and following the discussion in the previous section, we may treat the mentalistic attributions as names for scattered causes that operate via a complex web of states distributed throughout the brain (and, perhaps, the body and world—see Chapters 4 through 8).

This response exploits the fact, nicely noted by Rudder-Baker (1994, p. 342) that "one could be a realist about belief and identify a belief with a complex state of a subject and the environment." The problem, then, is to distinguish the idea of beliefs as scattered causes from "special pleading" and "ill-motivated protectionism." When is a cause real but scattered, as opposed to not being real at all?

This is a nice question and one that demands a much more extensive discussion than can be provided here. Some useful questions to consider might include: does the (putative) scattered cause figure in a *wide range* of effective predictions, counterfactuals, and explanations? Does it figure in any kind of *articulated theory* of a domain? Does it allow theories in one domain to be *linked* to theories in other domains? Do we have any positive reasons to *reject* the claim that we here confront a case of scattered causation? And so on.

The folk discourse actually fares rather well in the face of such questioning. As Fodor insists, it does indeed support a wide range of predictions, counterfactuals, and explanations. It implicitly specifies a fairly deep and articulated theory of daily behavior. It allows theories in social psychology, economics, politics, and sociology to interrelate in various ways. And, pace Churchland, I see no positive evidence against it. There is, of course, the apparent lack of neat inner brain states directly corresponding to the folk items—but this is obviously powerless as evidence against the image of the folk items as scattered causes.

C. UPGRADING THE BASIC BELIEVER

The intentional stance, we saw, works for all kinds of objects and systems—some more intuitively intentional than others. The human is ascribed the desire to fetch a cold beer, the cat to find a mouse, and the desk to stay still and support the notepaper! The apparent promiscuity of the intentional stance has worried many commentators, and rightly so. Certainly our preferred reconstruction of Dennett's position as a kind of realism about scattered causes looks to be clearly contraindicated by the acceptance of the desk (or lectern, or whatever) into the True Believers Hall of Fame. It is important to notice, however, that it is no part of Dennett's project to deny the very real *differences* between the various cases (such as the human, the car, and the desk). Indeed, Dennett's writings are increasingly concerned with these differences, depicted as a kind of cascade of upgrades to the simplest biological minds.

At the baseline, according to Dennett, lie any entities that might be classed as "smart agents" (Dennett, 1996, p. 34). In this low-key sense, a thermostat or an amoeba are smart insofar as they respond to their worlds in ways that are not random but respect certain basic hard-wired "goals." With respect to such entities, we can usefully predict their behavior by assuming they will act so as to "try" to achieve these goals. This, then, is the bedrock scenario for taking the intentional stance.

Above this bedrock lies an extended sequence (though not a strict hierarchy) of design innovations that allows entities to pursue and achieve ever more complex goals and to maintain increasingly more complex relations with their environments. Inner maps, speech, labeling, and self-reflection are all instances of important design innovations. Speech, for Dennett, is especially important in laying the ground for human-style cognition. During a discussion of what chimpanzees can and cannot do, he suggests that perhaps

> thinking—our kind of thinking—had to wait for talking to emerge. (Dennett, 1996, p. 130)

He also lays great stress on the way we off-load cognitive tasks onto the environment, using labels, notes, maps, signs, and a host of other technologies.

Given these currents in Dennett's thought, it seems unfair to accuse him of undervaluing "real" intentionality by allowing the promiscuous use of the intentional stance. Dennett's point, I think, is that despite the very many important differences among humans, amoeba, and thermostats, there remains an important commonality, viz. that we, like these simpler systems, succumb to the intentional stance because we are well-designed entities pursuing certain goals. If that were not the case, the intentional idiom would simply fail and we might "do any dumb thing at all" (Dennett, 1996, p. 34).

In light of all this, it is not clear what would be lost if we were simply to say that humans (and perhaps some other entities incorporating enough design innovations) really do have beliefs and desires, but that (1) there is no clean dividing line in nature—just a bag of design innovations that may be more or less shared with other entities, and (2) there is no reason to suppose that to each ascribed belief (etc.) there corresponds some simple neural state or "inner sentence." Why not, in short, reconstruct Dennett's position as a kind of fuzzy,[4] scattered realism? Dennett is, after all, willing to assert that "our kind of thinking" depends on a rich set of perfectly real, objective, and distinctive design features, and that mentalistic discourse talk picks our real patterns in the fabric of causation.

Can Dennett's position be thus reconstructed without causing trouble for it elsewhere? Should it be? Is scattered causation really an alternative to ungrounded counterfactual accounts or does it confront the same problems further down the line? Our discussion raises more problems than it solves. The complex issues concerning the fate and status of folk psychology remain among the most vexed and elusive in contemporary philosophy of mind.

3.3 Suggested Readings

On *computational realism about commonsense psychological talk*, see J. Fodor. "Introduction: The persistence of the attitudes" and "Appendix: Why there still has to be a language of thought." These are the opening and closing chapters of his *Psychosemantics: The Problem of Meaning in the Philosophy of Mind* (Cambridge, MA: MIT Press, 1987, pp. 1–26, 135–154). The opening chapter displays the appeal of strong realism about folk psychological expla-

---

[4]That is, realism without the idea of a clean break between the true believers and the rest (just as one can believe that some folk are really bald without believing that there is a clean line between the bald and the hirsute).

nation, whereas the closing chapter offers some more technical arguments in favor of a certain type of articulated inner code.

For a *more liberal view*, according to which the folk concepts are compatible with multiple cognitive scientific models, see G. Graham and T. Horgan, "Southern fundamentalism and the end of philosophy." In M. DePaul and W. Ramsey (eds.), *Rethinking Intuition* (Oxford, England: Rowman and Littlefield, 1999).

On eliminativism, see P. M. Churchland, "Eliminative materialism and the propositional attitudes" and "Folk psychology and the explanation of numan behavior." Both in his *A Neurocomputational Perspective* (Cambridge, MA: MIT Press, 1989, pp. 1–22, 111–128). The former presents Churchland's original, preconnectionist formulation of some grounds for skepticism about the folk psychological framework. The latter adds comments on connectionism and the debate with Dennett.

On instrumentalism and *the reality of patterns*, try D. Dennett, "Real patterns." *Journal of Philosophy*, 88, 27–51, 1991. [The current flagship statement of the intentional stance. See also the previous flagship, "True believers: The intentional strategy and why it works" in D. Dennett, *The Intentional Stance* (Cambridge, MA: MIT Press, 1987).]

For some criticism, see L. Rudder-Baker, "Instrumental intentionality. In S. Stich and T. Warfield (eds.), *Mental Representation: A Reader* (Oxford, England: Blackwell, 1994, pp. 332–344). (A clear and direct response to the "True Believers" argument.)

To continue the debate, see D. Dennett, "Back from the drawing board." In B. Dahlbom (ed.), *Dennett and His Critics* (Oxford, England: Blackwell, 1993, pp. 203–235). This is Dennett's response to a wide variety of critiques, all of which appear in the same volume. See especially the sections called "Labels: Am I a behaviorist? An ontologist?" (pp. 210–214), "Intentional laws and computational psychology" (pp. 217–222), and the reply to Millikan (pp. 222–227).

For a wonderful extended analysis, see B. McLaughlin and J. O'Leary-Hawthorn, "Dennett's logical behaviorism." *Philosophical Topics*, 22, 189–259, 1994. (A very thorough and useful critical appraisal of Dennett's problematic "behaviorism." See also Dennett's response in the same issue, pp. 517–522.)

A difficult but rewarding engagement with the "real patterns" ideas is to be found in J. Haugeland, "Pattern and being." In B. Dahlbom (ed.), *Dennett and His Critics* (Oxford, England: Blackwell, 1993, pp. 53–69).

And *for a taste of something different*, see R. G. Millikan, "On mentalese orthography." In B. Dahlbom (ed.), *Dennett and His Critics* (Oxford, England: Blackwell, 1993, pp. 97–123). (A different kind of approach to all the issues discussed above. Not easy, but your efforts will be rewarded.)

CONNECTIONISM

4.1 Sketches

The computational view of mind currently comes in two basic varieties. The basic physical symbol system variety, already encountered in Chapter 2, stresses the role of symbolic atoms, (usually) serial processing, and expressive resources whose combinational forms closely parallel those of language and logic. The other main variety differs along all three of these dimensions and is known variously as connectionism, parallel distributed processing, and artificial neural networks.

These latter models, as the last name suggests, bear some (admittedly rather distant) relation to the architecture and workings of the biological brain. Like the brain, an artificial neural network is composed of many simple processors linked in parallel by a daunting mass of wiring and connectivity. In the brain, the "simple processors" are neurons (note the quotes: neurons are much more complex than connectionist units) and the connections are axons and synapses. In connectionist networks, the simple processors are called "units" and the connections consists in numerically weighted links between these units—links known, unimaginatively but with pinpoint accuracy, as connections. In both cases, the simple processing elements (neurons, units) are generally sensitive only to local influences. Each element takes inputs from a small group of "neighbors" and passes outputs to a small (sometimes overlapping) group of neighbors.

The differences between simple connectionist models and real neural architectures remain immense and we will review some of them later in this chapter. Nonetheless, something of a common flavor does prevail. The essence of the common flavor lies mostly in the use of large-scale parallelism combined with local computation, and in the (related) use of a means of coding known as distributed representation. To illustrate these ideas, consider the now-classic example of NETtalk.

NETtalk (Sejnowski and Rosenberg, 1986, 1987) is an artificial neural network, created in the mid-1980s, whose task was to take written input and turn it into coding for speech, i.e., to do grapheme-to-phoneme conversion. A successful classical program, called DECtalk, was already in existence and performed the same task courtesy of a large database of rules and exceptions, hand coded by a team of human programmers. NETtalk, by contrast, instead of being explicitly programmed, *learned* to solve the problem using a learning algorithm and a substantial corpus of example cases—actual instances of good text-to-phoneme pairings. The output of the network was then fed to a fairly standard speech synthesizer that took the phonetic coding and transformed it into real speech. During learning, the speech output could be heard to progress from initial babble to semirecognizable words and syllable structure, to (ultimately) a fair simulacrum of human speech. The network, it should be emphasized, was not intended as a model of language understanding but only of the text-to-speech transition—as such, there was no semantic database tied to the linguistic structures. Despite this lack of semantic depth, the network stands as an impressive demonstration of the power of the connectionist approach. Here, in briefest outline, is how it worked.

The system, as mentioned above, is comprised of a set of simple processing units. Each unit receives inputs from its neighbors (or from the world, in the case of so-called input units) and yields an output according to a simple mathematical function. Such functions are often nonlinear. This means that the numerical value of the output is not directly proportional to the sum of the inputs. It may be, for example, that a unit gives a proportional output for an intermediate range of total input values, but gives a constant output above and below that range, or that the unit will not "fire" until the inputs sum to a certain value and thereafter will give proportional outputs. The point, in any case, is that a unit becomes activated to whatever degree (if any) the inputs from its local neighbors dictate, and that it will pass on a signal accordingly. If unit A sends a signal to unit B, the strength of the signal arriving at B is a joint function of the level of activation of the "sender" unit and the numerical weighting assigned to the connection linking A to B. Such weights can be positive (excitatory) or negative (inhibitory). The signals arriving at the receiving units may thus vary, being determined by the product of the numerical weight on a specific connection and the output of the "sender" unit.

NETtalk (see Box 4.1) was a fairly large network, involving seven groups of input units, each group comprising some 29 individual units whose overall activation specified one letter. The total input to the system at each time step thus specified seven distinct letters, one of which (the fourth) was the target letter whose phonemic contribution was to be determined and given as output. The other six letters provided essential contextual information, since the phonemic impact of a

Box 4.1

THE NETTALK ARCHITECTURE

The specific architecture of NETtalk (see Figure 4.1) involved three layers of units (a typical "first-generation" layout, but by no means obligatory). The first layer comprised a set of "input" units, whose task was to encode the data to be processed (information about letter sequences). The second layer consisted of a group of so-called hidden units whose job was to effect a partial recoding of the input data. The third layer consisted of "output" units whose activation patterns determine the system's overall response to the original input. This response is specified as a vector of numerical activation values, one value for each output unit. The knowledge that the system uses to guide the input–output transitions is thus encoded to a large extent in the weights on the various interunit connections. An important feature of the connectionist approach lies in the use of a variety of potent (though by no mean omnipotent!) learning algorithms. These algorithms (see text and Box 4.2) adjust the weights on the interunit connections so as to gradually bring the overall performance into line with the target input–output function implicit in a body of training cases.

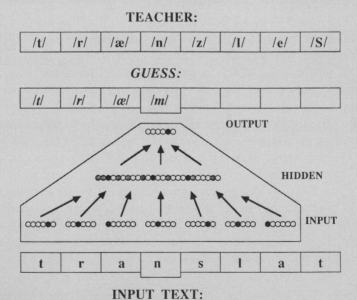

Figure 4.1 Schematic of NETtalk architecture showing only some units and connectivity. Each group of 29 input units represents a letter. The 7 groups of input units were transformed by 80 hidden units. These hidden units then projected to 26 output units, which represented 54 phonemes. There were a total of 18,629 weights in the network. (From Sejnowski and Rosenberg, 1987, by permission.)

Box 4.2	

GRADIENT DESCENT LEARNING

The learning routine involves what is known as gradient descent (or hill climbing, since the image can be systematically inverted!). Imagine you are standing somewhere on the inner slopes of a giant pudding basin. Your task is to find the bottom—the point corresponding to the lowest error and hence the best available solution. But you are blindfolded and cannot see the bottom and cannot run directly to it. Instead, you take a single step and determine whether you went up or down. If you went up (a local error), you go back and try again in the opposite direction. If you went down, you stay where you are. By repeating this procedure of small steps and local feedback, you slowly snake toward the bottom and there you halt (since no further step can take you any lower). The local feedback, in the case of the neural network, is provided by the supervisory system that determines whether a slight increase or decrease in a given weight would improve performance (assuming the other weights remain fixed). This procedure, repeated weight by weight and layer by layer, effectively pushes the system down a slope of decreasing error. If the landscape is a nice pudding-basin shape with no nasty trenches or gorges, the point at which no further change can yield a lower error signal will correspond to a good solution to the problem.

given letter (in English) varies widely according to the surrounding letters. The input units were connected to a layer of 80 hidden units, and these connected in turn to a set of 26 output units coding for phonemes. The total number of interunit links in the overall network summed to 18,829 weighted connections.

Given this large number of connections, it would be impractical (to say the least) to set about finding appropriate interunit connection weights by hand coding and trial and error! Fortunately, automatic procedures (learning algorithms) exist for tuning the weights. The most famous (but probably biologically least realistic) such procedure is the so-called back-propagation learning algorithm. In back-propagation learning, the network begins with a set of randomly selected connection weights (the layout, number of units, etc. being fixed by the designer). This network is then exposed to a large number of input patterns. For each input pattern, some (initially incorrect) output is produced. An automatic supervisory system monitors the output, compares it to the target (correct) output, and calculates small adjustments to the connection weights—adjustments that would cause slightly improved performance were the network to be reexposed to the very same input pattern. This procedure (see Box 4.2) is repeated again and again for a large (and cycling) corpus of training cases. After sufficient such training, the network often (though not always) learns an assignment of weights that effectively solves the problem—one that reduces the error signal and yields the desired input–output profile.

Such learning algorithms can discover solutions that we had not imagined. Researcher bias is thus somewhat decreased. Moreover, and perhaps more importantly, the way the trained-up network *encodes* the problem-solving information is quite unlike the more traditional forms of symbol-string encoding characteristic of the work discussed in Chapter 2. The connectionist system's long-term knowledge base does not consist in a body of declarative statements written out in a formal notation based not on the structure of language or logic. Instead, the knowledge inheres in the set of connection weights and the unit architecture. Many of these weighted connections participate in a large number of the system's problem-solving activities. Occurrent knowledge—the information active during the processing of a specific input—may usefully be equated with the transient activation patterns occurring in the hidden unit layer. Such patterns often involve *distributed* and *superpositional* coding schemes. These are powerful features, so let's pause to unpack the jargon.

An item of information is here said to have a distributed representation if it is expressed by the simultaneous activity of a number of units. But what makes distributed representation computationally potent is not this simple fact alone, but the systematic use of the distributions to encode further information concerning subtle similarities and differences. A distributed pattern of activity can encode "microstructural" information such that variations in the overall pattern reflect variations in the content. For example, a certain pattern might represent the presence of a black cat in the visual field, whereas small variations in the pattern may carry information about the cat's orientation (facing ahead, side-on, etc.). Similarly, the activation pattern for a black panther may share some of the substructure of the cat activation pattern, whereas that for a white fox may share none. The notion of superpositional storage is precisely the notion of such partially overlapping use of distributed resources, in which the overlap is informationally significant in the kinds of way just outlined. The upshot is that semantically related items are represented by syntactically related (partially overlapping) patterns of activation. The public language words "cat" and "panther" display no such overlap (though *phrases* such as "black panther" and "black cat" do). Distributed superpositional coding may thus be thought of as a trick for forcing still more information into a system of encodings by exploiting even more highly structured syntactic vehicles than words. This trick yields a number of additional benefits, including economical use of representational resources, "free" generalization, and graceful degradation. Generalization occurs because a new input pattern, if it resembles an old one in some aspects, will yield a response rooted in that partial overlap. "Sensible" responses to new inputs are thus possible. "Graceful degradation," alluring as it sounds, is just the ability to produce sensible responses given some systemic damage. This is possible because the overall system now acts as a kind of pattern completer—given a large enough fragment of a familiar pattern, it will recall the whole thing. Generalization, pattern completion, and damage tolerance are thus all reflections of the same powerful computational strategy: the use of distributed, superpositional storage schemes and partial cue-based recall.

Two further properties of such coding schemes demand our attention. The first is the capacity to develop and exploit what Paul Smolensky (1988) has termed "dimension shifted" representations. The second is the capacity to display fine-grained context sensitivity. Both properties are implied by the popular but opaque gloss on connectionism that depicts it as a "subsymbolic paradigm." The essential idea is that whereas basic physical symbol system approaches displayed a kind of semantic transparency (see Chapter 2) such that familiar words and ideas were rendered as simple inner symbols, connectionist approaches introduced a much greater distance between daily talk and the contents manipulated by the computational system. By describing connectionist representation schemes as dimension shifted and subsymbolic, Smolensky (and others) means to suggest that the features that the system uncovers are finer grained and more subtle than those picked out by single words in public language. The claim is that the contentful elements in a subsymbolic program do not directly recapitulate the concepts we use "to consciously conceptualize the task domain" (Smolensky, 1988, p. 5) and that "the units do not have the same semantics as words of natural language" (p. 6). The activation of a given unit (in a given context) thus signals a semantic fact: but it may be a fact that defies easy description using the words and phrases of daily language. The semantic structure represented by a large pattern of unit activity may be very rich and subtle indeed, and minor differences in such patterns may mark equally subtle differences in contextual nuance. Unit-level activation differences may, thus, reflect minute details of the visual tactile, functional, or even emotive dimensions of our responses to the same stimuli in varying real-world contexts. The pioneer connectionists McClelland and Kawamoto (1986) once described this capacity to represent "a huge palette of shades of meaning" as being "perhaps . . . the paramount reason why the distributed approach appeals to us" (p. 314).

This capacity to discover and exploit rich, subtle, and nonobvious schemes of distributed representation raises an immediate methodological difficulty: how to achieve, after training, some understanding of the knowledge and strategies that the network is actually using to drive its behavior? One clue, obviously, lies in the training data. But networks do not simply learn to repeat the training corpus. Instead they learn (as we saw) general strategies that enable them to group the training instances into property-sharing sets, to generalize to new and unseen cases, etc. Some kind of knowledge organization is thus at work. Yet it is impossible (for a net of any size or complexity) to simply read this organization off by, e.g., inspecting a trace of all the connection weights. All you see is numerical spaghetti!

The solution to this problem of "posttraining analysis" lies in the use of a variety of tools and techniques including statistical analysis and systematic interference. Systematic interference involves the deliberate damaging or destruction of groups of units, sets of weights, or interunit connections. Observation of the network's "postlesion" behavior can then provide useful clues to its normal operating strategies. It can also provide a further dimension (in addition to brute performance) along which to assess the "psychological reality" of a model, by comparing the way the network reacts to damage to the behavior patterns seen in humans suffering from various forms of local brain damage and abnormality (see, e.g., Patterson, Seidenberg, and McClelland, 1989; Hinton and Shallice, 1989). In practice, however, the most revealing forms of posttraining analysis have involved not artificial lesion studies but the use of statistical tools (see Box 4.3) to generate a picture of the way the network has learned to negotiate the problem space.

So far, then, we have concentrated our attention or what might be termed "first-generation" connectionist networks. It would be misleading to conclude, however, without offering at least a rough sketch of the shape of more recent developments.

Second-generation connectionism is marked by an increasing emphasis on temporal structure. First-generation networks, it is fair to say, displayed no real capacity to deal with time or order. Inputs that designated an ordered sequence of letters had to be rendered using special coding schemes that artificially disambiguated the various possible orderings. Nor were such networks geared to the production of output patterns extended in time (e.g., the sequence of commands needed to produce a running motion)[1] or to the recognition of temporally extended patterns such as the sequences of facial motion that distinguish a wry smile from a grimace. Instead, the networks displayed a kind of "snapshot reasoning" in which a frozen temporal instant (e.g., coding for a picture of a smiling person) yields a single output response (e.g., a judgment that the person is happy). Such networks could not identify an instance of pleasant surprise by perceiving the gradual transformation of puzzlement into pleasure (see e.g., Churchland, 1995).

To deal with such temporally extended data and phenomena, second-generation connectionist researchers have deployed so-called recurrent neural networks. These networks share much of the structure of a simple three-layer "snapshot" network, but incorporate an additional feedback loop. This loop (see Figure 4.3) recycles some aspect of the networks activity at time t_1 alongside the new inputs arriving at time t_2. Elman nets (see Elman, 1991b) recycle the hidden unit activation pattern from the previous time slice, whereas Jordan (1986) describes a net that recycles its previous output pattern. Either way, what is preserved is some kind of

---

[1]These issues are usefully discussed in Churchland and Sejnowski (1992, pp. 119–120). For a more radical discussion, see Port, Cummins, and McCauley (1995).

Box 4.3

CLUSTER ANALYSIS

Cluster analysis is an example of an analytic technique addressing the crucial question "what kinds of representation has the network acquired?" A typical three-layer network, such as NETtalk, uses the hidden unit layer to partition the inputs so as to compress and dilate the input representation space in ways suited to the particular target function implied by the training data. Thus, in text-to-phoneme conversion, we want the rather different written inputs "sale" and "sail" to yield the same phonetic output. The hidden units should thus compress these two input patterns into some common intermediate form. Inputs such as "shape" and "sail" should receive different, though not unrelated, codings, whereas "pint" and "hint," despite substantial written overlap, involve widely variant phonemic response and should be dilated—pulled further apart. To perform these tricks of pulling together and pushing apart, NETtalk developed 79 different patterns of hidden unit activity. Cluster analysis then involved taking each such pattern and matching it with its nearest neighbor (e.g., the four-unit activation pattern 1010 is nearer to 1110 than to 0101, since the second differs from the first in only one place whereas the third differs in four). The most closely matched pairs are then rendered (by a process of vector averaging) as new single patterns and the comparison process is repeated. The procedure continues until the final two clusters are generated, representing the grossest division of the hidden unit space learned by the system. The result is an unlabeled, hierarchical tree of hidden unit activity. The next task is to label the nodes. This is done as follows. For each of the original 79 activation patterns, the analyst retains a trace of the input pattern that prompted that specific response. She then looks at the pairs (or pairs of pairs, etc.) of inputs that the network "chose" to associate with these similar hidden unit activation patterns so as to discern what those inputs had in common that made it *useful* for the network to group them together. The result, in the case of NETtalk, is a branching hierarchical tree (see Figure 4.2) whose grossest division is into the familiar groupings of vowels and consonants and whose subdivisions include groupings of different ways of sounding certain input letters such as *i, o* etc. In fact, nearly all the phonetic groupings learned by NETtalk turned out to correspond closely to divisions in existing phonetic theory. One further feature discussed in Section 4.2 is that various versions of NETtalk (maintaining the same architecture and learning routine and training data but beginning with different assignments of random weights) exhibited, after training,

very different sets of interunit weightings. Yet these superficially different solutions yield almost identical cluster-analytic profiles. Such nets use different numerical schemes to encode what is essentially the *same* solution to the
text-to-phoneme conversion problem.

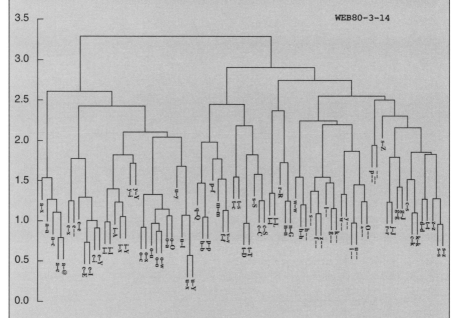

Figure 4.2 Hierarchical cluster analysis of the average activity levels on the hidden
units for each letter-to-sound correspondence (*l–p* for letter *l* and phoneme *p*). The
closest branches correspond to the most nearly similar activation vectors of the hidden units. (From Sejnowski and Rosenberg, 1987. Parallel networks that learn to pronounce English text. *Complex Systems*, 1, 145–168. Reproduced by kind permission
of T. Sejnowski.)

on-going trace of the network's last activity. Such traces act as a kind of short-term
memory enabling the network to generate new responses that depend both on the
current input and on the previous activity of the network. Such a set-up also allows output activity to continue in the complete absence of new inputs, since the
network can continue to recycle its previous states and respond to them.

For example, Elman (1991b) describes a simple recurrent network whose goal
is to categorize words according to lexical role (noun, verb, etc.). The network was
exposed to grammatically proper sequences of words (such as "the boy broke the
window"). Its immediate task was to predict the next word in the on-going sequence. Such a task, it should be clear, has no unique solution insofar as many
continuations will be perfectly acceptable grammatically. Nonetheless, there are

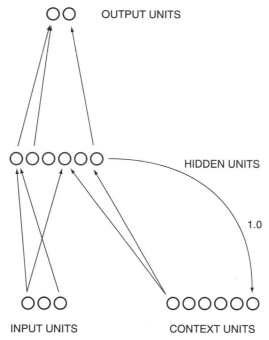
OUTPUT UNITS

HIDDEN UNITS

1.0

INPUT UNITS   CONTEXT UNITS

Figure 4.3 A three-layer recurrent network. The context units are activated, one by one, by the corresponding hidden units. For simplicity, not all the activation is shown. (After Elman, 1991b, with permission.)

whole classes of words that cannot be allowed to follow. For example, the input sequence "the boy who" cannot be followed by "cat" or "tree." These constraints on acceptable successor words reflect grammatical role and the training regime thus provides data germane to the larger goal of learning about lexical categories.

Elman's network proved fairly adept at its task. It "discovered" categories such as verb and noun and also evolved groupings for animate and inanimate objects, foods, and breakable objects—properties that were good clues to grammatical role in the training corpus used. To determine exactly what the network learned, Elman used another kind of posttraining analysis (one better suited to the special case of recurrent nets) called "principal component analysis" (PCA). The details are given in Clark (1993, pp. 60–67) and need not detain us here. It is worth noting, however, that whereas cluster analysis can make it seem as if a network has merely learned a set of static distributed symbols and is thus little more than a novel implementation of the classical approach, principal component analysis reveals the role of even deeper dynamics in promoting successful behavior. The key idea is that whereas cluster analysis stresses relations of similarity and difference between static states ("snapshots"), PCA reflects in addition the ways in which being in one state (in a recurrent network) can promote or impede movement into future states. Standard cluster analysis would not reveal these constraints on processing trajectories. Yet the grammatical knowledge acquired by the recurrent net inheres quite profoundly in such temporally rich information-processing detail.[2]

The more such temporal dynamics matter, the further we move (I contend) from the guiding image of the basic physical symbol system hypothesis. For at the heart of that image lies the notion of essentially static symbol structures that retain stable meanings while being manipulated by some kind of central processor. Such a picture, however, does not usefully describe the operation of even the simple recurrent networks previously discussed. For the hidden unit activation patterns (the nearest analogue to static symbols) do not function as fixed representations of word-role. This is because each such pattern reflects something of the prior context,[3] so that, in a sense, "every occurrence of a lexical item has a separate internal representation" (Elman, 1991b, p. 353). Elman's model thus uses so-called dynamic representations. Unlike the classical image in which the linguistic agent, on hearing a word, retrieves a kind of general-purpose lexical representation, Elman is suggesting a dynamic picture in which

> There is no separate stage of lexical retrieval. There are no representations of words in isolation. The representations of words (the internal states following input of a word) always reflect the input taken together with the prior state . . . the representations are not propositional and their information content changes constantly over time . . . words serve as guideposts which help establish mental states that support (desired) behavior. (Elman, 1991b, p. 378)

Elman thus invites us to see beyond the classical image of static symbols that persist as stored syntactic items and that are "retrieved" and "manipulated" during processing. Instead, we confront an image of a fluid inner economy in which representations are constructed on the spot and in light of the prevailing context and in which much of the information-processing power resides in the way current states constrain the future temporal unfolding of the system.

Third-generation connectionism continues this flight from the (static) inner symbol by laying even greater stress on a much wider range of dynamic and time-involving properties. For this reason it is sometimes known as "dynamical connectionism." Dynamical connectionism (see Wheeler, 1994, p. 38; Port and van Gelder, 1995, pp. 32–34) introduces a number of new and more neurobiologically realistic features to the basic units and weights paradigm, including special purpose units (units whose activation function is tailored to a task or domain), more complex connectivity (multiple recurrent pathways and special purpose wiring), computationally salient time delays in the processing cycles, continuous-time processing, analog signaling, and the deliberate use of noise. Artificial neural networks

---

[2]See Elman (1991b, p. 106).

[3]Even the first word in a sentence incorporates a kind of "null" context that is reflected in the network state.

exhibiting such nonstandard features support "far richer intrinsic dynamics than those produced by mainstream connectionist systems" (Wheeler, 1994, p. 38). We shall have more to say about the potential role of such richer and temporally loaded dynamics in future chapters. For the moment, it will suffice to note that second- and third-generation connectionist research is becoming progressively more and more dynamic: it is paying more heed to the temporal dimension and it is exploiting a wider variety of types of units and connectivity. In so doing, it is moving ever further from the old notion of intelligence as the manipulation of static, atemporal, spatially localizable inner symbols.

The connectionist movement, it is fair to conclude, is the leading expression of "inner symbol flight." The static, chunky, user-friendly, semantically transparent (see Chapter 2) inner symbols of yore are being replaced by subtler, often highly distributed and increasingly dynamic (time-involving) inner states. This is, I believe, a basically laudable transition. Connectionist models profit from (increasing) contact with real neuroscientific theorizing. And they exhibit a profile of strengths (motor control, pattern recognition) and weaknesses (planning and sequential logical derivation) that seems reassuringly familiar and evolutionarily plausible. They look to avoid, in large measure, the uncomfortable back-projection of our experiences with text and words onto the more basic biological canvass of the brain. But the new landscape brings new challenges, problems, and uncertainties. Time to meet the bugbears.

4.2 Discussion

A. CONNECTIONISM AND MENTAL CAUSATION

Connectionism, according to some philosophers, offers a concrete challenge to the folk psychological image of mind. The leading idea, once again, is that folk psychology is committed to the causal efficacy of the mental states named in ordinary discourse, and that there is now a tension between such imagined causal efficacy and the specific connectionist vision of inner processing and storage.

The key move in this argument is the insistence that the folk framework is indeed committed to a strong and direct notion of causal efficacy. In this vein, Ramsey, Stich, and Garon (1991) insist that the commonsense understanding of mind involves a crucial commitment to what they term "propositional modularity." This is the claim that the folk use of propositional attitude talk (talk of Pepa's believing that the wine is chilled and so on) implies a commitment to "*functionally discrete, semantically interpretable* states that play a *causal role* in the production of other propositional attitudes and ultimately in the production of behavior" (Ramsey, Stich, and Garon, 1991, p. 204, original emphasis). Ramsey, Stich, and Garon argue that distributed connectionist processing does not support such propositional modularity and hence that if human minds work like such devices, then the folk vision is fundamentally inaccurate.

Why suppose that the folk are committed to propositional modularity anyway? The evidence is in part anecdotal (we do talk of people gaining or losing beliefs one at a time and in that sense we seem to depict the beliefs, etc., as discrete
items—Ramsey, Stich, and Garon, 1991, p. 205) and in part substantive. The substantive evidence is that the very usefulness of the folk framework seems to depend
on our being able to cite specific beliefs as explanatory of specific actions. Pepa
may believe that the cat wants feeding, that Rome is pretty, and that the wine is
chilled, but we reserve the right to explain her going into the kitchen as a direct
result of her belief about the wine. The cat belief, though real and capable of
prompting the same behavior, may be imagined to be inactive at that moment.
And the Rome belief strikes us as simply irrelevant. In thus highlighting one belief
in the explanation of Pepa's action, we are committing ourselves, the authors argue, to the idea that individual beliefs can function as the discrete *causes* of specific actions.

This commitment sits comfortably with the traditional kind of A.I. model in
which specific inner syntactic states correspond to specific items of information
pitched at the level of daily talk and concepts. But this combination of inner discretion[4] and "semantic transparency" (see Chapter 2) is not, it seems, to be found
in distributed connectionist models. One major reason (the only one that will concern us here: for a full discussion see Clark (1993, Chapter 10) turns on the connectionist's use of overlapping ("superpositional") modes of information storage.
To focus the problem, Ramsey, Stich, and Garon ask us to consider two networks,
each of which is trained to give a yes/no answer to the same set of 16 questions.
To the input "dogs have fur" it must output a signal for "yes," to "fish have fur,"
"no," and so on. To perform the task, the net must find a single weight matrix that
supports the desired functionality. The use of distributed storage techniques (see
discussion above) means, however, that many of the weights and units implicated
in the encoding of the knowledge that dogs have fur will also figure in the encoding of the knowledge that cats have fur and so on. Here, then, is a first (putative)
conflict with propositional modularity. The conflict comes about because

> The information encoded . . . is stored holistically and distributed throughout the net-
> work. Whenever information is extracted . . . many connection strengths, many biases
> and many hidden units play a role. (Ramsey, Stich, and Garon, 1991, p. 212)

The idea, then, is that the use of overlapping storage leads to a kind of inner
mush such that, as far as the innards are concerned, it is no more defensible to say
that the knowledge that dogs have fur caused the response "yes," than to say that
the cause was the knowledge that fish have gills! This is the threat of what Stich

---

[4]Note, however, that even in the classical case the inner discretion is functional not physical. Many
models that are functionally classical are also physically nonlocal in their storage of information. For
some discussion, see Clark (1993, Chapter 10).

(1991, p. 181) once termed *total causal holism*. Total causal holism, it should be clear, is not prima facie compatible with the idea of individual beliefs as discrete causes. A second types of conflict (Ramsey, Stich, and Garon, 1991, p. 213) is re- vealed if we compare the original 16-proposition net to another net trained on one additional item of knowledge. Such a 17-proposition network accommodates the additional knowledge by making small changes to a lot of weights. The folk see a lot of commonality between the two nets. Both nets share, e.g., the belief that dogs have fur. But this commonality is said to be invisible at the level of units and weights. The two nets, thus described, may have no subset of weights in common. Once again, the folk image sits uneasily beside its inner-oriented scien- tific cousin.

There are three main ways to respond to these worries about surface incom- patibility. The first is to insist that the incompatibility is indeed merely surface and that more sensitive probing will reveal the inner scientific analogue to the folk vi- sion. The second is to question the commitment of the folk framework to the ex- istence of such inner analogues in the first place (see discussion in Section 3.2). The third is to accept the incompatibility and conclude that *if* distributed connec- tionist networks are good models of human cognition, then the folk framework is false and should be rejected. We have already discussed some of these issues in Chapter 3. So I shall add just a few comments aimed at the specific connectionist incarnation just described.

It is important, at the outset, that we should not be overly impressed by ar- guments that focus on the units and weights description of connectionist networks. We already saw, in our discussion of cluster analysis (Section 4.1 and Box 4.3), that there may be scientifically legitimate and functionally illuminating descriptions of connectionist networks pitched at much higher levels than that of units and weights. Thus recall that the various versions of NETtalk (beginning with different assign- ments of random weights) ended up with very different weight matrixes yet yielded almost identical cluster analytic profiles. Such higher-level commonality may like- wise unite e.g., the 16 and 17 proposition networks mentioned above. By the same token, the worry about total causal holism looks wildly overstated. It is simply not the case that all the units and all the weights participate equally in every input-to- output transition. Techniques such as cluster analysis help reveal the precise ways in which these complex networks make different uses of their inner resources in the course of solving different problems.

A revealing exchange, which turns entirely on this possibility, can be traced through Ramsey, Stich, and Garon (1991), Clark (1990), Stich and Warfield (1995), Fodor and LePore (1993) and P. M. Churchland (1993). In barest essence, the story goes like this. Clark (1990) discussed the possibility of finding higher level com- monalities (via techniques of statistical analysis) between superficially disparate network: commonalities that revealed folk-identified types (specific beliefs, etc.) hidden among the numerical spaghetti. Stich and Warfield (1995) reject this, noting that the common cluster analysis of versions of NETtalk were all based on nets with identical architectures (numbers of units, layers, etc.) and just different initial weights. Yet, the differences between biological brains that solve similar problems may surely be much more profound, involving different network architectures, numbers of units, etc. So such analytic techniques look unlikely to apply. Fodor and LePore (1993) raise a similar worry for the more general idea of what Paul Churchland (1993) dubbed a "state-space semantics," viz. a way of understanding semantic similarity and differences rooted in geometric analysis of connectionist-style representational systems. Most recently, Churchland (1998), drawing on new work by Laakso and Cottrell (1998), argued that there now exists "a large family of mathematical measures of conceptual similarity, measures that see past differences—even extensive differences—in the connectivity, the sensory inputs and the neural dimensionality of the systems being compared" (Churchland and Churchland, 1998, p. 81). Without pursuing this rather complex exchange any further here, I simply note that these recent results suggest that pace Stich and Warfield, the empirical possibility highlighted in Clark (1990) remains a live and analytically tractable option. Connectionist networks, it is thus increasingly clear, by no means present the kind of analytic mush that some philosophers once feared.

B. SYSTEMATICITY

The most famous argument against connectionist models of human thought goes like this:

Thought is systematic;

So internal representations are structured;

Connectionist models lack structured internal representations;

So connectionist models are not good models of human thought.

Classical artificial intelligence, by contrast, is said to posit structured internal representations and thus to have the necessary[5] resources to explain human thought. Such, at least, is the view of Fodor and Pylyshyn (1988), whose so-called systematicity argument against connectionism (qua psychological model) is displayed above. Let us put some flesh on the bones.

   The argument pivots on the claim that thought is systematic. The idea of systematic thought is best explained by analogy with systematic linguistic competence. A speaker who knows English and can say "the cat loves John" will usually be equally capable of forming the sentence "John loves the cat." This is because to know a language is to know its parts and how they fit together. The very same competence (with "John" "loving" "cat" and subject–object formations) thus yields the capacity to generate a variety of sentences involving those parts. The phenomenon

---

[5]Though not yet sufficient. See Fodor (1991, pp. 279–280).

of systematicity is thus observed whenever we find a set of capacities that appear to be compositional variations on a single structured substrate [think of the capacity of a cook, armed with a set of basic ingredients, to prepare a wide variety of related pizzas: cheese and red pepper, tuna and red pepper, tuna and cheese (yuck!) and so on]. Linguistic competence provides a clear example. But thought itself (so Fodor and Pylyshyn argue) is another. Beings who can think that John loves Mary can usually think (if the occasion arises) that Mary loves John. And the explanation, so the argument goes, is the same. The systematicity of thought is an effect of the compositionally structured inner base, which includes manipulable inner expressions meaning "John" "loves" and "Mary" and resources for combining them. The systematicity of thought is thus presented as an argument in favor of a classical vision of the inner economy, and against the connectionist alternative.

This argument has spawned a mass of widely differing (but usually negative) responses.[6] But the two most important, it seems to me, are (1) the reply that classical symbol systems are not the only way to support systematically structured cognition and (2) the suggestion that human thought may actually inherit such systemacity as it actually displays from the grammatical structure of human language itself.

The search for a genuinely connectionist (hence nonclassical) model of systematic cognitive capacities has been most persuasively pursued by Paul Smolensky who investigated connectionist techniques such as tensor product encodings. The idea here[7] is to decompose target knowledge into roles and fillers. Thus to represent the ordered string $\langle A,B,C \rangle$ you represent both a set of three roles, which indicate position in the string, i.e., [position 1, position 2, position 3] and three fillers, the letters $[A]$, $[B]$, and $[C]$. Each letter and position (role and filler) get a distinct connectionist "vectorial" representation and the two are bound together by a process known as vector multiplication. The result is that such a system can differentially represent $\langle A,B,C \rangle$ and $\langle B,C,A \rangle$. Yet the resultant representations do not simply mimic the classical trick of stringing constituents together. Instead the structural representation is just another vector (a sequence of numbers) resulting from the multiplication of the base vectors. It is for this reason that such a system [as van Gelder (1990) nicely explains] does not simply amount to a variant implementation of the original classical strategy.

Chalmers (1990) offers another connectionist angle on systematic structure. He uses a technique called recursive autoassociative memory[8] (or RAAM) to develop compressed representations of sentence structure trees. Chalmers showed that a connectionist network could learn to operate directly upon these compressed

---

[6]See the various essays in MacDonald and MacDonald (1995, Part I), Ramsey, Stich, and Rumelhart (1991), Chalmers (1990), and van Gelder (1990).

[7]See Smolensky (1991) and van Gelder (1990).

[8]See Pollack (1988).

descriptions and hence perform structure-sensitive transformations (such as turning an active sentence into a passive one) without first unpacking the RAAM encoding into its original constituents. The conclusion was that compositional structure, of the kind highlighted by Fodor and Pylyshyn, could be encoded in a
distinctively connectionist way (the RAAM encodings) and directly exploited in
that form.

Further discussion of the details and the problems afflicting these approaches
can be found in Clark (1993, Chapter 6). The present point, however, is just this:
it is an empirical question whether there can be a distinctively connectionist account of cognitive systematicity, and there are already some signs of progress. I
would just add, however, that the notion that the root issue concerns the use of
highly structured inner encodings may itself be something of a distortion. The
deeper challenge (and one that is still largely unmet) is to discover connectionist
methods that support the *multiple usability* of bodies of stored information. Current networks tend to be very task specific. Yet human agents can call on the same
body of knowledge in the service of many different types of projects. This capacity (which looks closely related to, yet not identical with, systematicity as invoked
by Fodor and Pylyshyn) is currently being studied using techniques such as "gating," in which the flow of information is varied using subnetworks whose job is to
open and close channels of internal influence (see, e.g., Van Essen et al., 1994; Jacobs, Jordan, and Barto, 1991).

The other major response to the problem of systematicity is to downplay the
extent and importance of cognitive systematicity itself. This response is deeply com-
plimentary to the more technical ones just sketched since the technical tricks look
set to buy a degree of systematicity, multiusability etc., but may well still fall short
of providing the equivalent of an extreme version of classical inner symbol manipulability. In place of such extreme manipulability (the kind bought by a common central database and unitary symbolic code—see Chapter 2) we will probably confront a more modular system, with no central symbolic code, but with a
dynamically reconfigurable web of inner channels of influence. Such systems must
build task flexibility on top of a mass of relatively special-purpose adaptations. The
trouble with this kind of "bag-of-tricks" response is that it is not clear how it can
scale up to explain the full gamut of human thought and reason. One possible
way to fill in the gaps is to stress (Dennett, 1991, 1995; Clark 1997, 1998a) the
cognition-enhancing and cognitive-transforming powers of public language itself.
The presence of a public code in which real chunky external symbols are indeed
widely recombinable and highly manipulable adds whole new dimensions to basic
biological cognition. [This is demonstrated in careful empirical detail for the special case of mathematical knowledge in Dehaene (1997).] Perhaps, then, it is these
new (and relatively recent) dimensions that give human thought the appearance
of such deep systematicity. We possess a new tool—language—that sculpts and
guides our thought in new ways. Fodor and Pylyshyn believe that our basic cog-

nitive architecture, the one we share with nonlinguistic animals such as dogs and rabbits, itself takes the form of a symbol-manipulating classical system. Their claim is not about us alone but about intelligent creatures in general. Yet as Dennett (1991b, p. 27) points out, it is not at all obvious that (nonhuman) animal thought is systematic in the Fodor and Pylyshyn sense. The lion that can think "I want to eat the puppy" may well be congenitally unable to think that "the puppy wants to eat me." It seems at least possible that it is our experiences with public language that equip us to think such an open-ended variety of thoughts and hence that cognitive systematicity may be both nonpervasive and rather closely tied to our linguistic abilities themselves.

In sum, the systematicity argument draws attention to two important phenomena: the capacity to make multiple use of stored bodies of information and the capacity to encode knowledge in structured ways. But genuinely connectionist proposals exist addressing both of these needs to a limited extent. In addition, it remains unclear whether full systematicity, as treated by Fodor and Pylyshyn, reflects facts about our basic cognitive architecture or about the effects of a more recent linguistic overlay.

C. BIOLOGICAL REALITY?

The most telling criticisms of first wave connectionism were those that questioned its biological plausibility. Such criticisms were sometimes misguided, to be sure. Any model must simplify in order to explain. But three species of biologically based criticism seem to hit the mark.

One worry concerns the use of artificial tasks, and the choice of input and output representations. For although such networks learned their own solutions to given problems, what they learned remained heavily tainted by a variety of choices made by the human experimentalist. Such choices included, especially, the choice of problem domain and the choice of training materials. As far as problem domains went, the trouble was that much of the classical conception of the nature of the problems themselves was retained. Many networks were devoted to investigating what have been termed "horizontal microworlds": small slices of human-level cognition such as the capacity to produce the past tense of English verbs (Rumelhart and McClelland, 1986) or to learn simple grammars (Elman, 1991a). Even when the tasks looked more basic (e.g., balancing building blocks on a beam that pivots on a movable fulcrum—McClelland, 1989; Plunkett and Sinha, 1992), the choice of input and output representations was often very artificial. The output of the block-balancing program, for example, was not real motor action involving robot arms, nor even coding for such action. Rather, it was just the relative activity of two output units interpreted so that equal activity on both indicates an expectation of a state of balance and excess activity on either unit indicates an expectation that the beam will overbalance in that direction. The inputs to the system, likewise, were artificial—an arbitrary coding for weight along one input channel and for distance from the fulcrum along another. It is not unreasonable to suppose that this way of setting up the problem space might well lead to nonrealistic, artifactual solutions. An alternative and perhaps better strategy would surely be to set up the system to take more biologically realistic inputs (e.g., using cameras) and to yield real actions as outputs (moving real blocks to a point of balance). Of course, such a set-up requires the solution of many additional problems, and science must always simplify experiments when possible. The suspicion, however, is that simplifications that take the real world and the acting organism out of the loop are ones that cognitive science can no longer afford. For such simplifications may obscure the kinds of solutions to ecologically realistic problems that characterize the intelligence of active embodied agents such as ourselves. The aspirations of cognitive science to illuminate real biological cognition may thus not be commensurate with a continuing strategy of abstraction away from the real-world anchors of perception and action. Such abstraction also deprives our artificial systems of the opportunity to simplify or otherwise transform their information-processing tasks by the direct exploitation of real-world structure. Examples of such exploitation include using the world as its own model (see, e.g., Brooks, 1991) and physically restructuring the environment so as to reduce the computational complexity of problem solving (see Chapters 5–8).

A second problem is that early connectionist networks tended to use relatively small resources of units and connections (compared to the brain) to tackle relatively discrete and well-defined problems. Nets tend, as we commented earlier, to be trained on artificial versions of real-world problems: versions that dramatically downsize the input and output vectors that real sensory data and motor control would demand. Moreover, they are usually focused on a single problem. Nature's neural networks, by contrast, must deal with very high dimensional inputs and outputs, and must somehow cope with the fact that we are often assailed by batches of data that will pertain to multiple problems and thus require internal sorting and distribution. As Churchland and Sejnowski (1992, p. 125) comment, "visual information concerning motion, stereo, shape, etc. has to be separated by the nervous system and objects do not arrive at the retina bagged and labeled." The flip side of this kind of separation is also observed. Biological neural nets will usually contribute to several kinds of problem-solving tasks, at least as we intuitively identify such tasks. The "one net, one task" ethos may thus constitute a substantial distortion of the biological facts (see Karmiloff-Smith, 1992).

Solutions that work well for small networks with a narrow focus thus often fail dismally to scale-up to deal with large input spaces and multiple tasks. Speech recognition networks can deal with a single voice enunciating staccato words. But any attempt to deal with multiple voices producing continuous speech can cause havoc in such networks. Nor does simply expanding the network generally solve the problem. Bigger networks require more training time and data. And even these will often fail due to the phenomenon of "unlearning." Here, the attempt to accommodate a new pattern of data (involving, say, recognition of vowel sounds in a child's speech) results in the network overwriting (and hence forgetting) other information (e.g., how to recognize the same sounds in male adult speech)—see French (1992, 1999).

How might real neural networks cope? One reasonably well-understood strategy involves using a network of networks in place of a single resource. Complex real-world problems, it seems, often demand highly articulated processing architectures. For example, the problem of multispeaker vowel recognition yields to an architecture involving a group of smaller networks, each of which learns to specialize in the processing of a particular type of voice (e.g., adult male, adult female, child—see Churchland and Sejnowski, 1992, pp. 125–130; Jacobs, Jordan, Nowlan, and Hinton, 1991). Moreover, the idea that the brain may operate using a wide multiplicity of relatively special purpose subnetworks is one that finds increasing support in contemporary neuroscience (see Chapter 5).

The third problem is that most artificial neural networks remain rather distant from the details of real neuroscientific research. Real neuronal assemblies exhibit a wide variety of properties missing from (most) connectionist models. These include nonlocal effects [e.g., the modification of the response of a whole population of neurons by the diffusion of a gas or chemical over a wide area—see discussion in Brooks (1994) and the work on "Gas nets" by Husbands et al. (1998)], continuous-time processing, the use of a variety of different types of activation function, and of heavily recurrent but nonsymmetrical connectivity. Models that incorporate such features exhibit a whole range of dynamic properties[9] not found in simple first-wave systems.

In addition, more sustained attention to the details of gross neuroanatomy may, at times, pay dividends. Thus McClelland et al. (1995) ask the question "why have a hippocampus?" This paper constitutes a nice example of how connectionist thinking and neuroscientific research may fruitfully coevolve. It sets out to determine a possible computational role for a known neural structure by hypothesizing that that structure (the hippocampus) is able to slowly train a further resource (the neocortex) on newly acquired patterns, thus sidestepping the endemic problem (see above) of unlearning or catastrophic forgetting. This hypothesis lies squarely at the intersection between basic connectionist principles and problems (the tendency of new patterns to overwrite old ones) and neuroscientific data and neuroanatomy. Such coevolution of connectionist and neuroscientific conjecture suggests one major way in which connectionists can begin to face up to the challenges of understanding real biological cognition.

The first wave of connectionist research played, I conclude, a crucial role in the expansion of our computational horizons. It showed, in real detail, that it is

[9]See Wheeler (1994).

possible to solve complex problems without the standard symbol-manipulating apparatus associated with the original physical symbol system hypothesis. To complete the revolution, however, we must both expand and tune the new perspective. The tuning involves the incorporation of a wider range of features and dynamics, and is pursued in Chapters 5 through 8. The expansion involves recognizing the profound roles played by external and nonbiological resources in the promotion of cognitive success. Such resources include bodily action, instruments and artifacts, the local environment, and external symbol structures. The result is a vision of cognitive agency in which the inner and the outer play complementary and deeply interwoven roles and in which the inner computational story is almost maximally distant from the classical vision explored in previous chapters. This alternative vision is biologically plausible, conceptually attractive, and computationally economical. But it brings with it a new and fascinating set of hurdles and problems, as we shall soon see.

4.3 Suggested Readings

On *connectionism*. J. McClelland, D. Rumelhart, and the PDP Research Group (eds.), *Parallel Distributed Processing: Explorations in the Microstructure of Cognition* (Cambridge, MA: MIT Press, 1986, Vols. I and II) is still the best introduction to the connectionist research program. User-friendly treatments include A. Clark, *Microcognition*, (Cambridge, MA: MIT Press, 1989) and *Associative Engines* (Cambridge, MA: MIT Press, 1993). P. M. Churchland's *The Engine of Reason: The Seat of the Soul* (Cambridge, MA: MIT Press, 1995) is a superbly accessible account of the connectionist paradigm. It includes substantial discussion of recurrent nets and ends with some chapters on moral and social implications. S. Franklin's *Artificial Minds* (Cambridge, MA: MIT Press, 1995), has useful chapters on connectionism and the connectionist/classicist debate (Chapters 6 and 7). For a more advanced treatment, see P. S. Churchland and T. J. Sejnowski, *The Computational Brain* (Cambridge, MA: MIT Press, 1992, Chapter 3).

    An illuminating recent exchange concerning *connectionism and symbolic rules* can be found in G. Marcus et al., "Rule learning by 7 month old infants." *Science*, 283, 77–80, 1999; J. McClelland and D. Plaut "Does generalization in infants learning implicate abstract algebra-like rules?" *Trends in Cognitive Sciences*, 3(5), 166–168, 1999, and the reply by G. Marcus in the same issue.

    On *folk psychology and systematicity*. The collection edited by C. McDonald and G. McDonald, *Connectionism: Debates on Psychological Explanation* (Oxford, England: Blackwell, 1995) is excellent and fairly comprehensive. A wider ranging discussion is found in W. Ramsey, S. Stich, and D. Rumelhart (eds.), *Philosophy and Connectionist Theory* (Hillsdale, NJ: Erlbaum, 1991). The roles of *language and of external symbol structures* are discussed in D. Dennett, *Darwin's Dangerous Idea* (New York: Simon & Schuster, 1995) and in A. Clark, *Being There* (Cambridge, MA: MIT Press, 1997).

    On *biological plausibility*. For an honest and sophisticated discussion of the neural plausibility of connectionist models, see P. S. Churchland and T. J. Sejnowski's *The Computational Brain* (Cambridge, MA: MIT Press, 1992). For a critical assault, see G. Reeke and G. Edelman, "Real brains and artificial intelligence." *Daedalus*, Winter, 143–173, 1988, reprinted in S. R. Graubard (ed.), *The Artificial Intelligence Debate* (Cambridge, MA: MIT Press, 1988).

On the questions of *state-space semantics and of measures of conceptual similarity across networks of differing gross architectures*, see the exchanges between Fodor and LePore and P. M. Churchland in R. McCauley (ed.), *The Churchlands and Their Critics* (Oxford, England: Blackwell, 1996, Chapter 6) and reply C, the exchange between Clark and Stich and Warfield in C. MacDonald and G. MacDonald (eds.), *Connectionism: Debates on Psychological Explanation* (Oxford, England: Blackwell, 1995, Chapters 9 and 11) and Paul Churchland's recent reply to Fodor and LePore in P. M. Churchland and P. S. Churchland, *On the Contrary: Critical Essays 1987–1997* (Cambridge, MA: MIT Press, 1998, Chapter 7). All three of the volumes can also be recommended for a general overview of the intense philosophical controversies surrounding connectionist approaches.

Finally, to get a sense of just how far connectionism has progressed from its origins in simple, three-layer feedforward networks, take a look at the special edition of *Connection Science* on Biorobotics: *Connection Science*, 10(314), 1998.

PERCEPTION, ACTION, AND THE BRAIN

5.1 Sketches

It is time to revisit one of the guiding motivations behind the computational approach to understanding cognition. The motivation was nicely expressed in the 1980s by David Marr, a major figure in the history of artificial intelligence. Reflecting on typical neuroscientific studies of neural organization and structure (work in which Marr had been personally involved) he suggested that there remained a need for

> [some] additional level of understanding at which the character of the information-processing tasks carried out . . . are analyzed and understood in a way that is independent of the particular mechanisms and structures that implement them in our heads (Marr, 1982, p. 19)

The strategy that Marr proposed was to divide the explanatory task into three. First, and most important, there was to be a (level one) general analysis of the *task* being performed [e.g., localizing a prey via sonar, identifying three-dimensional (3D) objects via two-dimensional (2D) visual input, doing addition, sorting a set of numbers into sequence, whatever]. This would involve pinning down a precise input–output function, and addressing the question of what subtasks would need to be carried out in solving the problem. Then, with the task thus a little better understood, you could (level two) go on to describe a scheme for *representing* the inputs and outputs, and a *sequence of mechanical steps* that would carry out the task. And finally (level three), having achieved such a clear but still abstract understanding of both the task and a sequence of steps to carry it out, you could address the most concrete question: how do we actually *build* a device capable of running through the sequence of steps. These three levels of analysis were dubbed the levels of computational theory (or better, task analysis), of representation and algorithm, and of implementation, respectively. Merely understanding what the neural structures underlying, say, vision were and how the neurons fired and were organized would amount only to an appreciation of the implementation of a *still-not-understood abstract strategy* for, e.g., transforming 2D retinal inputs into a 3D model of the visual scene. What is missing—and explanatorily crucial—is an understanding of the details of the task (level one) and the set of information-processing steps (the level two algorithm) involved.

Until the late 1980s many cognitive scientists took the Marr framework as a license to ignore or downplay the importance of understanding the biological brain. It is not hard to see why. The brain, it was agreed, is in some sense the physical engine of cognition and mindfulness. But everything that really *mattered* about the brain (qua mind-producing engine) seemed to turn not on the physical details but on the computational and information-processing strategies (level one and two) that the brain ("merely") implemented. In addition, the state of neuroscientific understanding in those early days was widely perceived as too undeveloped to afford much in the way of real constraints on computational theorizing—although some of Marr's own early work, interestingly, makes among the best and most computationally informative uses of the neuroscientific data that was then available.[1]

Marr's three-level framework now looks to have been just a little bit *too* neat. In the real world, as we shall see, the distinctions among task, algorithm, and implementation are not always crystal clear. More importantly, the process of *discovering* good computational or information-processing models of natural cognition can and should be deeply informed by neuroscientific understanding. Indeed the two forms of understanding should ideally coevolve in a richly interanimated style.

What was *correct* about the Marr framework was surely this: that *merely* understanding the physiology was not enough. To grasp the origins of mindfulness in the organization and activity of neural matter we need to understand how the system is organized at higher, more abstract levels, and we may need to associate aspects of that organization with the computation of cognitively relevant functions. This point is forcefully made by the cognitive scientist Brian Cantwell Smith (1996, p. 148) who draws a parallel with the project of understanding ordinary computer systems. With respect to, e.g., a standard PC running a tax-calculation program, we could quite easily answer all the "physiological" questions (using source code and wiring diagrams) yet still lack any real understanding of what the program does or even how it works. To really understand how mental activity yields mental states, many theorists believe, we must likewise understand something of the computational/information-processing organization of the brain. Physiological

---

[1]See Marr (1969) and various papers in Vaina (1991).

studies may contribute to this understanding. But even a full physiological story would not, in and of itself, reveal how brains work *qua* mind-producing engines.

The danger, to repeat, was that this observation could be used as an excuse to downplay or marginalize the importance of looking at the biological brain *at all*. But although it is true that a computational understanding, when we have it, is in principle independent of the details of any specific implementation in hardware (or wetware), the project of *discovering* the relevant computational description (especially for biological systems) is quite definitely not.

One key factor here is evolution. Biological brains are the product of biological evolution and as such often fail to function in the ways we (as human designers) might expect.[2] The abstract "design stance" (see Dennett, 1987, and Chapter 3) that we are invited to take at Marr's levels one and two is hostage to both our intuitive ideas about what the cognitive tasks really are (is vision really about achieving a mapping from 2D input onto a 3D world model? We will later find cause for doubt) and to our relatively prejudiced sense of the space of possible designs. Biological evolution, by contrast, is both constrained and liberated in ways we are not. It is *constrained* to build its solutions incrementally on top of simpler but successful ancestral forms. The human lung, to give one example, is built via a process of "tinkering" (Jacob, 1977) with the swim bladder of the fish. The human engineer might design a better lung from scratch. The tinkerer, by contrast, must take an existing device and subtly adapt it to a new role. From the engineer's ahistorical perspective, the tinkerer's solution may look bizarre. Likewise, the processing strategies used by biological brains may surprise the computer scientist. For such strategies have themselves been evolved via a process of incremental, piecemeal, tinkering with older solutions.

More positively, biological evolution is *liberated* by being able to discover efficient but "messy" or unobvious solutions that may, for example, exploit environmental interactions and feedback loops so complex that they would quickly baffle a human engineer. Natural solutions (as we will later see) can exploit just about any mixture of neural, bodily, and environmental resources along with their complex, looping, and often nonlinear interactions. Biological evolution is thus able to explore a very different solution space (wider in some dimensions, narrower in others) than that which beckons to conscious human reason.

Recent work in cognitive neuroscience emphasizes the distance-separating biological and "engineered" problem solutions, and displays an increasing awareness of the important interpenetration—in biological systems—of perception, thought, and action. Some brief examples should help fix the flavor.

As a gentle entry point, consider some recent work on the neural control of monkey finger motions. Traditional wisdom depicted the monkey's fingers as individually controlled by neighboring groups of spatially clustered neurons. Ac-

---

[2]See, e.g., Simon (1969), Dawkins (1986), and Clark (1997, Chapter 5).

cording to this story, the neurons (in Motor Area 1, or M1) were organized as a "somatotopic map" in which a dedicated neural subregion governed each individual digit, with the subregions arranged in spatial sequence just like the fingers on each hand. This is a tidy, easily conceptualized solution to the problem of finger control. But it is the engineer's solution, not (it now seems) that of Nature.

Schieber and Hibbard (1993) have shown that individual finger movements are accompanied by activity spread pretty well throughout the M1 hand area, and that precise, single-digit movements actually require *more* activity than some multidigit whole hand actions (such as grasping an object). Such results are inconsistent with the hypothesis of digit-specific local neuronal groups. From a more evolutionary perspective, however, the rationale is obvious. Schieber (1990, p. 444) conjectures that the basic ancestral need was for whole hand-grasping motions (used to grab branches, to swing, to acquire fruits, etc.) and that the most fundamental neural adaptations are thus geared to allow simple commands to exploit naturally selected inbuilt synergies[3] of muscle and tendon so as to yield such coordinated motions. The "complex" coordinated case is thus evolutionarily basic and neurally simpler. The "simple" task of controlling, e.g., an individual digit represents the harder problem and requires more neural activity, viz. the use of some motor cortex neurons to *inhibit* the naturally coordinated activity of the other digits. Precise single-digit movements thus require the neural control system to tinker with whole-hand commands, modifying the basic coordinated dynamics (of mechanically linked tendons, etc.) geared to the more common (whole-hand) tasks.

Consider next a case of perceptual adaptation. The human perceptual system can, we know (given time and training), adapt in quite powerful ways to distorted or position-shifted inputs. For example, subjects can learn how to coordinate vision and action while wearing lenses that invert the entire visual scene so that the world initially appears upside down. After wearing such lenses for a few days, the world is seen to flip over—various aspects of the world now appear to the subject to be in the normal upright position. Remove the lenses and the scene is again inverted until readaptation occurs.[4] Thach et al. (1992) used a variant of such experiments to demonstrate the motor specificity of some perceptual adaptations. Wearing lenses that shifted the scene *sideways* a little, subjects were asked to throw darts at a board. In this case, repeated practice led to successful adaptation,[5] but of a motor-loop-specific kind. The compensation did not "carry over" to tasks in-

---

[3]The notion of synergy aims to capture the idea of links that constrain the collective unfolding of a system comprising many parts. For example, the front wheels of a car exhibit a built-in synergy that allows a single driver "command" (at the steering wheel) to affect them both at once. Synergetic links may also be learned, as when we acquire an automated skill, and may be neurally as well as brute-physiologically grounded. See Kelso (1995, pp. 38, 52).

[4]For a survey of such experiments, see Welch (1978).

[5]In this case, *without* any perceived change in phenomenology.

volving the use of the nondominant hand to throw, or to an underarm variant of the usual overarm throw. Instead, adaptation looked to be restricted to a quite specific combination of gaze angle and throwing angle: the one used in overarm, dominant-hand throwing.

Something of the neural mechanisms of such adaptation is now understood.[6] The general lesson, however, concerns the nature of the perception–action system itself. For it increasingly appears that the simple image of a general purpose perceptual system delivering input to a distinct and fully independent action system is biologically distortive. Instead, perceptual and action systems work together, in the context of specific tasks, to promote adaptive success. Perception and action, in this view, form a deeply interanimated unity.

Further evidence for such a view comes from a variety of sources. Consider, for example, the fact that the primate visual system relies on processing strategies that are not strictly hierarchic but instead depend on a variety of top-to-bottom and side-to-side channels of influence. These complex inner pathways allow a combination of multiple types of information (high-level intentions, low-level perception, and motor activity) to influence all stages of visual processing. (see Box 5.1)

Such complex connectivity opens up a wealth organizational possibilities in which multiple sources of information combine to support visually guided action. Examples of such combinations are provided by Churchland, Ramachandran, and Sejnowski (1994), who offer a neurophysiologically grounded account of what they term "interactive vision." The interactive vision paradigm is there contrasted with approaches that assume a simple division of labor in which perceptual processing yields a rich, detailed inner representation of the 3D visual scene, which is then given as input to the reasoning and planning centers, which in turn calculate a course of action and send commands to the motor effectors. This simple image (of what roboticists call a "sense–think–act" cycle) is, it now seems, not true to the natural facts. In particular:

1. Daily agent–environment interactions seem not to depend on the construction and use of detailed inner models of the full 3D scene.

2. Low-level perception may "call" motor routines that yield *better perceptual input* and hence improve information pick-up.

3. Real-world actions may sometimes play an important role in the computational process itself.

4. The internal representation of worldly events and structures may be less like a passive data structure or description and more like a direct recipe for action.

---

[6]It is known, for example, that the adaptation never occurs in patients with generalized cerebellar cortical atrophy, and that inferior olive hypertrophy leads to impaired adaptation. On the basis of this and other evidence, Thach et al. (1992) speculate that a learning system implicating the inferior olive and the cerebellum (linked via climbing fibers) is active both in prism adaptation and in the general learning of patterned responses to frequently encountered stimuli.

Box 5.1

MACAQUE VISUAL SYSTEM: THE SUBWAY MAP

The Macaque monkey (to take one well-studied example) possesses about 32 visual brain areas (see Figure 5.1) and over 300 connecting pathways (see Figure 5.2). The connecting pathways go both upward and downward (e.g., from V1 to V2 and back again) and side to side (between subareas in V1)— see, e.g., Felleman and Van Essen (1991). Individual cells at "higher" levels of processing, such as V4 (visual area 4), do, it is true, seem to specialize in the recognition of specific geometric forms. But they will also respond, in some degree, to many other stimuli. The cells thus function not as simple feature detectors but as filters tuned along a whole range of stimulus dimensions (see Van Essen and Gallant, 1994). The most informationally significant facts thus often concern the patterns of activity of whole populations of such tuned filters—an image much more in line with the connectionist vision of Chapter 4 than the symbolic one of Chapters 1 and 2. To add further complication, the responses of such cells now look to be modifiable both by attention and by details of local task-specific context (Knierim and Van

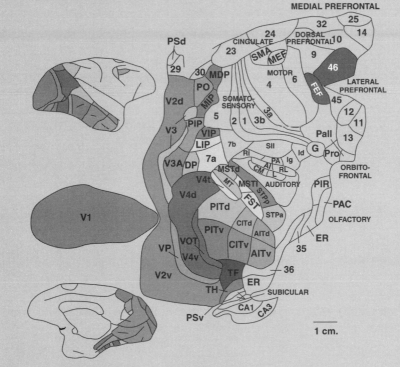

Figure 5.1 Map of cortical areas in the macaque.

Essen, 1992). In fact, back-projecting (corticocortical) connections tend, in the monkey, to outnumber forward ones, i.e., there are more pathways leading from deep inside the brain outward *toward* the sensory peripheries than vice versa (though much of the connectivity is reciprocal. See Van Essen and Anderson (1990) and Churchland et al. (1994, p. 40). Visual processing thus involves a wide variety of criss-crossing influences that could only roughly, if at all, be described as a neat progression through a lower-to-higher (perception to cognition) hierarchy.

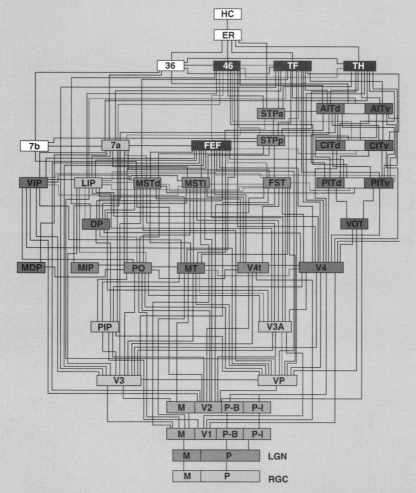

Figure 5.2 Hierarchy of visual areas. This hierarchy shows 32 visual cortical areas, subcortical visual stages (the retinal ganglion cell layer and the LGN), plus several nonvisual areas [area 7b of somatosensory cortex, perirhinal area 36, the ER, and the hippocampal complex)]. These areas are connected by 197 linkages, most of which have been demonstrated to be reciprocal pathways. [From Felleman and Van Essen (1991). Reproduced by courtesy of David Van Essen.]

Evidence for proposition 1 comes from a series of experiments in which subjects watch images on a computer screen. As the subject's eyes saccade around the scene (focusing first on one area, then another) changes are made to the display. The changes are made during the visual saccades. It is an amazing fact that, for the most part,[7] quite large changes go unnoticed: changes such as the replacement of a tree by a shrub, or the addition of a car, deletion of a hat, and so on. Why do such gross alterations remain undetected? A compelling hypothesis is that the visual system is not even attempting to build a rich, detailed model of the current scene but is instead geared to using frequent saccades to retrieve information *as and when it is needed* for some specific problem-solving purpose. This fits nicely with Yarbus' classic (1967) finding that the pattern of such saccades varies (even with identical scenes) according to the type of task the subject has been set (e.g., to give the ages of the people in a picture or to guess the activity they have been engaged in, etc.). According to both Churchland et al. (1994) and Ballard (1991), we are prone to the illusion that we constantly command a rich inner representation of the current visual scene precisely because we are able to perform these fast saccades, retrieving information as and when required. (An analogy[8]: a modern store may present the illusion of having a massive amount of goods stocked on the premises, because it always has what you want when you want it. But modern computer-ordering systems can automatically count off sales and requisition new items so that the necessary goods are available just when needed and barely a moment before. This just-in-time ordering system offers a massive saving of on-site storage while tailoring supply directly to customer demand.)

Contemporary research in robotics (see Chapter 6) avails itself of these same economies. One of the pioneers of "new robotics," Rodney Brooks (see, e.g., Brooks, 1991) coined the slogan, "the world is its own best model" to capture just this flavor. A robot known as Herbert (Connell, 1989), to take just one example, was designed to collect soft drink cans left around a crowded laboratory. But instead of requiring powerful sensing capacities and detailed advance planning, Herbert got by (very successfully) using a collection of coarse sensors and simple, relatively independent, behavioral routines. Basic obstacle avoidance was controlled by a ring of ultrasonic sound sensors that brought the robot to a halt if an object was in front of it. General locomotion (randomly directed) was interrupted if Herbert's simple visual system detected a roughly table-like outline. At this point a new routine kicks in and the table surface is swept using a laser. If the outline of a can is detected, the whole robot rotates until the can is centered in its field of vision. This physical action simplifies the pick-up procedure by creating a standard action-frame in which the robot arm, equipped with simple touch sensors, gently skims

---

[7]The exception is if subjects are told in advance to watch out for changes to a certain feature. See McConkie (1990) and Churchland et al. (1994).

[8]Thanks to David Clark for pointing this out.

the table surface dead ahead. Once a can is encountered, it is grasped, and collected and the robot moves on. Notice, then, that Herbert succeeds without using any conventional planning techniques and without creating and updating any detailed inner model of the environment. Herbert's world is composed of undifferentiated obstacles and rough table-like and can-like outlines. Within this world the robot also exploits its own bodily actions (rotating the torso to center the can in its field of view) so as to greatly simplify the computational problems involved in eventually reaching for the can. Herbert is thus a simple example of both a system that succeeds using minimal representational resources and one in which gross motor activity helps streamline a perceptual routine [as suggested in proposition (2) above].

The "interactive vision" framework envisages a more elaborate natural version of this same broad strategy, viz. the use of a kind of perceptuomotor loop whose role is to make the most of incoming perceptual clues by combining multiple sources of information. The idea here is that perception is not a passive phenomenon in which motor activity is only initiated at the end point of a complex process in which the animal creates a detailed representation of the perceived scene. Instead, perception and action engage in a kind of incremental game of tag in which motor assembly begins long before sensory signals reach the top level. Thus, early perceptual processing may yield a kind of protoanalysis of the scene, enabling the creature to select actions (such as head and eye movements) whose role is to provide a slightly upgraded sensory signal. That signal may, in turn, yield a new protoanalysis indicating further visuomotor action and so on. Even whole-body motions may be deployed as part of this process of improving perceptual pick-up. Foveating an object can, for example, involve motion of the eyes, head, neck, and torso. Churchland et al. (1994, p. 44) put it well: "watching Michael Jordan play basketball or a group of ravens steal a caribou corpse from a wolf tends to underscore the integrated, whole-body character of visuomotor coordination." This integrated character is consistent with the neurophysiological and neuroanatomical data that show the influence of motor signals in visual processing.[9]

Moving on to proposition (3) (that real-world actions may sometimes play an important role in the computational process itself), consider the task of distinguishing figure from ground (the rabbit from the field, or whatever). It turns out that this problem is greatly simplified using information obtained from head movement during eye fixation. Likewise, depth perception is greatly simplified using cues obtained by the observer's own self-directed motion. As the observer moves, close objects will show more relative displacement than farther ones. That is prob-

_____

[9]There are—to take just two further examples—neurons sensitive to eye position in V1, V3, and LGN (lateral geniculate nucleus), and cells in V1 and V2 that seem to know in advance about planned visual saccades (showing enhanced sensitivity to the target). See Churchland et al. (1994, p. 44) and Wurtz and Mohler (1976).

ably why, as Churchland et al. (1994, p. 51) observe, head bobbing behavior is frequently seen in animals: "a visual system that integrates across several glimpses to estimate depth has computational savings over one that tries to calculate depth from a single snapshot."

And so to proposition (4): that the neural representation of worldly events may be less like a passive data structure and more like a recipe for action. The driving force, once again, is computational economy. If the goal of perception and reason is to guide action (and it surely is, evolutionary speaking), it will often be simpler to represent the world in ways rather closely geared to the kinds of actions we want to perform. To take a simple example, an animal that uses its visual inputs to guide a specific kind of reaching behavior (so as to acquire and ingest food) need not form an object-centered representation of the surrounding space. Instead, a systematic metrical transformation (achieved by a point-to-point mapping between two internal maps) may transform the visual inputs directly into a recipe for reaching out and grabbing the food. In such a set-up, the animal does not need to do additional computational work on an action-neutral inner model so as to plan a reaching trajectory. The perceptual processing is instead tweaked, at an early stage, in a way dictated by the particular use to which the visual input is dedicated.[10]

In a related vein, Maja Mataric of the MIT Artificial Intelligence Laboratory has developed a neurobiologically inspired model of how rats navigate their environments. This model exploits the kind of layered architecture[11] also used in the robot Herbert. Of most immediate interest, however, is the way the robot learns about its surroundings. As it moves around a simple maze, it detects landmarks that are registered (see Figures 5.3, 5.4, and 5.5) as a combination of sensory input and current motion. A narrow corridor thus registers as a combination of forward motion and short lateral distance readings from sonar sensors. Later, if the robot is required to find its way back to a remembered location, it retrieves[12] an interlinked set of such combined sensory and motor readings. The stored "map" of the environment is thus immediately fit to act as a recipe for action, since the motor signals are part of the stored spatial knowledge. The relation between two locations is directly encoded as the set of motor signals that moved the robot from one to the other. The inner map is thus *itself* the recipe for the necessary motor actions. By contrast, a more classical approach would first generate a more objective map, which would then need to be *reasoned over* to plan the route.

[10]This strategy is described in detail in Churchland's (1989, Chapter 5) account of the "connectionist crab," in which research in artificial neural networks (see Chapter 4) is applied to the problem of creating efficient point-to-point linkages between deformed inner "topographic" maps.

[11]This is known as a "subsumption" architecture, because each of the layers constitutes a complete behavior-producing system and interacts only in simple ways such as by one layer subsuming (turning off) the activity of another (see Brooks, 1991).

[12]By a process of spreading activation among landmark encoding nodes—see Mataric (1991).

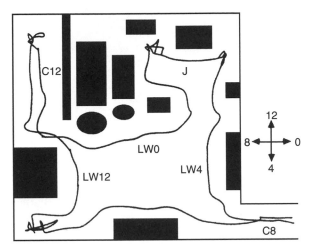

Figure 5.3 Example of a robot's reflexive navigation behavior in a cluttered office environment. Labels include landmark type and compass bearing (LW8, left wall heading south; C0, corridor heading north; J, long irregular boundary). (*Source*: Mataric, 1991. Used by kind permission of M. Mataric and MIT Press.)

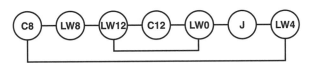

Figure 5.4 A map constructed by a robot in the environment shown in Figure 5.3. Topological links between landmarks indicate physical spatial adjacency. (*Source*: Mataric, 1991. Used by kind permission of M. Mataric and MIT Press.)

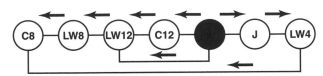

Figure 5.5 The map actively carries out path finding. The shaded node is the goal node. Arrows indicate the spreading of activation from the goal. (*Source*: Mataric, 1991. Used by kind permission of M. Mataric and MIT Press.)

Box 5.2

MIRROR NEURONS

As a last nod in that same direction, consider the fascinating case of so-called mirror neurons (Di Pellegrino et al., 1992). These are neurons, in monkey ventral premotor cortex, that are action oriented, context dependent, and implicated in both self-initiated activity and passive perception. These neurons are active both when the monkey *observes* a specific action (such as someone grasping a food item) and when the monkey *performs* the same kind of action (in this case, the grasping of a food item—see also Rizzolatti et al., 1996). The implication, according to the psychologist and neuroscientist Marc Jeannerod, is that "the action . . . to be initiated is stored in terms of an action code, not a perceptual one" (Jeannerod, 1997, p. 191).

The Mataric robot (which is based on actual rat neurobiology—see McNaughton and Nadel, 1990) exemplifies the attractions of what I call "action-oriented representations" (Clark, 1997, p. 49): representations that describe the world by depicting it in terms of possible actions.[13] This image fits nicely with several of the results reported earlier, including the work on monkey finger control and the motor loop specificity of "perceptual" adaptation. The products of perceptual activity, it seems, are not always action-neutral descriptions of external reality. They may instead (and see Box 5.2) constitute direct recipes for acting and intervening. We thus glimpse something of the shape of what Churchland et al. (1994, p. 60) describe as a framework that is "motocentric" rather than "visuocentric."

Putting all this together suggests a much more integrated model of perception, cognition, and action. Perception is itself often tangled up with possibilities for action and is continuously influenced by cognitive, contextual, and motor factors. It need not yield a rich, detailed, and action-neutral inner model awaiting the services of "central cognition" so as to deduce appropriate actions. In fact, these old distinctions (between perception, cognition, and action) may sometimes obscure, rather than illuminate, the true flow of events. In a certain sense, the brain is revealed not as (primarily) an engine of reason or quiet deliberation, but as an organ of *environmentally situated control.*

---

[13]Such representations bear some resemblance to what the ecological psychologist J.J. Gibson called "affordances," although Gibson himself would reject our emphasis on inner states and encodings. An affordance is the potential of use and activity that the local environment offers to a specific kind of being: chairs afford sitting (to humans), and so on. See Gibson (1979). The philosopher Ruth Millikan has developed a nice account of action-oriented representation under the label "pushmipullyu representation"—see Millikan (1996).

5.2 Discussion

A. MARR'S LEVELS AND THE BRAIN

Consider once again Marr's three-way distinction among task, algorithm, and implementation. We have seen how details of bodily mechanics (synergies of tendons, etc.) and embodied action taking (moving, visual saccades, etc.) can radically transform the shape of the computational problems faced by a real-world agent. This fact alone puts pressure on the practical value of the three-level schema. The task of visual processing may have pretheoretically seemed to require an algorithm for mapping passively received 2D information onto a 3D inner model of the current scene. But reflection on the role of motion and action and on our specific behavioral needs at any given moment suggests, we saw, a much more minimalist picture—one in which a mobile, embodied system actively seeks the kinds of limited information and visual cues than will enable it to fulfill a specific current goal, and no more. Our notions of *what* top-level task needs to be performed, and of what kinds of algorithm are adequate to perform it, are thus deeply informed by reflection on details of bodily implementation, current needs, and action-taking potential.

Such observations[14] do not directly undermine the task/algorithm/implementation distinction itself. But they do reveal the possibility of an upward cascade of influence in which even isolating the right task depends on an appreciation of details of body and implementation. More radically still, a closer confrontation with natural systems casts some doubt on the biological applicability of the three-way distinction itself. The root of the problem hereabouts concerns the proper way to map the three analytic levels (task/algorithm/implementation) onto actual details of neural organization. Thus Churchland and Sejnowski (1990, p. 249) observe that there are many levels of neural organization, including "the biochemical . . . the membrane, the single cell, and the circuit, and perhaps . . . brain subsystems, brain systems, brain maps and the whole central nervous system." Which of these various levels of organization is the level of implementation? Obviously, the answer depends on exactly what function or task we are studying. One result of this multiplicity of possible targets, however, is that what is an algorithmically interesting detail relative to one task may well be "mere implementation detail" relative to another. To understand circuit x, you may need to know that x uses a specific algorithm to, e.g., choose the greatest of eight magnitudes. But to understand the subsystem of which x is a part, all you need to know is that x selects the greatest magnitude—the rest is "mere implementation detail." Explaining fine-grained patterns of breakdown may, however, yet again force attention onto details that were previously regarded as merely implementational—details of the timing of events, the temperature range for normal functioning of components, and so on.

---

[14]See, e.g., Churchland and Sejnowski (1990, p. 248).

The issue of timing, will, in fact, loom rather large in some of our later discussions (see Chapter 7). For timing considerations are absolutely crucial to many aspects of neural functioning, including sensorimotor control and even "passive" information processing. Yet details of real timing and dynamics are inevitably washed out in pure algorithmic descriptions, since these specify only the input and output representations and the sequence of transformations that mediates between them. Crucial explanatory work thus remains to be done even when a full algorithmic understanding is in place. Once again, the notion that understanding natural cognition is simply understanding the algorithms that the brain happens to implement is called into question.

Finally, recall the discussion of connectionism from Chapter 4. One feature of those models was the apparent collapse of the data/algorithm distinction itself. The connection weights, in such models, act as both knowledge store and knowledge-manipulation algorithm. If real neural computation is indeed anything like connectionist computation, the standard notion of an algorithm as a recipe for acting on an independent data set also seems strictly inapplicable.

Overall, then, we may agree with Churchland and Sejnowski (1990, p. 249) that "Marr's *three levels of analysis* and the brain's *levels of organization* do not appear to mesh in a very useful or satisfying manner." In particular, implementation level knowledge may be essential for understanding what tasks the neural system confronts. We may also need to recognize a multiplicity of roughly algorithmic "levels," and (perhaps) to seek types of understanding that are not easily classed as algorithmic at all.

B. COMPUTATION AND IMPLEMENTATION

Proceeding from the worries raised in the previous section, consider next the task of *distinguishing* "computational" from "implementational" features in the first place. For most human-designed computer systems this distinction is easy to draw. But this probably reflects the nature of the conscious design process, in which the engineer or programmer first conceives of a problem solution in terms of an abstract sequence of simpler steps and then implements the sequence by associating each step with a distinct and mechanistically tractable operation. This strategy typically results in what might be termed "neatly decomposable" systems in which there is a nice clear mapping between a step-wise problem solution and the functionality of a set of relatively independent mechanical or electronic components. [The construction of semantically transparent systems (see Chapter 2) is plausibly seen as one expression of this general tendency in the special case of systems designed to model reason-guided behavior.]

By contrast, biological evolution (as we observed earlier) is not thus bound by the process of conscious, step-by-step design. There is incrementality in biological evolution, to be sure (see, e.g., Simon, 1962). But there is no need for biological design to conform to the principle of neat functional decomposition. Instead, evo-lutionary search (by processes such as random variation and differential selection) can uncover problem solutions that depend crucially on complex interactions be-tween multipurpose circuits. This is a corner of design space curiously opaque to conscious human reason, which is far and away most comfortable with simple lin-ear interactions between multiple single-purpose components.

There are, however, ways around this apparent mismatch. Computationalists lately exploit so-called genetic algorithms[15] (see Box 5.3) that roughly mimic the process of evolutionary search and allow the discovery of efficient but sometimes strange and highly interactive adaptive strategies and problem solutions. A recent extension of such approaches uses a variant[16] kind of genetic algorithm to search for new kinds of *hardware* design that are freed from the "simplifying constraints normally imposed to make design by humans tractable" (Thompson et al., 1996, p. 1). Thompson and his colleagues used a special form of genetic algorithm to evolve real electronic circuits whose task was to use sonar echo information to drive the wheels of a mobile robot so as to avoid crashing into walls. The genetic algo-rithm worked on a "population" of real electronic circuits driving real robot wheels. Unhindered by the various constraints that the process of conscious human design imposes on circuit specification, the genetic algorithm found highly efficient solu-tions to the control problem. Human designed circuits, for example, often rely heavily on the use of a global clock to ensure that the output of a state transition is not "listened to" by other components until it has had time to settle into a fully on or fully off state. By contrast, the evolved circuitry was able to exploit even the transient (unsettled) dynamics so as to achieve efficient behavior using very mod-est resources (32 bits of RAM and a couple of flip-flops). In another experiment, a problem solution was found that depended on the slightly different input–output time delays of components. These delays were originally randomly fixed, but rerandomization at the end of the evolutionary search now destroyed success-ful performance, showing that the circuits had, unexpectedly, come to exploit those specific (and randomly chosen) delays as part of the problem-solving configura-tion. The authors comment that, in general:

> it can be expected that all of the detailed physics of the hardware will be brought to bear on the problem at hand: time delays, parasitic capacitances, cross-talk, meta-stability constraints and other low-level characteristics might all be used in generating the evolved behavior (Thompson et al., 1996, p. 21)

More recently, the same group has used hardware evolution to develop a chip that distinguishes two tones (1 and 10 kHz). Conventional solutions again rely

---

[15]For a review, see Clark (1997, Chapter 5).

[16]Standard GAs (genetic algorithms) require a fixed-dimensional search space. The variation required for efficient hardware evolution involves the relaxation of this constraint, so that the number of com-ponents required to solve a problem need not be fixed in advance. See Thompson, Harvey, and Hus-bands (1996) and Thompson (1997).

Box 5.3

GENETIC ALGORITHMS

Genetic algorithms (GAs) were introduced by John Holland (1975) as a computational version of (something akin to) biological evolution. The idea was to take a population of computational "chromosomes"—bit strings—and to subject them to a regime of trial, variation, selective retention, and reproduction. The bit strings would encode, or at least be capable of encoding, possible solutions to some prespecified problem. A fitness function (a measure of how well each bit string is able to perform the task) identifies which members of a varied initial population perform best. These form the "breeding stock" for the next generation, created by processes of crossover (mixing parts of 2 bit strings to form a new one) and random mutation (flipping some values in a bit string, for example). Each new generation is again tested against the fitness function, and over hundreds of thousands of generations performance (often) dramatically improves, to the point where highly evolved bit strings solve the problem in robust and efficient ways. Genetic algorithms have been successfully used for a variety of practical and theoretical purposes, including the evolution of good weight assignments for neural networks, of scheduling systems pairing tasks and resources (e.g., efficiently assigning unpainted cars and trucks to automated paint booths in a production line), of control architectures for robotic devices, and (see text) of efficient special-purpose silicon chips. For the classic introduction, see Holland (1975). For some user-friendly guides, see Holland (1992), Franklin (1995, Chapter 8), and Mitchell (1995).

heavily on a global clock that synchronizes the action of many logic blocks. The evolved chip dispenses with the clock and makes full use of the low-level properties of the physical device. Once again, the result is an amazingly efficient design that uses 21 logic blocks compared to many hundreds in the conventional chip.

What this work (and work in so-called neuromorphic VLSI[17]) shows is that low-level physical properties, of the kind associated with actual physical implementation rather than abstract computational designs, can be coopted (by natural or artificial evolution) into doing very substantial problem-solving work. When a system fully exploits such low-level physical features, it is capable of solving specific problems with an efficiency close to that determined by the limits of physics itself. It remains a vexed question whether we should say in such cases that the system is solving the problem by non-computational means or whether we should

[17]Very large-scale integrated circuits. For "neuoromorphic" VLSI see Mead (1989).

say, rather, that nature is able to put these unexpectedly subtle and low-level properties to good computational use.

It seems clear that restricting ourselves to the level of familiar kinds of algorithmic specification is a poor strategy if we hope to understand the way biological brains guide intelligent action. Instead, we must pay close and constant attention to the nature and properties of neural circuits and to the complex interactions among brain, body, and environment. The strategy of focusing attention on a kind of disembodied "pure software" level, floating high above the messy material realm, works well when we confront computational systems of our own design. But it works because of the simplifications, regimentations, and neat decompositions *we* artificially impose on the electronic circuitry so as to make it tractable to the process of conscious design in the first place. Understanding the intricate, unexpected, yet often stunningly efficient products of blind natural evolution calls for other techniques and ways of thinking. It is only by coevolving ideas about wetware, computational profile, and environmental interactions that this rather opaque region of design space will come into better focus.

C. INTERNAL FRAGMENTATION AND COORDINATED ACTION

There is something deeply fragmentary about the vision of neural architecture scouted earlier. The images of multiple processing streams and of special-purpose, action-oriented representations combine to yield a distinctive vision of the natural roots of intelligent behavior in which efficient response depends on the presence of what the cognitive neuroscientist V.S. Ramachandran calls a "bag of tricks." The idea, then, is that intelligence does not depend on the translation of incoming information into some unitary inner code that is then operated on by general purpose logical inference (the classical image pursued in research programs such as the SOAR project—see Chapter 2). Instead, we confront a mixed bag of relatively special-purpose encodings and stratagems whose overall effect is to support the particular needs of a certain kind of creature occupying a specific environmental niche. We shall consider further evidence for such a view in subsequent chapters. But we have already seen enough to raise a difficult issue. How might large-scale coherent behavior arise from the operation of such an internally fragmented system?

There are (at least) three different ways in which such coordination might be achieved. They are (1) by internal signaling, (2) by global dissipative effects, and (3) by external influence. The first is the most obvious route. There are, however, two quite distinct visions of how such signal-based coordination might be achieved. One vision depicts the neural components as passing rich messages in a general purpose code. This vision does not fit well with the "bag of tricks" style of operation posited earlier—an approach predicated on the efficiency gains associated with special-purpose styles of problem solution. A somewhat different vision, however, comports much better with the new approach. This is a vision of simple signal

Box 5.4

SUBSUMPTION ARCHITECTURE

In a subsumption architecture, there are several "layers" of circuitry each of which offers a complete route from input to motor action. Each layer is, if you like, functionally equivalent to a simple whole robot, capable of performing just one task. The robot Herbert (discussed in the text) comprises a multiplicity of such simpler devices: some for obstacle avoidance, some for exploring, some for table recognition, etc. Obviously, there needs to be some kind of coordination between the layers. This is achieved not by the internal transmission of complex messages but by the transmission of simple signals that turn one device on or off when another achieves a certain state (e.g., the total cessation of wheel motion initiates grasping, the detection of an obstacle inhibits forward motion, etc.).

passing, in which there is no rich trade in messages, but rather an austere trade in signals that either encourage or inhibit the activity of other components. [In the robotics literature, this vision is cashed in the idea of a *subsumption architecture* (Brooks, 1991)—see Box 5.4.]

Attractive as the simple signaling model is, more complex behaviors will surely require additional kinds of internal coordination. Contemporary neuroscientific theory displays a variety of proposals that fall midway along the spectrum of internal communicative complexity. Thus Van Essen et al. (1994) posit neural "gating" mechanisms whose task is to regulate the flow of information between cortical areas, whereas Damasio and Damasio (1994) posit a series of "convergence zones": areas in which multiple feedback and feedforward connections converge and that act as switching posts so as to bring about the simultaneous activity of the multiple brain areas implicated in certain tasks. In both these cases, there is no sense in which the inner control system (the gating neurons or the convergence zone) has access to all the information flowing through the system. These are not executive controllers privy to all the information in the system, so much as simple switching agents, opening and closing channels of influence between a wide variety of inner processors and components. One might also consider the use of so-called dissipative effects. The idea here (see Brooks, 1994; Husbands et al., 1998) is to exploit the capacity of a released substance (e.g., a chemical neuromodulator) to affect the processing profile of a large chunk of the system. Such substances would be released, have their effects, and then dissipate, returning the system to normal.

The coordinated behavior of multiple inner components can also sometimes be achieved not via the use of inner signals or diffuse chemical influences but by the action of the external environment itself. Much of Herbert's coordinated activity (see text and Box 5.4) depends on the flow of actual environmental triggers, e.g., encountering a table and then switching into can-seeking mode. A more advanced twist on this strategy occurs when we actively structure our environments in ways designed to off-load control and action selection (as when we place reminders in select locations, or when we lay out the parts of a model plane in the correct order for assembly). This devolution of control to the local environment is a topic to which we shall return.

In sum, it remains unclear how best to press coordinated behavior from a "bag of tricks" style of cognitive organization. But preserving the gains and advantages that such a style of organization offers precludes the use of a central executive and a heavy duty, message-passing code. Instead, appropriate coordination must somehow emerge from the use of simpler forms of internal routing and signaling and (perhaps) from the structure of the environment itself.

5.3 Suggested Readings

For a *general introduction to the contemporary neuroscience of perception and action*, try M. Jeannerod *The Cognitive Neuroscience of Action* (Oxford, England: Blackwell, 1997). This covers work on reaching and grasping, and is an especially clear introduction to the interface between psychology and neuroscience. See also A. D. Milner and M. Goodale, *The Visual Brain in Action* (Oxford, England: Oxford University Press, 1995) for a clear but provocative story about vision and action. The review article by T. Decety and T. Giezes, "Neural mechanisms subserving the perception of human actions." *Trends in Cognitive Sciences*, 3(5), 172–178, 1999, is also a useful resource.

For a philosophically, computationally, and neuroscientifically informed discussion of the *questions about levels of analysis and explanation*, see P. S. Churchland and T. J. Sejnowski, *The Computational Brain* (Cambridge, MA: MIT Press, 1992), a dense but accessible treatment of contemporary computational neuroscience, with especially useful discussions of the issues concerning levels of analysis and levels of description, and P.S. Churchland, *Neurophilosophy* (Cambridge, MA: MIT Press, 1986), which also contains a useful and accessible primer on basic neuroscience and neuroanatomy.

The work on *interactive vision and change-blindness* is nicely described in P. S. Churchland, V. S. Ramachandran, and T. Sejnowski, "A critique of pure vision." In C. Koch and T. Davis (eds.), *Large-Scale Neuronal Theories of the Brain* (Cambridge, MA: MIT Press, 1994, pp. 23–60). See also the review articles by D. Simons and D. Levin, "Change blindness." *Trends in Cognitive Sciences*, 1, 261–267, 1997; and D. Ballard, "Animate vision." *Artificial Intelligence*, 48, 57–86, 1991. The latter is just about the perfect introduction to computational work on real-world, real-time vision.

For a nice review of the work on *real-world robotics*, see J. Dean, "Animats and what they can tell us." *Trends in Cognitive Science*, 2(2), 60–67, 1998. For a longer treatment, integrating themes in philosophy, robotics, and neuroscience, see A. Clark, *Being There: Putting Brain, Body and World Together Again* (Cambridge, MA: MIT Press, 1997).

And finally, the various essays in *Daedalus*, 127(2), 1998 (special issue on the brain) range over a variety of topics relating to the *current state of mind/brain research* and include useful general introductions to work on vision, sleep, consciousness, motor action, and lots more.

ROBOTS AND ARTIFICIAL LIFE

6.1 Sketches

In Chapter 5, we began to encounter our first examples of work in robotics—work that falls broadly within the field that has come to be known as artificial life. This work is characterized by three distinct, but interrelated themes:

1. An interest in complete but low-level systems (whole, relatively autonomous artificial organisms that must sense and act in realistic environments).

2. Recognition of the complex contributions of body, action, and environmental context to adaptive behavior.

3. Special attention to issues concerning emergence and collective effects.

In this sketch, I introduce these topics using two concrete examples: cricket phonotaxis and termite nest building.

The interest in complete but low-level systems is most famously illustrated by Rodney Brooks' work on mobile robots (mobots), and by robots such as Herbert, whom we already met in Chapter 5. But the idea of building such creatures goes back at least to the early 1950s when W. Grey Walter created a pair of cybernetic turtles named Elmer and Elsie. In 1978, the philosopher Daniel Dennett published a short piece called "Why Not the Whole Iguana" that likewise argued in favor of studying whole simple systems displaying integrated action, sensing, and planning routines (contrast this with the stress on isolated aspects of advanced cognition such as chess playing, story understanding, and medical diagnosis displayed by classical artificial intelligence—see Chapters 1 and 2). One powerful reason for such a switch, as we have noted before, is that biological solutions to these more advanced problems may well be profoundly shaped by preexisting solutions to more basic problems of locomotion, sensing, and action selection. Moreover, the idea that it is fruitful to separate basic functions such as vision, planning, and action taking is itself open to doubt: these functions (as we also saw in the previous chapter) look to be quite intimately interrelated in naturally intelligent systems. As an example of the whole system approach in action, let us consider (partly by way of variety—Brooks' robots are a nice, but overused, example) Barbara Webb's recent work on cricket phonotaxis.

Female crickets are able to identify a male of the same species by his song, and are able to use the detected song as a signal allowing the female to find the male. The term "phonotaxis" names this capacity to detect and reliably move toward a specific sound or signal. The male cricket's song is produced by rubbing its wings together and consists in a carrier frequency (a simple tone) and a rhythm (the way the tone is broadcast in discrete bursts, separated by silence, as the wings open and close). The repetition rate of the bursts (or "syllables") is an important indicator of species, whereas the loudness of the song may help to pick out the most desirable male from a group. The female cricket must thus

1. hear and identify the song of her own species,

2. localize the source of the song, and

3. locomote toward it.

This way of describing the problem may, however, be misleading, and for some increasingly familiar reasons. The hear–localize–locomote routine constitutes a neat task decomposition and identifies a sequence of subtasks that would plainly solve the problem. But it is again hostage to a nonbiological vision of single functionality and sequential flow. Webb, heavily inspired by what is known of real cricket anatomy and neurophysiology, describes the following alternative scenario, which was successfully implemented in a robot cricket.

The cricket's ears are on its forelegs and are joined by an inner tracheal tube that also opens to the world at two other points (called spiracles) on the body (see Figure 6.1). External sounds thus arrive at each ear via two routes: the direct external route (sound source to ear) and an indirect internal route (via the other ear, spiracles, and tracheal tube). The time taken to travel through the tube alters the phase of the "inner route" sound relative to the "outer route" sound on the side (ear) nearest to the sound source (since sound arriving at the ear *closer* to the external source will have traveled a much shorter distance than sound arriving at the same ear via the inner route). As a result, simple neural or electronic circuitry can be used to sum the out-of-phase sound waves, yielding a vibration of greater amplitude (heard as a louder sound) at the ear nearest the sound source. Orientation in the direction of the male is directly controlled by this effect. Each of the two in-

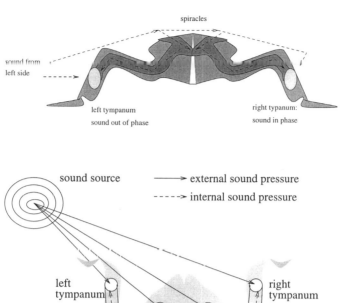

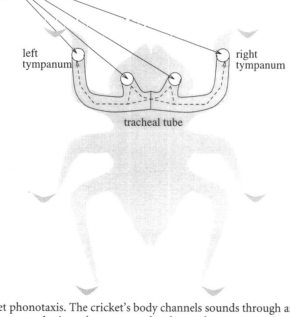

Figure 6.1 Cricket phonotaxis. The cricket's body channels sounds through an internal tracheal tube that connects the insect's ears to each other and to two openings, called spiracles, at the top of the body. Each ear is near a knee on a front leg. Because of the tube, sound reaches each ear in two ways: directly from the sound source, and indirectly, via the tube, from the spiracles and other ear. At the ear closer to the sound source, the sound that has traveled directly to the outside of the eardrum has traveled a shorter distance than the sound arriving through the tube at the inside of the eardrum. Because of this difference in distance, the sound arriving at one side of this eardrum is out of phase with respect to the sound arriving at the other side. At this eardrum the out-of-phase waves are summed, causing a vibration of greater amplitude, sensed as a louder sound. (Pictures courtesy of Barbara Webb.)

terneurons (one connected to each ear) fires when the input (vibration amplitude) reaches a critical level. But the one connected to the ear nearest the sound source will reach this threshold first. The cricket's nervous system is set up so as to reliably turn the cricket to the side on which the dedicated interneuron fires first. As a result, the insect responds, at the start of each burst of male song, by turning and moving in the direction of the sound (hence the importance of syllable *repetition* in attracting a mate). Notice, finally, that in this story the particularities of the tracheal tube are especially crucial to success. As Webb puts it:

> One of the fundamental principles of this system is that the cricket's tracheal tube transmits sounds of the desired calling song frequency, and the phase shifts in this transmission are suited to that particular wavelength. (Webb, 1996, p. 64)

The result is that the robot cricket (see Figure 6.2) does not possess any *general* mechanism for identifying the direction of sounds, nor does it need to *actively* discriminate the song of its own species from other songs. For other sounds are structurally incapable of generating the directional response. The robot cricket does not succeed by tailoring general purpose capacities (such as pattern recognition and sound localization) to the special case of mate detection: instead, it exploits *highly efficient but (indeed, because) special-purpose strategies*. It does not build a rich model of its environment and then apply some logicodeductive inference system to generate action plans. It does not even possess a central sensory information store capable of integrating multimodel inputs.

As a result, it is not at all obvious that the robot cricket uses anything worth calling internal representations. Various inner states do correspond to salient outer parameters, and certain inner variables to motor outputs. But Webb argues:

> It is not necessary to use this symbolic interpretation to explain how the system functions: the variables serve a mechanical function in connecting sensors to motors, a role epistemologically comparable to the function of the gears connecting the motors to the wheels. (Webb, 1994, p. 53)

In fact, understanding the behavior of the robot cricket requires attention to details that (from the standpoint of classical cognitive science) look much more like descriptions of implementation and environmental context than substantive features of an intelligent, inner control system. Key factors include, as noted, the fixed-length trachea and the discontinuity and repetition of the male song. The explanation of real-life cricket phonotaxis, if the Webb model is anywhere near correct,[1] involves a complex interaction among brain, body, and world, with no single component bearing the brunt of the problem-solving burden.

---

[1]The issue of biological plausibility has been addressed in two ways. First, by direct confrontation with cricket physiology and neuroanatomy (Webb, 1996) and second, by reimplementing the robotic solution so as to allow phonotaxis to real cricket song—a nice (though nonconclusive) test previously ruled out by details of size and component speed. Once reimplemented, the robot was indeed able to direct and locate real singing males (see Lund et al., 1997).

Figure 6.2 Two versions of the robot cricket: the original LEGO version and a newer version based on the Khepera robot platform. (Photos courtesy of Barbara Webb.)

One major strand of work in artificial life thus stresses the importance of real-time, real-world activity and the distribution of problem-solving contributions across body, brain, and local environment. Another strand, to which we now turn, stresses issues concerning emergence and collective effects in large ensembles. To get the flavor, consider Craig Reynolds groundbreaking work on flocking. Reynolds (1987) showed that the fluid and elegant flocking behavior of birds and other animals could be replicated (in computer animation) using a group of simulated agents (boids) each of which followed just three simple, local rules.

The rules were, roughly, to try to stay near a mass of other boids, to match your velocity to that of your neighbors, and to avoid getting too close to any one neighbor. When each boid followed these rules, patterns of on-screen activity ensued that quite closely resembled the flocking behavior of real birds, schooling fish, and other animals. Widely spaced boids immediately closed ranks, then group motion ensued with each boid making subtle speed and position adjustments as needed. And unexpectedly, when the mobile flock ran into an obstacle, it simply parted, washed around it, and reformed elegantly on the other side!

The boid work, although initially conceived as a simple tool for computer animation, clearly offered possible insight into the mechanisms of flocking in real animals. More importantly, for current purposes, it exemplified several themes that have since become central to work in artificial life. It showed that interesting collective effects can emerge as a result of the interactions between multiple simple agents following a few simple rules. It showed that the complexity and adaptability of such emergent behavior can often exceed our untutored expectations (witness the elegant obstacle-avoidance behavior). And it began to raise the question of what is real and what is mere simulation: the boids were not real animals, but the *flocking* behavior, it was later claimed (Langton, 1989, p. 33) was still an instance of *real flocking*. (We will return to this issue in the discussion.)

The boid research, however, really addresses only patterns emergent from agent–agent interaction. An equally important theme (and one also foregrounded in the kind of robotics work discussed earlier) concerns agent–environment interactions. Thus consider the way (real) termites build nests. The key principle behind termite nest building is the use of what have become known as "stigmergic" routines. In a stigmergic routine, repeated agent–environment interactions are used to control and guide a kind of collective construction process [the word derives from "stigma" (sign) and "ergon" (work) and suggests the use of work as a signal for more work—see Grasse (1959) and Beckers et al. (1994)]. A simple example is the termite's construction of the arches that structure the nests. Here, each termite deploys two basic strategies. First, they roll mud up into balls that are simultaneously impregnated—by the termite—with a chemical trace. Second, they pick up the balls and deposit them wherever the chemical trace is strongest. At first, this leads to random depositing. But once some impregnated mudballs are scattered about, these act as attractors for further deposits. As mudballs pile up, the attractive force increases and columns form. Some of these columns are, as luck would have it, fairly proximal to one another. In such cases, the drift of scent from a nearby column inclines the termites to deposit new mudballs on the side of the column nearest to the neighboring column. As this continues, so the columns gently incline together, eventually meeting in the center and creating an arch. Similar stigmergic routines then lead to the construction of cells, chambers, and tunnels. Recent computer-based simulations have replicated aspects of this process, using simple rules to underpin the piling of "wood chips" (Resnick, 1994, Chapter 3). And experiments using groups of small real-world robots have shown similar effects in laboratory settings (Beckers et al., 1994). The moral, once again, is that apparently complex problem solving need not always involve the use of heavy-duty individual reasoning engines, and that coordinated activity need not be controlled by a central plan or blueprint, nor by a designated "leader." In the termite studies just described no termite knows much at all: simply how to respond to an encountered feature of the local environment, such as the chemical trace in the mudballs. The collective activity is not even orchestrated by regular signaling or communication—instead, signals are channeled through the environmental structures, with one agent's work prompting another to respond according to some simple rule. (In Chapter 8, we will discuss some closely related ideas in the realm of advanced human problem solving).

In sum, work on artificial life aims to reconfigure the sciences of the mind by emphasizing the importance of factors other than rich, individual computation and cogitation. These factors include (1) the often unexpected ways in which multiple factors (neural, bodily, and environmental) may converge in natural problem solving, (2) the ability to support robust adaptive response without central planning or control, and (3) the general potency of simple rules and behavioral routines operating against a rich backdrop of other agents and environmental structure.

6.2 Discussion

A. THE ABSENT AND THE ABSTRACT

Work in artificial life and real-world robotics often has a rather radical flavor. This radicalism manifests itself as a principled antipathy toward (or at least agnosticism about) the invocation of internal representations, central planning, and rich inner models in cognitive scientific explanations of intelligent behavior.[2] Such radicalism looks, however, somewhat premature given the state of the art. For the notions of internal representation, inner world models and their ilk were introduced to help explain a range of behaviors significantly different from those studied by most roboticists: behaviors associated with what might reasonably[3] be called "advanced reason." Such behaviors involve, in particular:

1. The coordination of activity and choice with distal, imaginary, or counterfactual states of affairs.

2. The coordination of activity and choice with environmental parameters whose ambient physical manifestations are complex and unruly (e.g., open-endedly disjunctive—we will review examples below).

---

[2]See, e.g., Thelen and Smith (1994), Brooks (1991), van Gelder (1995), Keijzer (1998), and Beer (1995) among many others.

[3]This is not to downplay the difficulty or importance of basic sensorimotor routines. It is meant merely to conjure those distinctive skills by which some animals (notably humans) are able to maintain cognitive contact with distal, counterfactual, and abstract states of affairs.

It is these kinds of behavior, rather than locomotion, wall following, mate detection, and the like, for which the representationalist approach seems best suited.

Thus consider the first class of cases, the ones involving the coordination of activity and choice across some kind of physical disconnection.[4] Examples might include planning next year's family vacation, plotting the likely consequences of some imagined course of action, using mental imagery to count the number of windows in your London apartment while sitting at your desk in St. Louis, Missouri, or doing mental arithmetic. In all these cases, the objects of our cognitive activity are physically absent. By contrast, almost all[5] the cases invoked by the new roboticists involve behavior that is continuously driven and modified by the relevant environmental parameter—a light source, the physical terrain, the call of the male cricket, etc. Yet these kinds of problem domain, it seems clear, are simply not sufficiently "representation hungry" (Clark and Toribio, 1994) to be used as part of any *general* antirepresentationalist argument. This is why the best examples of representation-sparse real-world robotics strike us as rather poor examples of genuinely cognitive phenomena. Paradigmatically cognitive capacities involve the ability to generate appropriate action and choice despite physical disconnection. And this requires, prima facie, the use of some inner item or process whose role is to stand in for the missing environmental state of affairs and hence to support thought and action in the absence of on-going environmental input. Such inner stand-ins *are* internal representations, as traditionally understood.

The point here—to be clear—is *not* to argue that the capacity to coordinate action despite physical disconnection strictly implies the presence of anything like traditional internal representations. For it is certainly possible to *imagine* systems that achieve such coordination without the use of any stable and independently identifiable inner states whose role is to act as stand-ins or surrogates for the absent states of affairs [see Keijzer (1998) for a nice discussion]. The point is rather that it is dialectically unsound to argue *against* the representationalist by adducing cases where there is no physical disconnection. Such cases are interesting and informative. But they cannot speak directly against the representationalist vision.

Similar issues can be raised by focusing on our second class of cases. These involve not full-scale physical disconnection so much as what might be termed "attenuated presence." The issue here is related to a concern often voiced by Jerry Fodor, viz. that advanced reason involves selective response to nonnomic properties (see Box 6.1) of the stimulus–environment (see Fodor, 1986). Nomic properties are those that fall directly under physical laws. Thus detecting light intensity is detecting a nomic property. Humans (and other animals) are, however, capable of selective response to "nonnomic" properties such as "being a crumpled shirt"—a

---

[4]For an extended discussion of the themes of connection, and disconnection see Smith (1996).

[5]A notable exception is Lynne Stein's work on imagination and situated agency. See Stein (1994) and comments in Clark (1999b).

Box 6.1

NONNOMIC PROPERTIES

Nomic properties are properties of an object such that possession of the properties causes the object to fall under specific scientific laws. The physical and chemical properties of a Picasso are thus nomic, whereas the property of "being admired by many" is not. The property of being worth a million dollars is likewise nonnomic, as is the property (according to Fodor—see text) of being a crumpled shirt. The parts of the physical universe that are, indeed, crumpled shirts are (of course) fully bound by physical laws. But such laws apply to them *not* because they are crumpled shirts (or even shirts) but because they, e.g., weigh 2 pounds or have such and such a mass, etc. For a nice discussion of the issues arising from Fodor's suggestion that selective response to nonnomic properties is the cash value of the use of mental representations, see Antony and Levine (1991) and Fodor's reply in the same volume.

property that (unlike, e.g., the shirt's mass) does not characterize the object in a way capable of figuring in physical laws. Ditto for "being a genuine dollar bill" or "being a labour victory in the 1996 election." Fodor's (1986, p. 14) view was that "selective response to [such] non-nomic properties is the great evolutionary problem that mental representation was invented to solve."

The nomic/nonnomic distinction does not, however, fully serve Fodor's purposes. For it is clearly possible to respond selectively to "nonnomic" properties such as "shirtness" (we do it all the time). If this is to be physically explicable, there must be *some* kind of (perhaps complex and multifaceted) lawful relation linking our reliable selective responses to shirt-presenting circumstances. The real issue, as Fodor (1991, p. 257) more recently acknowledges, is not whether shirt detection falls under laws, but "that there is no non-inferential way of detecting shirtness."

The deep issue, as Fodor now sees it, thus concerns what we might call "simple sensory transducability." To track a property such as "being a shirt" we seem to need to use an indirect route—we directly track a complex of other features that cumulatively signifies shirthood. No one could build a simple sensory transducer (where a transducer is loosely conceived as a device that takes sensory input and converts it into a different form or signal used for further processing) that (even roughly) itself isolated all and only those energy patterns that signify the presence of shirts. Instead, you need to detect the obtaining of properties such as "is shirt shaped," "could be worn by a human," etc. and then (or so Fodor insists) *infer* the presence of a shirt. It is the presence of inferred representations and the associated capacity to go beyond simple, direct transduction that Fodor (1991, p. 257) now sees as the source of a "principled distinction" between very simple minds (such as that of a paramecium) and the minds of advanced reasoners (such as ourselves).

I think there is something in this. There certainly seems to be a large gap between systems that track directly transducible environmental features (such as the presence of sugar or the male cricket song) and ones that can respond to more arcane features, such as the carrying out of a charitable action or the presence of a crumpled shirt. Prima facie, the obvious way to support selective response to ever-more arcane features is to detect the presence of multiple other features and to develop deeper inner resources that covary with the obtaining of such multiple simple features: complex feature detectors, in short. But internal states developed to serve such a purpose would, at least on the face of it, seem to count as internal representations in good standing.

The proper conclusion here, once again, is not that it is simply inconceivable that coordination with what is absent, counterfactual, nonexistent, or not directly transducible is *impossible* without deploying inner states worth treating as internal representations. Rather, it is that existing demonstrations of representation-free or representation-sparse problem solving should not be seen as directly arguing for the possibility of a more general antirepresentationalism. For the problem domains being negotiated are not, in general, the kind most characteristic of advanced "representation-hungry" reason.

All this, to be sure, invites a number of interesting (and sometimes potent) replies. This discussion continues in Chapters 7 and 8.

B. EMERGENCE[6]

The artificial life literature gives special prominence to the notions of emergence and collective effects. But the notion of emergence is itself still ill understood. Nor can it be simply identified with the notion of a collective effect, for not every collective effect amounts intuitively to a case of emergence, nor does every case of emergence seem (again, intuitively) to involve a collective effect. Thus consider the way a collection of small identical weights (billiard balls perhaps) may collectively cause a balance-beam to tip over onto one side. This is a collective effect all right (it needs, let us imagine, at least 30 billiard balls to tip the scale). But we seem to gain nothing by labeling the episode as one of "emergent toppling." Or consider, by contrast, the case of the simple robot described in Hallam and Malcolm (1994). This robot follows walls encountered to the right by means of an inbuilt bias to move to the right, and a right-side sensor, contact activated, that causes it to veer slightly to the left. When these two biases are well calibrated, the robot will follow the wall by a kind of "veer and bounce" routine. The resultant behavior is described as "emergent wall following," yet the number of factors and forces involved seems

---

[6]This section owes a lot to discussions with Pim Haselager and Pete Mandik.

too low, and the factors too diverse, to count this as a collective effect of the kind mentioned in our earlier sketch.

Relatedly, we need to find an account of emergence that is neither so liberal as to allow just about everything to count as an instance of emergence (a fate that surely robs the notion of explanatory and descriptive interest), nor so strict as to effectively rule out any phenomenon that can be given a scientific explanation (we do not want to insist that only currently unexplained phenomena should count as emergent, for that again robs the notion of immediate scientific interest). Rather it should pick out a distinctive way in which basic factors and forces may conspire to yield some property, event, or pattern. The literature contains a number of such suggestions, each of which cuts the emergent/nonemergent cake in somewhat different ways. As a brief rehearsal of some prominent contenders, consider the following.

1. Emergence as Collective Self-Organization. This is the notion most strongly suggested by the earlier examples of flocking, termite nest building, etc. As a clinically pure example, consider the behavior of cooking oil heated in a pan. As the heat is applied it increases the temperature difference between the oil at the top (cooler) and at the bottom (hotter). Soon, there appears a kind of rolling motion known as a convection roll. The hotter, less dense oil rises, to be replaced by the cooler oil, which then gets hotter and rises, and so on. Of such a process, Kelso (1995, pp. 7–8) writes:

> The resulting convection rolls are what physicists call a collective or cooperative effect, which arises without any external instructions. The temperature gradient is called a control parameter [but it does not] prescribe or contain the code for the emerging pattern. . . . Such spontaneous pattern formation is exactly what we mean by self-organization: the system organized itself, but there is no 'self', no agent inside the system doing the organizing.

The proximal cause of the appearance of convection rolls is the application of heat. But the *explanation* of the rolls has more to do with the properties of an interacting mass of simple components (molecules) that, under certain conditions (viz. the application of heat), feed and maintain themselves in a specific patterned cycle. This cycle involves a kind of "circular causation" in which the activity of the simple components leads to a larger pattern, which then *enslaves* those same components, locking them into the cycle of rising and falling. (Think of the way the motion of a few individuals can start a crowd moving in one direction: the initial motion induces a process of *positive feedback* as more and more individuals then influence their own neighbors to move in the same direction, until the whole crowd moves as a coherent mass.)

Such collective effects, with circular causation and positive feedback, can be usefully understood using the notion of a "collective variable"—a variable whose changing value reflects the interactive result of the activities of multiple systemic elements. Examples include the temperature and pressure of a gas, the rate of acceleration and direction of motion of the crowd, the amplitude of the convection rolls, and so on. Dynamic systems theory (which we will introduce in the next chapter) specializes in plotting the values of such collective variables as systemic behavior unfolds over time, and in plotting the relations between the collective variables and any control parameters (such as the temperature gradient in the oil). An emergent phenomenon, according to our first account, is thus any interesting behavior that arises as a direct result of multiple, self-organizing (via positive feedback and circular causation) interactions occurring in a system of simple elements.

Problems? This story works well for systems comprising large numbers of essentially identical elements obeying simple rules. It thus covers flocking, termite nest building, convection rolls, etc. But it is less clearly applicable to systems comprising relatively few and more heterogeneous elements (such as the robot cricket and the bounce and veer wall follower).

2. *Emergence as Unprogrammed Functionality.* By contrast, the idea of emergence as something like "unprogrammed functionality" is tailor-made for the problem cases just mentioned. In such cases we observe adaptively valuable behavior arising as a result of the interactions between simple on-board circuitry and bodily and environmental structure. Such behaviors (wall following, cricket phonotaxis) are not supported by explicit programming or by any fully "agent-side" endowment. Instead, they arise as a kind of *side-effect* of some iterated sequence of agent–world interactions. The point is not that such behaviors are necessarily unexpected or undesigned—canny roboticists may well set out to achieve their goals by orchestrating just such interactions. It is, rather, that the behavior is not subserved by an internal state encoding either the goals (follow walls, find males, etc.) or how to achieve them. Such behaviors thus depend on what Steels (1994) calls "uncontrolled variables"—they are behaviors that can only be very *indirectly* manipulated, since they depend not on central or explicit control structures but on iterated agent–environment interactions.

Problems? As you might guess, this story works well for the cases just mentioned. But it seems less clearly applicable to cases of collective self-organization. For cases of the latter kind clearly do allow for a form of direct control by the manipulation of a single parameter (such as the heat applied to the cooking oil).

3. *Emergence as Interactive Complexity.* I think we can do some justice to *both* the proceeding accounts by understanding emergent phenomena as the effects, patterns, or capacities made available by a certain class of complex interactions between systemic components. Roughly, the idea is to depict emergence as the process by which complex, cyclic interactions give rise to stable and salient patterns of systemic behavior. By stressing the complexity of the interactions we allow emergence

Box 6.2

NONLINEAR INTERACTIONS

A nonlinear interaction is one in which the value of x does not increase proportionally to the value of y. Instead, x may (for example) remain at zero until y reaches a critical value and then increase unevenly with an increase in the value of y. The behavior of a standard connectionist unit (see Chapter 4) is nonlinear since the output is not simply the weighted sum of the inputs but may involve a threshold, step function, or other nonlinearity. A typical example is a unit having a sigmoid activation function, in which certain input values (high positive or negative values, for example) yield a sharp response, causing the unit to output 0 (for high negative input) or 1 (for high positive input). But for certain intermediate input values (mildly positive or mildly negative ones), such a unit gives a more subtly gradated response, gradually increasing the strength of the output signal according to the current input. See Figure 6.3.

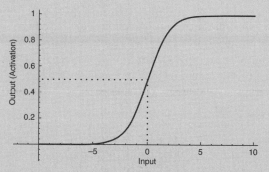

Figure 6.3 Nonlinear response in a connectionist unit. Notice that the unit responds with 0 to all high negative input values, with 1 to all high positives, with 0.5 when the input is zero, and with subtly gradated responses for all intermediate values. (Adapted from Elman et al., 1996, Fig. 2.2, p. 53.)

to come (obtain) in degrees. Phenomena that depend on repeated linear interactions with only simple kinds of feedback loop (e.g., a strict temporal sequence in which x affects y which then affects x) will count as, at best, only weakly emergent. In such cases it is usually unclear whether talk of emergence is explanatorily useful. By contrast, phenomena that depend on multiple, nonlinear (see Box 6.2), temporally asynchronous, positive feedback involving interactions will count as strongly emergent. Bounce-and-veer wall following is thus a case of weak emergence, whereas the convection roll example, when fully described, turns out to be

> ## Box 6.3
>
> # A Case in Which Prediction
> # Requires Simulation
>
> Consider the decimal expansion of $\sqrt{2} - 1$. This (see Franklin, 1995, p. 282) defines an irrational number. The resulting sequence is unpredictable except by direct step-by-step calculation. To find the next digit you must always calculate the proceeding digit. By contrast, some functions rapidly converge to a fixed point or a repeating pattern. In these cases (e.g., the infinite sequence .33333 recurring) we can predict the nth number in the sequence without calculating $n - 1$ and applying a rule. Such sequences afford short-cuts to prediction. Mathematical chaos represents a kind of middle option— sequences of unfolding that exhibit real *local* patterning but that resist long-term prediction (see Stewart, 1989).

a classic case of strong emergence (see Kelso, 1995, pp. 5–9). Emergent phenomena, thus defined, will typically reward understanding in terms of the changing values of a collective variable—a variable (see above) that tracks the pattern resulting from the interactions of multiple factors and forces. Such factors and forces may be wholly internal to the system or may include selected elements of the external environment.

4. *Emergence as Uncompressible Unfolding.* Finally (and for the sake of completeness), I should note another (and I think quite different) sense of emergence represented in the recent literature. This is the idea of emergent phenomena as those phenomena for which *prediction* requires *simulation*—and especially those in which *predication* of some macrostate P requires simulation of the complex interactions of the realizing microstates M_1–M_n. (See Box 6.3 for an example.) Bedau (1996, p. 344) thus defines a systemic feature or state as emergent if and only if you can predict it, in detail, *only* by modeling all the interactions that give rise to it. In such cases, there is no substitute for actual simulation if we want to predict, in detail, the shape of the macroscopic unfolding.

Problems? This definition of emergence strikes me as overly restrictive. For example, even in cases involving multiple, complex, nonlinear, and cyclic interactions, it will often be possible to model systemic unfolding by simulating only a *subset* of actual interactions. Convection roll formation, for example, succumbs to an analysis that (by exploiting collective variables) allows us to predict how the patterns (given a set of initial conditions) will form and unfold over time. Bedau's proposal, in effect, restricts the notion of emergence to phenomena that resist all such attempts at low-dimensional modeling. My intuition, by contrast, is that emergent phenomena are often *precisely* those phenomena in which complex interactions yield robust, salient patterns capable of supporting prediction and explanation, i.e., that lend themselves to various forms of low-dimensional projection.

C. LIFE AND MIND[7]

Work in artificial life also raises some fundamental questions concerning the very idea of life and the relationship between life and mind. On the very idea of life, the challenge is direct and simple: could life be actually instantiated (rather than simply modeled) in artificial media such as robots or computer-based ecosystems? Consider, for example, the virtual ecosystem named Tierra (Ray, 1991, 1994). Here, digital organisms (each one a kind of small program) compete for CPU time. The, "organisms" can reproduce (copy) and are subject to change via random mutations and occasionally incorrect copying. The system is implemented in the memory of the computer and the "organisms" (code fragments or "codelets") compete, change, and evolve. After a while, Ray would stop the simulation and analyze the resultant population. He found a succession of successful (often unexpected) survival strategies, each one exploiting some characteristic weakness in the proceeding dominant strategy. Some codelets would learn to exploit (piggyback on) the instructions embodied in other organisms' code, as "virtual parasites." Later still, codelets evolved capable of diverting the CPU time of these parasites onto themselves, thus parasitizing the parasites, and so on. The following question then arises: Are these *merely* virtual, simulated organisms or is this a *real* ecosystem populated by *real* organisms "living" in the unusual niche of digital computer memory? Ray himself is adamant that, at the very least, such systems can genuinely support several properties characteristic of life—such as real self-replication, real evolution, real flocking, and so on (see Ray, 1994, p. 181).

One debate, then, concerns the effective definition of life itself, and perhaps of various properties such as self-replication. In this vein, Bedau (1996, p. 338) urges a definition of life as "supple adaptation"—the capacity to respond appropriately, in an indefinite variety of ways, to an unpredictable (from the perspective of the organism) variety of contingencies. Such a definition [unlike, for example, one focused on the metabolization of matter into energy—see Schrödinger (1969) and Boden (1999)] clearly allows events and processes subsisting in electronic and other media to count as instances of life properly so-called. Other authors focus on still other properties and features, such as autopoiesis (autopoietic systems actively create and maintain their own boundaries, within which complex circular interactions support the continued production of essential chemicals and materials—see Varela, Maturana, and Uribe, 1974), autocatalysis (sets of

---

[7]Thanks to Brian Keeley for insisting on the importance of these topics, and for helping me to think about them.

elements—chemical or computational—that catalyze their own production from available resources—see Kauffman, 1995), self-reproduction, genetics, and metabolization (Crick, 1981), and so on. A very real possibility—also mentioned by Bedau (1996)—is that "life" is a so-called cluster concept, involving multiple typical features none of which is individually necessary for a system to count as alive, and multiple different subsets of which could be sufficient.

There is also a debate about the relations between life and mind. One way to resist the worry (see Section A) that these simple, life-like systems tell us little about really *cognitive* phenomena is to hold that life and mind share deep organizational features and that the project of understanding mind is thus continuous with the project of understanding life itself. The position is nicely expressed by Godfrey-Smith (1996a, p. 320) in his description[8] of the thesis of "strong continuity":

> Life and mind have a common abstract pattern or set of basic organizational proper ties. The functional[9] properties characteristic of mind are an enriched version of the functional properties that are fundamental to life in general. Mind is literally life-*like*.

This, as Godfrey-Smith notes, is a deep claim about the phenomenon of mind itself. It thus goes beyond the more methodological claim that the scientific investigation of mind should proceed by looking at whole, embodied life-forms, and asserts that the central *characteristics* of mind are, in large part, those of life in general. This is not to imply, of course, that life and mind are exactly equivalent—just that if we understood the deep organizing principles of life in general, we would have come a very long way in the project of understanding mind. In more concrete terms, the thesis of strong continuity would be true if, for example, the basic concepts needed to understand the organization of life turned out to be self-organization, collective dynamics, circular causal processes, autopoiesis, etc., and if *those very same concepts and constructs* turned out to be central to a proper scientific understanding of mind. A specific—and currently quite popular—version of the strong continuity thesis is thus the idea that the concepts and constructs of dynamic systems theory will turn out to be the best tools for a science of mind, and will simultaneously reveal the fundamental organizational similarity of processes operating across multiple physical, evolutionary, and temporal scales. The danger, of course, is that by stressing unity and similarity we may lose sight of what is special and distinctive. Mind may indeed participate in many of the dynamic processes characteristic of life. But what about our old friends, the funda-

---

[8]As far as I can tell, Godfrey-Smith remains agnostic on the truth of the strong continuity thesis. He merely presents it as one of several possible positions and relates it to certain trends in the history of ideas. See Godfrey-Smith (1996a,b).

[9]It may be that Godfrey-Smith overplays the role of functional description here. Recall our discussions of function versus implementation in Chapters 1 through 6. For a version of strong continuity without the functional emphasis, see Wheeler (1997).

mentally reason-based transitions and the grasp of the absent and the abstract characteristic of advanced cognition?

Balancing these explanatory needs (the need to see continuity in nature and the need to appreciate the mental as somehow *special*) is perhaps the hardest part of recent cognitive scientific attempts to naturalize the mind.

6.3 Suggested Readings

Useful general introductions to work in robotics and artificial life include S. Levy, *Artificial Life* (London: Cape, 1992), a journalistic but solid introduction to the history and practice of artificial life, and S. Franklin, *Artificial Minds* (Cambridge, MA: MIT Press, 1995). C. Langton (ed.), *Artificial Life: An Overview* (Cambridge, MA: MIT Press, 1995) reprints the first three issues of the journal *Artificial Life* and includes excellent, specially commissioned overview articles covering robotics, collective effects, evolutionary simulations, and more. It includes one of Ray's papers on the Tierra project, as well as excellent introductory overviews by (among other) Luc Steels, Pattie Maes, and Mitchel Resnick.

For an excellent treatment of the issues concerning *emergence and collective effects*, the reader is strongly encouraged to look at M. Resnick, *Turtles, Termites and Traffic Jams* (Cambridge, MA: MIT Press, 1994). This is a delightful, simulation-based introduction to the emergence of complex effects from the interaction of simple rules. Software is available on the web.

For the *philosophical issues concerning emergence, representation, and the relation of life to mind*, see various essays in M. Boden (ed.), *The Philosophy of Artificial Life* (Oxford, England: Oxford University Press, 1996), especially the papers by Langton, Wheeler, Kirsh, and Boden. A. Clark, *Being There: Putting Brain, Body and World Together Again* (Cambridge, MA: MIT Press, 1997) is an extended treatment of many of the core issues.

For work on *real-world robotics and the importance of physical implementation*, see H. Chiel and R. Beer "The brain has a body." *Trends in Neuroscience*, 20, 553–557, 1997. This is an excellent short summary of evidence in favor of treating the nervous system, body, and environment as a unified system. R. McClamrock, *Existential Cognition: Computational Minds in the World* (Chicago: University of Chicago Press, 1995) is a well-executed philosophical argument for viewing the mind as essentially environmentally embedded, and B. Webb "A Cricket Robot." *Scientific American*, 275, 62–67, 1996, is a user-friendly account of the work on the robot cricket.

Volumes of conference proceedings probably offer the best view of the actual practice of artificial life. See, e.g., *Artificial Life I–VII* (and counting) published by MIT Press, Cambridge, MA.

DYNAMICS 7

7.1 Sketches

Cognitive science, we have seen, is involved in an escalating retreat from the inner symbol: a kind of inner symbol flight. The original computational vision (Chapters 1 and 2) displayed no such qualms and happily tied syntax to semantics using static inner items that could stand for semantic contents. Such items were invariant ("token identical") across different contexts and were easily thought of as inner symbols. Connectionist approaches (Chapter 4) expanded our conception of the syntax/semantics link, allowing context-sensitive coalitions of unit activity to bear the semantic burden and producing sensible behaviors and judgments without the use of static, chunky, easy-to-interpret inner states. Connectionism, we might say, showed us how to believe in internal *representations* without quite believing in traditional internal *symbols*. Recent work in neuroscience, animate vision, robotics, and artificial life (Chapters 5 and 6) has expanded our conceptions still further, by displaying an even wider range of neural dynamics and possible coding strategies and by stressing the profound roles of timing, body, motion, and local environment in biological problem solving.

But as the complexity and environmental interactivity of our stories increase, so the explanatory leverage provided by the original complex of theoretical notions (symbols, internal representations, computations) seems to diminish. Dynamic systems theory, as it is used in recent[1] cognitive science, can be seen as an attempt

---

[1]Dynamic approaches to cognition go back at least as far as the wonderful cybernetics literature of the 1940s and 1950s—see, e.g., Wiener (1948) and Ashby (1952, 1956). But the approach fell into disfavor in the early days of symbol system A.I. Its recent resurgence owes a lot to the efforts of theorists such as Kelso (1995), van Gelder (1995), Thelen and Smith (1994), Beer (1995), and van Gelder and Port (1995).

to find analytic tools better suited to the study of complex interactive systems. Whether such tools offer an out-and-out *alternative* to the traditional theoretical framework, or are better seen as a kind of subtle *complement* to that framework, are matters to which we will soon return. The first order of business is to clarify what a dynamic approach involves.

Dynamic systems theory is a well-established framework in physical science.[2] It is primarily geared to modeling and describing phenomena that involve change over time (and change in rate of change over time, and so on). Indeed, the broadest definition of a dynamic system is simply any system that changes over time. Just about every system in the physical world (including all computational systems) is thus a dynamic system. But it is only when the patterns of change over time exhibit a certain kind of complexity that the technical apparatus of dynamic systems theory really comes into its own. Some of the key features on which this special kind of explanatory power depends include

1. the discovery of powerful but low-dimensional descriptions of systemic unfolding,
2. the provision of intuitive, geometric images of the state space of the system,
3. the (closely related) practice of isolating *control parameters* and defining *collective variables* (see below), and
4. the use of the technical notion of *coupling* (see below) to model and track processes involving continuous circular causal influence among multiple subsystems.

Transposed into the cognitive scientific domain, these features make dynamic approaches especially attractive for understanding those aspects of adaptive behavior that depend on complex, circular causal exchanges in which some inner factor x is continuously affecting and being affected by some other (inner or outer) factor y (which may itself stand in similar relations to a factor z, and so on). Such complex causal webs, as we began to see in the previous chapter, are often characteristic of natural systems in which neural processing, bodily action, and environmental forces are constantly and complexly combined. To get the flavor of the dynamic approach in action, let us review a few examples.

Case 1: Rhythmic Finger Motion

Consider the case (Kelso, 1981, 1995, Chapter 2) of rhythmic finger motion. Human subjects, asked to move their two index fingers at the same frequency in a side-to-side "wiggling" motion, display two stable strategies. Either the fingers move in phase (the equivalent muscles of each hand contract at the same moment), or exactly antiphase (one contracts as the other expands). The antiphase solution, however, is unstable at high frequencies of oscillation—at a critical frequency it collapses into the phased solution.

[2]See, e.g., Abraham and Shaw (1992).

How should we explain and understand this patter of results? One strategy is to seek a more illuminating description of the behavioral events. To this end, Kelso and his colleagues plotted the phase relationship between the two fingers. This variable is constant for a wide range of oscillation frequencies but is subject to a dramatic shift at a critical value—the moment of the antiphase/phase shift. Plotting the unfolding of the relative phase variable is plotting the values of what is known as a "collective variable," whose value is set by a *relation* between the values of other variables (the ones describing individual finger motions). The values of these collective variables are fixed by the frequency of motion, which thus acts as a so-called control parameter. The dynamic analysis is then fleshed out by the provision of a detailed mathematical description—a set of equations displaying the space of possible temporal evolutions of relative phase as governed by the control parameter. This description fixes, in detail, the so-called state space of the system. A systemic state is defined by assigning a value to each systemic variable, and the overall state *space* (also known as phase space) is just the set of all possible values for these variables—all the value combinations that could actually come about. Dynamicists often think about target systems in terms of possible trajectories through such state spaces—possible sequences of states that could take the system from one location in state space to another. The set of possible trajectories through a state space is called the "flow." Finally, certain regions of the state space may exhibit notable properties (see Box 7.1). An *attractor* is a point or region such that any trajectory passing close by will be drawn into the region (the area of such influence being known as the basin of attraction). A *repellor* is a point or region that deflects incoming trajectories. A *bifurcation* occurs when a small change in parameter values can reshape the flow within the state space and yield a new landscape of attractors, repellors, and so on. Dynamic systems approaches thus provide a set of mathematical and conceptual tools that helps display the way a system changes over time.

In the case of rhythmic finger motion, Haken, Kelso, and Bunz (1985) use a dynamic analysis to display how different patterns of finger coordination (inphase/antiphase, etc.) result from different values of the control parameter (frequency of oscillation). This detailed dynamic model was capable of (1) accounting for the observed phase transitions without positing any special "switching mechanism"—instead, the switching emerges as a natural product of the normal, self-organizing evolution of the system, (2) predicting and explaining the results of selective interference with the system (as when one finger is temporarily forced out of its stable phase relation), and (3) generating accurate predictions of, e.g., the time taken to switch from antiphase to phase. For a nice review of the model, see (Kelso, 1995, pp. 54–61).

A good dynamic explanation is thus perched midway between what, to a more traditional cognitive scientist, may at first look like a ("mere") *description* of a pattern of events and a real *explanation* of why the events unfold as they do. It is not a mere description since the parameters need to be very carefully chosen so that the resulting model has predictive force: it tells us enough about the system to know

Box 7.1

NUMERICAL DYNAMICS

Stan Franklin (1995), in his *Artificial Minds* (Chapter 12), offers a useful introductory example of a dynamical analysis. Consider the real numbers (with infinity). And imagine that the global dynamics of the number space are set by a squaring function so that for any number x, given as input (initial state), the next state of the system will be x^2. Now consider what happens assuming different initial states. If the initial state is the input 0, the numerical unfolding stays at 0: this is an example of "converging to a fixed point attractor." For initial state 2, the numerical unfolding continues 4, 16, 256, converging to infinity. For initial state -1, the system goes to 1 and stops. But initial points close to 1 (0.9, etc.) move rapidly away. 0 and infinity are thus the attractors to which many initial states converge. 1 is a repellor; a point from which most initial states move away. Since all initial states between 0 and 1 head progressively toward 0 (as the numbers become smaller and smaller with each application of the squaring function), 0 has a basin of attraction that includes all these points (in fact, all the real numbers between -1 and 1). Infinity has a basin of attraction that includes all points greater than 1 or less than -1. The general situation is illustrated in Figure 7.1. To produce so-called periodic behavior, it is necessary to alter the global dynamics, e.g., to the square of the input number, minus 1. An initial state of -1 will then display the repeating (periodic) trajectory: 0, -1, 0, -1, etc.

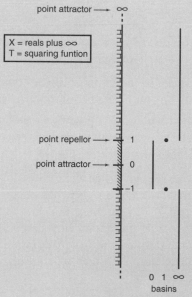

Figure 7.1 Basins of attraction. [From Franklin (1995, p. 283). By permission of MIT Press.]

how it would behave in various nonactual circumstances. But it differs from more traditional cognitive scientific explanations in that it greatly abstracts away from the behavior of individual systemic components.

Case 2: Treadmill Stepping[3]

Consider the phenomenon of learning to walk. Learning to walk involves a regular pattern of developmental events that includes (1) the ability, present at birth, to produce coordinated stepping motions when held upright in the air, (2) the disappearance, at about 2 months, of this response, (3) its reappearance at around 8–10 months when the child begins to support its own weight on its feet, and (4) the appearance, at around 1 year old, of independent coordinated stepping (walking).

At one time, it was thought that the best explanation of this overall pattern would depict at as the expression of a prior set of instructions, complete with timing, encoded in (perhaps) a genetically specified central pattern generator (see Thelen and Smith, 1994, pp. 8–20, 263–266). Thelen and Smith (1994) argue, however, that there is no such privileged, complete, and prespecified neutral control system, and that learning to walk involves a complex set of interactions between neural states, the spring-like properties of leg muscles, and the local environment. Walking, according to Thelen and Smith, emerges from the balanced interplay of multiple factors spanning brain, body, and world, and is best understood using a dynamic approach that charts the interactions between factors and that identifies crucial elements on "control parameters."

Thelen and Smith conducted a fascinating sequence of experiments yielding broad support for such a view. Two especially significant findings were

1. that stepping motions can be induced during the "nonstepping" window (2–8 months) by simply holding the baby upright in warm water (instead of air) and

2. that nonstepping 7 month olds held upright on a motorized treadmill perform coordinated alternating stepping motion, and are even able to compensate for twin belts driving each leg at a different speed!

The explanation, according to Thelen and Smith (1994, Chapters 1 and 4), is that stepping is dynamically assembled rather than being the expression of a simple inner command system. Bodily parameters such as the leg weight, which is effectively manipulated by partial immersion in water, and environmental factors (such as the presence of the treadmill) seem equally implicated in the observed behaviors. In the case of the treadmill, further experiments revealed that the crucial

---

[3]This case is treated in more detail in Clark (1997).

factor was the orientation of leg and foot to the treadmill. Infants who made flat-foot belt contact exhibited treadmill stepping, whereas those that made only toe contact failed to step. Thelen and Smith (1994, pp. 111–112) explain this by hypothesizing that the infant leg, when stretched out, is acting like a spring. At full back stretch, the spring uncoils and swings the leg forward. Flat-foot belt contact precociously ensures this full back stretch and hence initiates stepping. Relative flexor or extensor tendencies in the legs thus contribute heavily to the emergence of coordinated stepping in the normal case (Thelen and Smith, 1994, p. 113). The treadmill stepping task provides an especially useful window onto the dynamic construction of infant walking, as it highlights the complex and subtle interplay between intrinsic dynamics, organic change, and external task environment. In dynamic terms, the treadmill looks to be acting as a real-time control parameter that prompts the phase shift, in 7 month olds, from nonstepping to smooth alternating stepping motions. Stepping behavior thus "emerges only when the central elements cooperate with the effecters—the muscles, joints, tendons—in the appropriate physical context" (Thelen and Smith, 1994, p. 113).

Case 3: The Watt Governor

Consider finally a classic example recently deployed by Tim van Gelder (1995)—the operation of the Watt (or centrifugal) governor. The job of the governor is to keep constant the speed of a flywheel that drives industrial machinery and is itself driven by a steam engine. Given variations in steam pressure and current workload (number of machines being driven, etc.), the flywheel speed tends to fluctuate. To keep it smooth and constant, the amount of steam entering the pistons is controlled by a throttle valve. More steam results in more speed; less steam results in less speed. At one time, a human engineer had the unenviable task of making these constant corrections. How might such a process be automated?

One solution (which van Gelder describes as the computational solution) would involve a sequence of steps and measurements. For example, we might program a device to measure the speed of the flywheel, compare this to some desired speed, measure the steam pressure, calculate any change in pressure needed to maintain the desired speed, adjust the throttle valve accordingly, then begin the whole sequence anew (see van Gelder, 1995, p. 348). What makes this kind of solution *computational*, van Gelder suggests, is a complex of familiar features. The most important one is representation: the device measures the speed of the flywheel, creates a token that stands for the speed, and performs numerous operations (comparisons, etc.) on this and other representations. These operations are discrete and occur in a set sequence, which then repeats itself. The sequence involves a perception/measurement–computation–action cycle in which the environment is measured ("perceived"), internal representations created, computations performed, and an action chosen. The overall device reflects a nicely decomposable problem solution. For it respects a division of the problem into these distinct subparts, each of which is dealt with independently, and which are coordinated by acts of communication (in which x tells y the value of z and so on). The features distinctive of the computational governor are thus (1) the use of internal representations and symbols, (2) the use of computational operations that alter and transform those representations, (3) the presence of a well-defined perception–computation–action cycle (what van Gelder calls "sequential and cyclic operation"), and (4) the susceptibility to step-wise information-processing decomposition (what van Gelder calls "homuncularity").

Now for the second solution, the one discovered by James Watt (see Figure 7.2). Gear a vertical spindle into the flywheel and attach two hinged arms to the spindle. To the end of each arm, attach a metal ball. Link the arms to the throttle valve so that the higher the arms swing out, the less steam is allowed through. As the spindle turns, centrifugal force causes the arms to fly out. The faster it turns, the higher the arms fly out. But this now reduces steam flow, causing the engine to slow down and the arms to fall. This, of course, opens the valve and allows more steam to flow. By clever calibration this centrifugal governor can be set up so as to maintain engine speed smoothly despite wide variations in pressure, workload, and so on. (This story is condensed from van Gelder, 1995, pp. 347–350.)

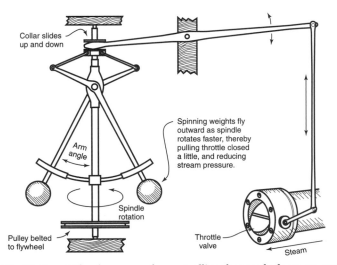

Figure 7.2 The Watt centrifugal governor for controlling the speed of a steam engine (Farey, 1827). [From van Gelder, T.J. (1997). "Dynamics and cognition." In J. Haugeland, ed., *Mind Design II: Philosophy, Psychology, and Artificial Intelligence*, rev. ed. Cambridge, MA: MIT Press. Reproduced by kind permission of the author and the publishers, MIT Press.]

This centrifugal governor, van Gelder claims, constitutes a control system that is noncomputational, nonrepresentational, and that simply cries out for dynamic analysis and understanding. In particular, only a dynamic analysis can explain the peculiarly complex, yet effective, relationship that is obtained between the arm angle and the engine speed. A mad-dog representationalist might, perhaps, try to claim that the best way to understand this relationship is by depicting the arm angle as a representation of the engine speed. But, van Gelder (1995, p. 353) insists, the real relationship is "much more subtle and complex than the standard notion of representation can handle." It is more subtle and complex because the arm angle is continuously modulating the engine speed at the same time as the engine speed is modulating the arm angle. The two quantities are best seen as being codetermined and codetermining—a relationship nicely captured using a dynamic apparatus (see below) of coupled differential equations. The Watt governor then fails to constitute a *computational* device for two reasons. First, because, on van Gelder's (1995, p. 353) account, computation requires the manipulation of token-like representations that seem notably absent here. And second, because there are no discrete operations in the governing processes and hence no distinct sequence of manipulations to identify with the steps in an algorithmic solution. The Watt governor thus fails to exhibit any of the features associated with the computational solution, and for a single deep reason: the continuous and simultaneous relations of causal influence that obtain among the various factors involved. It is this distinctive kind of causal profile that both invites treatment in terms of an alternative dynamic analysis and that causes problems for the traditional (computational and representational) approach.

The way to capture such a complex causal relationship, van Gelder asserts, is by using the dynamic notion of *coupling*. In a typical quantitative dynamic explanation, the theorist specifies a set of parameters whose collective evolution is governed by a set of differential equations. Such explanations allow distinct components (such as the arm and the engine) to be treated as a coupled system in a specific technical sense, viz. the equation describing the evolution of each component contains a slot that factors in the other one's current state (technically, the state variables of the first system are the parameters of the second and vice versa). Thus consider two wall-mounted pendulums placed in close proximity on a single wall. The two pendulums will tend (courtesy of vibrations running along the wall) to become swing-synchronized over time. This process admits of an elegant dynamic explanation in which the two pendulums are analyzed as a single coupled system with the motion equation for each one including a term representing the influence of the other's current state.[4] This kind of complex, constant, mutual interaction is, van Gelder and others claim,[5] much closer to the true profile of agent–

---

[4]See Salzman and Newsome (1994).

[5]For example, Beer and Gallagher (1992) and Wheeler (1994).

environment interactions than is the traditional vision of a simple perception–computation–action sequence.

With these comments and case studies in hand, it is now reasonably easy to construct the case for a dynamic cognitive science. The case turns on three basic assertions.

The first, relatively unproblematic, assertion is that body and world (and hence time, movement, and so on) all matter, and can play powerful roles in adaptive problem solving. We have seen several examples of this earlier in the text, e.g., the work on infant locomotion, cricket phonotaxis, and animate vision, as well as in a wealth of research in biology, cognitive neuroethology, and robotics.[6] The second assertion is that body and world matter not simply because they provide an arena for useful action and a sensitive perceptual front-end, but because neural, bodily, and environmental elements are intimately intermingled courtesy of processes of continuous reciprocal causation that criss-cross intuitive boundaries. This leads to the third and final assertion, that the traditional tools of computational and representational analysis (with the associated image of an input–compute–act cycle) cannot do justice to such a complex interactive process and that the mathematical and topological resources of dynamic systems theory are to be preferred. Such, it seems to me, is the central argument.[7] But is it really powerful enough to win the day?

7.2 Discussion

A. THE HIDDEN PREMISE

The most radical conclusion to be drawn from the dynamic considerations seems to go something like this:

> *The Radical Embodied Cognition Thesis*
> Structured, symbolic, representational, and computational views of cognition are mistaken. Embodied cognition is best studied using noncomputational and nonrepresentational ideas and explanatory schemes, and especially the tools of dynamic systems theory.

---

[6]For review, see Clark (1997).

[7]The centrality of the point about continuous reciprocal causation is evident from remarks such as these: "the . . . deepest reason for supposing that the centrifugal governor is not representational is that . . . arm angle and engine speed are at all times both determined by, and determining each other's behavior. [This relationship] is much more subtle and complex than the standard concept of representation can handle" (van Gelder, 1995, p. 353). Or again: "adaptive behavior is the result of the continuous interaction between the nervous system, the body and the environment . . . one cannot assign credit for adaptive behavior to any one piece of this coupled system" (Chiel and Beer, 1997, p. 555). See also van Gelder and Port (1995, pp. ix, 23), Schöner (1993), Kelso (1995), and the discussion in Clark (1998c).

Given the nature of the dynamic demonstrations, it seems initially surprising to find such radical and sweeping conclusions. What we seem to have before us is, surely, just an argument that some quite low-level sensorimotor engagements with the world (finger wiggling, infant walking, Watt governing, etc.) exhibit a complex causal structure that makes it hard to fully explain such engagements using standard notions of computations and representation, and the input–compute–act cycle. This seems compatible with (1) the idea that for *higher level* cognition, the standard framework is still the best and (2) the idea that even at the lower levels, *some aspects* of systemic unfolding might still reward a more traditional analysis.

Despite this, there can be little doubt that genuine and sweeping radical reform is in the air. Thelen and Smith clearly support the radical thesis, writing that:

> *Explanations in terms of structure in the head*—beliefs, rules, concepts and schemata—*are not acceptable.* . . . Our theory has new concepts at the center—nonlinearity, reentrance, coupling heterochronicity, attractors, momentum, state spaces, intrinsic dynamics, forces. These concepts are not reducible to the old ones. (Thelen and Smith, 1994, p. 339; my emphasis)

> We posit that development happens because of the time-locked pattern of activity across heterogenous components. We are not building representations of the world by connecting temporally contingent ideas. *We are not building representations at all! Mind is activity in time* . . . the real time of real physical causes. (Thelen and Smith, 1994, p. 338; my emphasis)

Scott Kelso, though more sympathetic to a (reconceived) notion of internal information bearers (representations?), asserts that

> The thesis here is that the human brain is *fundamentally* a pattern-forming, self-organized system governed by non-linear dynamical laws. *Rather than compute*, our brain dwells (at least for short times) in metastable states. (Kelso, 1995, p. 26; second emphasis mine)

Other writers who sometimes seem tempted by the radical thesis include Smithers (1994), Wheeler (1994), Maturana and Varela (1980), Skarda and Freeman (1987), and van Gelder (1995). The generally balanced and extended treatment in Keijzer (1998, p. 240) also leans toward the radical conclusion, suggesting that attempts (such as Clark, 1997) to preserve the use of a computational/representational framework amount to "the injection of a particular set of thought habits into a tentative and still fragile interactionist account of behavior."

The first order of business, then, is to somehow join the dots, to identify the additional ideas and premises that might link the rather limited empirical demonstrations to the sweeping radical conclusion. The most crucial linking theme, I now believe,[8] relates to the idea of the continuity of life and mind. We have already encountered this idea (in Chapter 6), so let us be brief.

---

[8]Thanks to Esther Thelen for insisting (personal communications) on the importance of this idea.

Consider—following Pollack (1994)—the history of flight. When we first encounter birds and wonder how they manage to fly, the most superficially salient feature might seem to be the flapping of wings. But, as we all now know, and as some early pioneers found out by bitter experience, powerful flapping is not really the key. Instead, as the Wright brothers finally figured out:

> most of the problem of flying is in finding a place within the weight/size dimension where gliding is possible, and getting the control systems for dynamical equilibrium right. Flapping is the last piece, the propulsive engine, but in all its furiousness it blocks our perception. (Pollack, 1994, p. 188)

Specifically, what the flapping obscures is the pivotal importance of what is known as the Aileron principle—the use of control cables and raisable and lowerable wing flaps to allow the pilot to balance the machine while gliding in the air.

> The analogical extension to dynamical approaches to cognition is pretty direct: Just like flapping, symbolic thought is the last piece [of the puzzle] . . . in all its furiousness it obscures our perception of cognition as an exquisite control system . . . governing a very complicated real-time physical system. (Pollack, 1994, p. 118)

Understanding that real-time physical system, Pollack believes, is pretty impossible as long as we focus on symbolic problem solving (flapping). Instead, we should (Pollack, 1994, p. 119) "unify cognition with nature"—look not at "software law" but at physical law. Only then will we begin to see how biological intelligence can be as robust and flexible as it is—how, for example, the injured cat can immediately adopt a successful three-legged gait courtesy of the complex, interactive dynamics linking neural nets with spring-like muscle and tendon systems. Such rich interactive dynamics have little, it seems, to do with explicit, symbol-using problem solving. Yet it is this rich nonsymbolic substrate that, it is argued, forms the essential basis for all aspects of biological intelligence (see, e.g., Thelen and Smith, 1994, p. xxiii). This substrate, as we saw, is characterized by processes of continuous reciprocal causal influence in which overall interaction dynamics (rather than some privileged, knowledge-based component) enable the organism to achieve its goals and to compensate for unwelcome environmental changes. It is in this way that the Watt governor, although clearly itself a noncognitive device, may be presented (van Gelder, 1995, p. 358) as "more relevantly similar" in its operation to (the fundamental, dynamical substrate of) human cognition than more traditional computation-and-representation invoking benchmarks such as SOAR (Chapter 2) or even NETtalk (Chapter 4).

B. STRONG AND WEAK CONTINUITY

The radical thesis is rooted, then, in a familiar observation: the shape and operation of higher level cognitive processes have probably been built, in some highly path-dependent fashion, on a more evolutionary basic substrate of perception and sensorimotor control. Connectionists, however (recall Chapter 4) have made similar points, as have theorists working in traditional artificial intelligence (e.g., Simon, 1996), and done so *without* calling into question the fundamental framework of computational and representational explanation. Where's the difference?

The difference again lies in the dynamicist's emphasis on interaction and continuous reciprocal causation; the idea that it is the on-going couplings between environment, body, and nervous system that form the basis of real-time adaptive response. Accepting both path dependence and the interactive nature of basic sensorimotor adaptation, however, *still* falls well short of establishing the thesis of radical embodied cognition.

Thus consider a traditional claim—that we sometimes solve problems by exploiting inner models that are designed (by learning or evolution) to function as off-line *stand-ins* for features of our real-world environment. In such cases, we temporarily abandon the strategy of directly interacting with our world so as to engage in more "vicarious" forms of exploration. It is certainly possible that such off-line problem solving is perfectly continuous with various on-line, highly environmentally interactive, motor control strategies. Thus Grush (1995) describes a piece of circuitry whose principal role is the fine-tuning of on-line reaching. The circuitry, however, involves the use of an inner model (an "emulator loop") that predicts sensory feedback in advance of the actual signals arriving (rather too slowly) from the bodily peripheries. This inner loop, once in place, supports the additional functionality of fully off-line deployment, allowing the system to rehearse motor actions entirely in its "imagination." Such cases suggest both a profound *continuity* between smooth motor control strategies and higher cognitive capacities such as off-line reasoning and imagination, and (simultaneously) a profound *discontinuity* in that the system is now using specific and identifiable inner states as full-blooded stand-ins for specific extraneural (in this case bodily) states of affairs. These are surely internal representations in quite a strong sense. At such times the system is *not* continuously assembling its behavior by balancing ongoing neural bodily and environmental influences. We thus preserve a kind of architectural continuity, but without the added commitment to the radical embodied cognition thesis (for a fuller treatment, see Clark and Grush, 1999).

C. REPRESENTATION AND COMPUTATION, AGAIN

Another worry concerns the nature (content) of any putative internal representations. For it looks as if the target of much dynamicist skepticism is not internal representation per se so much as a particular type of internal representation, viz. what are sometimes called "objectivist" representations—the kind that might be featured in a detailed, viewpoint-independent model of some aspect of the world. Notice, then, a second (and I believe, highly significant—see Clark, 1995) way in which higher level cognition may be continuous with its motor and developmental roots. It may be continuous insofar as it involves internal representations whose contents (unlike detailed "objectivist' representations) are heavily geared toward the support of typical or important kinds of real-world, real-time action. Such contents may (as in the previous example) sometimes be manipulated "off-line"—but they are nonetheless *types* of content (what I elsewhere call action-oriented contents) that are especially suited to the control and coordination of real action in real time. Cognition, on this model, need not always be *actually* interactive (involving brain, body, and world as equal partners). But the inner economy is deeply sculpted and shaped by the interactive needs and patterns of the organism.

Much dynamicist skepticism, on closer examination, looks to address only the notion of objectivist (detached, action-independent, highly-detailed, static, general-purpose) internal representations. Thus Thelen and Smith (1994, pp. 37–44) question all these ideas, suggesting instead that we treat knowledge as an action-guiding process continually organized against a contextual backdrop that brings forth its form, content, and use. The same emphases characterize Varela's notion of "enaction" in which "cognitive structures emerge from the recurrent sensorimotor patterns that enable action to be perceptually guided" (Varela, Thompson, and Rosch, 1991, p. 173). In a related vein, Agre (1995, p. 19) notes the importance of "indexical-functional representations" (such as "a few feet straight ahead")—these are ideal for the cheap control of individual action and are contrasted with objectivist map-like representations such as "at latitude 41, longitude 13." Perhaps, then, some of the disputes really concern the content, not the existence, of inner states whose role is to stand in for important extraneural states of affairs.

Related to this may be an assumption concerning the type of inner control implicated in broadly representationalist/computationalist accounts. The assumption, roughly, is that computational models involve the storage and use of complex inner control structures that plot, in *explicit detail*, all the values and settings of all the physical parameters involved in a given action. Something like this assumption would help explain why Thelen and Smith repeatedly associate the idea that the brain is a computational device with seemingly orthogonal ideas about detailed advance blueprints for behavior, complete with internal clocks, full specifications of all relevant parameter settings (joint-angle coordinates, muscle fixing patterns, etc.) for the limbs, and capable of controlling movement by "'pure' neural commands" (Thelen and Smith, 1994, p. 75, see also pp. xix, 62–63, 71, 264). They then *contrast* this vision of highly detailed, complete neural instruction sets with the ideas of collective states, phase shifts, and control parameters, as discussed earlier. Certain preferred collective states of the system are depicted as synergetic wholes that can be brought forth (but not "programmed") by the action of some control parameter (such as frequency of motion in the rhythmic finger motion case and flexor tone in the treadmill stepping case). Kelso's description of the brain itself as not a computing device but a "pattern-forming, self-organized system" (Kelso, 1995, p. 26) has the same flavor. The contrast is between systems whose behavior is fixed by complete encoded instruction sets and ones whose behavior emerges as a sequence of temporarily stable states of a complex system with richly interdependent intrinsic dynamics. The slogan may be "patterns without programs"; but the real target is the idea that we use complex neural instruction sets to force orderly behavior from multiple muscles, links, joints, etc. Such detailed forcing is not necessary, it is claimed, because the system self-organizes into a smaller set of preferred states whose flux may be controlled by the action of some simple parameter. (It is a little as if the "computationalist," faced with the problem of moving a crowd from A to B, were to encode an instruction for each person's trajectory, whereas the dynamicist simply finds a control parameter (maybe increasing the heat on one side of the crowd) that then exploits the intrinsic responses of those closest to it, whose motion in turn entrains the movements of their near neighbors, until the crowd moves as a unified whole in the desired direction).

This is an important and fascinating shift in emphasis, to be sure. But does it really amount to a rejection of the idea that the brain computes? I suggest that it cannot, since there is no necessary commitment on the part of the computationalist to the idea of highly detailed or complete instruction sets. A short piece of software, written in a high-level language, will not *itself* specify how or when to achieve many subgoals—these tasks are ceded to built-in features of the operating system or to the activity of a cascade of lower level code. Moreover, a program can perfectly well "assume" a necessary backdrop of environmental or bodily structures and dynamics. Jordan et al. (1994) describe a program for the control of arm motions, but one that assumes (for its success) a lot of extrinsic dynamics such as mass of arm, spring of muscle, and force of gravity.

Now it may be that so very much is done by the synergetic dynamics of the body–environment system that the neural contributions are indeed best treated, at times, as just the application of simple forces to a complex but highly interanimated system whose intrinsic dynamics then carry most of the load. But less radically, it may be that motor activity simply requires *less* in the way of detailed inner instruction sets than we might have supposed, courtesy of the existence of a small set of preferred collective states such that successful behavior often requires only the setting of a few central parameters such as initial stiffness in a spring-like muscle system and so on. Such sparse specifications may support complex global effects without directly specifying joint-angle configurations and the like.

The lack of a particularly detailed kind of neural instruction set does not then establish the total absence of stored programs. Such a characterization is compelling only at the most extreme end of a genuine continuum. Between the two extremes lies the interesting space of what I elsewhere (Clark, 1997) call "partial programs"—minimal instruction sets that maximally exploit the inherent (bodily and environmental) dynamics of the controlled system. The real moral of much actual dynamic systems-oriented research is, I suspect, that it is *in this space that we may expect to encounter nature's own programs.*

D. THE SPACE OF REASONS

The deepest problem with the dynamic alternative lies, however, in its treatment of the brain as *just one more factor* in the complex overall web of causal influences. In one sense this is obviously true. Inner and outer factors do conspire to support many kinds of adaptive success. But in another sense it is either false, or our world view will have to change in some very dramatic fashion indeed. For we do suppose that it is the staggering structural complexity and variability of the brain that are the key to understanding the specifically intelligence-based route to evolutionary success. And we do suppose that that route involves the ability, courtesy of complex neural events, to become appraised of *information* concerning our surroundings, and to use that information as a guide to present and future action. If these are not truisms, they are very close to being so. But as soon as we embrace the notion of the brain as the principal seat of information-processing activity, we are already seeing it as fundamentally different from, say, the flow of a river or the activity of a volcano. And this is a difference that needs to be reflected in our scientific analysis: a difference that typically *is* reflected when we pursue the kind of information-processing model associated with computational approaches, but that looks to be lost if we treat the brain in exactly the same terms as, say, the Watt governor, or the beating of a heart, or the unfolding of a basic chemical reaction.[9]

The question, in short, is how to do justice to the idea that there is a principled *distinction* between knowledge-based and merely physical-causal systems. It does not seem likely that the dynamicist will deny that there is a difference (though hints of such a denial[10] are sometimes to be found). But rather than responding by embracing a different vocabulary for the understanding and analysis of brain events (at least as they pertain to cognition), the dynamicist recasts the issue as the explanation of distinctive kinds of behavioral flexibility and hopes to explain that flexibility using the very same apparatus that works for other physical systems, such as the Watt governor.

Such apparatus, however, may not be intrinsically well suited to explaining the particular way certain neural processes contribute to behavioral flexibility. This is because it is unclear how it can do justice to the fundamental ideas of agency and of information-guided choice. Isn't there a (morally and scientifically) crucial distinction between systems that select actions for reasons and on the basis of acquired knowledge, and other (often highly complex) systems that do not display such goal-oriented behaviors? The image of brain, body, and world as a single, densely cou-

---

[9]For the last two cases, see Goodwin (1995, p. 60).

[10]For example, van Gelder's comments (1995, p. 358) on tasks that may only initially appear to require "that the system have knowledge of and reason about, its environment," and Thelen and Smith's (1994, p. xix) stress on the brain as a thermodynamic system. By contrast, the dynamicist Kelso (1995, p. 288) sees the key problem as "how *information* is to be conceived in living things, in general, and the brain in particular."

pled system threatens to eliminate the idea of purposive agency unless it is combined with some recognition of the special way goals and knowledge figure in the origination of some of our bodily motions.[11] The computational/information-processing approach provides such recognition by embracing a kind of dual-aspect account in which certain inner states and processes act as the vehicles of knowledge and information.

Perhaps, then, what is needed is a kind of dynamic computationalism in which the details of the flow of information are every bit as important as the larger scale dynamics, and in which some local dynamic features lead a double life as elements in an information-processing economy. Here, then, is one way in which dynamic and computational analyses may proceed hand in hand.[12] The dynamic analyses may help identify the complex and temporally extended physical processes that act as the *vehicles* of representational content. Traditional computationalism may have been just too narrow minded in its vision of the likely syntactic form of the inner bearers of information and content. Our fascination with the static characters and strings of natural language led us to expect simple, local, spatially extended states to function as inner content bearers. Connectionist approaches helped us see beyond that vision, by identifying the content bearers as distributed patterns of activity. But it may take the full firepower of dynamic systems theory to reveal the rich and complex space of possible content bearers.

E. COGNITIVE INCREMENTALISM: THE BIG ISSUE

The work in artificial life (Chapter 6) and dynamic systems raises, in an especially acute form, a puzzle that we have already touched on several times. I think it is worthwhile, however, to now make this puzzle as explicit and prominent as possible.

The puzzle is this: What, in general, is the relation between the strategies used to solve basic problems of perception and action and those used to solve more abstract or higher level problems? Can the capacity to solve more intuitively "cognitive" problems (such as planning next year's vacation, thinking about absent friends, and designing a particle accelerator) be understood in essentially the same terms as the capacity to follow walls, to coordinate finger motions, to generate rhythmic stepping, and so on? Certainly, much of the recent literature on "embodied cognition" seems committed to a notion that I am calling "cognitive incrementalism." This is the idea that you do indeed get full-blown, human cognition by gradually adding "bells and whistles" to basic (embodied, embedded) strategies of relating to the present at hand. It is just such a principle of continu-

---

[11]For a similar argument, see Keijzer and Bem (1996).

[12]Just such a union is pursued in Crutchfield and Mitchell (1995) and in Mitchell et al. (1994). van Gelder's own notion of "revisionary representationalism" and his discussion of decision field theory (van Gelder, 1995, p. 359–363) show that he is open to the idea of such a union.

ity that prompts Thelen and Smith, for example, to comment that "there is in principle no difference between the processes engendering walking, reaching, and looking for hidden objects and those resulting in mathematics and poetry—cognition [is] seamless and dynamic" (Thelen and Smith, 1994, p. xxiii). Much depends, of course, on what we are here to understand by the phrase "no difference between." For in many interesting instances (see also Section B) we can discern both a kind of (often structural) continuity alongside some quite radical functional discontinuity. As a result, some cognitive functions may depend *not* on the tweaking of basic sensorimotor processing, but on the development of relatively (functionally) independent and (functionally) novel kinds of neural processes.

A case in point looks to be the "two visual systems" hypothesis of Milner and Goodale (1995). Milner and Goodale's claim, very (very!) briefly is that on-line visuomotor action is guided by neural resources that are quite fundamentally distinct (see Box 7.2) from those used to support conscious visual experience, off-line visual reasoning, and visually based categorization and verbal report. The latter complex of activities depends, it is argued, on a ventral processing stream and the former on a largely independent dorsal stream. Milner and Goodale's (admittedly quite contentious) explanation thus invokes a quite radical *dissociation* of codings-for-on-line action and for off-line reason and imagination. Here, then, is one very concrete case in which we seem to confront not a simple incremental process in which off-line reason exploits the very same basic mechanisms as on-line action guidance, but something more dramatic and different: a case, perhaps, in which nature adds functionality by developing whole new ways of processing and exploiting sensory input.

Notice that the Milner and Goodale story (unlike the example in Section B) does *not* depict reflective thought as simply the "off-line" use of strategies and encodings developed to promote fluent action in the here and now. Instead, it depicts nature as building (though doubtless out of old parts!) a *new kind* of cognitive machinery, allowing certain animals to categorize and comprehend their world in novel ways that are geared to the conceptualization of sensory input via the extraction of viewer-independent information (concerning object shape, identity, function, and so on). Such modes of encoding format, package and poise sensory information for use in conceptual thoughts and reason, and create what Milner and Goodale (1998, p. 4) suggestively call a system for "insight, hindsight and foresight about the visual world."

It is not my purpose, here, to attempt to fully describe, or critically assess this proposal (see Clark, 1999a, for an attempt). Rather, I invoke it merely to illustrate the empirical uncertainties hereabouts. It may indeed be—as Thelen, Smith, and others suggest—that the neural mechanisms of higher thought and reason are fully continuous with mechanisms of on-line action control. But it may be quite otherwise. Most likely, what we confront is a subtle and complex mixture of strategies, in which new kinds of information-processing routine peaceably coexist with, and

Box 7.2

VISION FOR ACTION VERSUS VISION FOR PERCEPTION?

Milner and Goodale's (1995) controversial suggestion, briefly discussed in the text, is that the neural systems underlying visually guided action (such as reaching) are quite distinct from those underlying conscious visual recognition, categorization, experience, and imagination. A suggestive demonstration involves the so-called Tichener circles illusion (see Figure 7.3)—a case of illusory size distortions in which we regularly misjudge the sizes of the central discs. In the topmost drawing, the two central discs are (in fact) equal in size, whereas in the lower drawing they are different in size. The surrounding rings of large and small circles, in each case, lead us to perceptually misrepresent the actual size of the central discs, seeing them as different when they are the same (top case) and as the same when they are different (bottom case).

Perceptual experience here delivers a content that plainly misrepresents the actual size of the center discs. But there is a twist. Aglioti, Goodale, and Desouza (1995) set up a physical version of the illusion using thin poker chips as the discs, and then asked subjects to "pick up the target disc on the left if the two discs appeared equal in size and to pick up the one on the right if they appeared different in size" (Milner and Goodale, 1995, p. 167). The surprising result was that even when subjects were unaware of—but clearly subject to—the illusion, their motor control systems produced a precisely fitted grip with a finger-thumb aperture perfectly suited to the *actual* (non-illusory) size of the disc. This aperture was not arrived at by touching and adjusting, but was instead the direct result of the visual input. Yet, to repeat, it reflected not the illusory disc size given in the subject's visual experience, but the actual size. In short:

> Grip size was determined entirely by the true size of the target disc [and] the very act by means of which subjects indicated their susceptibility to the visual illusion (that is, picking up one of two target circles) was itself uninfluenced by the illusion. (Milner and Goodale, 1995, p. 168)

This is, indeed, a somewhat startling result. It suggests, to Milner and Goodale, that the processing underlying visual awareness may be operating quite independently of that underlying the visual control of action. Nor is this suggestion warranted only by the (interesting but perhaps somewhat marginal) case of these visual illusions. The general idea of a dissociation between systems for visual awareness and systems for visuomotor action is also suggested by anatomical data and data from brain-damaged patients. The patient DF, for example, suffers from ventral stream lesions and cannot visually identify objects or visually discriminate shapes. Nonetheless, she is able to pick up these very same objects—that she cannot visually identify—using fluent, well-oriented precision grips. Others, by contrast, suffer dorsal stream lesions and "have little trouble seeing [i.e., identifying objects in a visual scene] but a lot of trouble reaching for objects they can see. It is as though they cannot use the spatial information inherent in any visual scene" (Gazzaniga, 1998, p. 109).

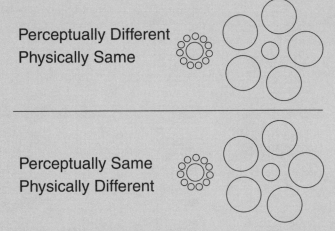

Figure 7.3 Diagram showing the Titchener circles illusion. In the top figure the two central discs are of the same actual size, but appear different; in the bottom figure, the disc surrounded by an annulus of large circles has been made somewhat larger in size in order to appear approximately equal in size to the other central disc. (From Milner and Goodale, 1995. By permission.)

at times exploit and coopt, more primitive systems (For some fascinating conjecture about the possible shape of such an interplay, see Damasio, 1999).

In sum, we must treat the doctrine of cognitive incrementalism with great caution. It is a doctrine that is both insufficiently precise (concerning what is to count as continuity, incremental change, etc.) and empirically insecure. Attention to the shape of nature's solution to basic problems of real-time response and sensorimotor coordination will surely teach us a lot. Whether it will teach us enough to understand mindfulness itself is still unknown.

7.3 Suggested Readings

For *accessible introductions to dynamical systems theory*, try R. Abraham and C. Shaw, *Dynamics—The Geometry of Behavior* (Redwood, CA: Addison Wesley, 1992); the chapter by A. Norton, "Dynamics: An introduction." In R. Port and T. van Gelder (eds.), *Mind as Motion* (Cambridge, MA: MIT Press, 1995); or (perhaps best of all for philosophers and cognitive scientists) Chapters 1–3 of J. A. Scott Kelso, *Dynamic Patterns: The Self-organization of Brian and Behavior* (Cambridge, MA: MIT Press, 1995, Chapters 1–3), which also contains descriptions of the work on *rhythmic finger motion*.

For the work on *infant stepping*, see E. Thelen and L. Smith, *A Dynamic Systems Approach to the Development of Cognition and Action* (Cambridge, MA: MIT Press, 1994), and critical discussion in A. Clark, "The dynamical challenge." *Cognitive Science*, 21(4), 461–481, 1997.

For the *Watt governor argument*, see T. van Gelder, "What might cognition be if not computation?" *Journal of Philosophy*, 92(7), 345–381, 1995, and critical discussion in A. Clark, "Time and mind." *Journal of Philosophy*, XCV(7), 354–376, 1998.

A good window on the *debate over internal representations* is provided by looking at on the one hand, A. Clark and J. Toribio, "Doing without representing?" *Synthese*, 101, 401–431, 1994, and on the other, F. Keijzer, "Doing without representations which specify what to do." *Philosophical Psychology*, 11(3), 267–302, 1998. The latter is a philosophically astute defense of a fairly radical dynamicist position, whereas the former is somewhat more skeptical.

The collection, by R. Port and T. van Gelder (eds.), *Mind as Motion* (Cambridge, MA: MIT Press, 1995) contains a number of interesting and provocative papers. I especially recommend the introduction "It's about time," by van Gelder and Port, "Language as a dynamical system," by Jeff Elman (a nice blend of connectionism and dynamics), and the robotics-oriented paper by R. Beer, "Computational-dynamical languages for autonomous agents."

For further discussion of the broad notion of *cognitive incrementalism*, see J. Fodor, *In Critical Condition*, (Cambridge, MA: MIT Press, 1998, Chapter 17, pp. 203–214).

8 COGNITIVE TECHNOLOGY
Beyond the Naked Brain

8.1 Sketches

We have come a long way. From the initial image of the mind as a symbol-crunching meat machine, to the delights of vector coding and subsymbolic artificial intelligence, on to the burgeoning complexities of real-world, real-time interactive systems. As the journey continued one issue became ever more pressing: how to relate the insights gained from recent work in robotics, artificial life, and the study of situated cognition to the kinds of capacity and activity associated with so-called higher cognition? How, in short, to link the study of "embodied, environmentally embedded" cognition to the phenomena of abstract thought, advance planning, hypothetical reason, slow deliberation, and so on—the standard stomping grounds of more classical approaches.

In seeking such a link, there are two immediate options:

1. To embrace a deeply hybrid view of the inner computational engine itself. To depict the brain as the locus both of quick, dirty "on line," environment-exploiting strategies and of a variety of more symbolic inner models affording varieties of "off-line" reason.

2. To bet on the basic "bag-of-tricks" kind of strategy *all the way up*—to see the mechanisms of advanced reason as deeply continuous (no really new architectures and features) with the kinds of mechanisms (of dynamic coupling, etc.) scouted in the last two chapters.

In this final section, I investigate a third option—or perhaps it is really just a subtly morphed combination of the two previous options.

3. To depict much of advanced cognition as rooted in the operation of the same basic kinds of capacity used for on-line, adaptive response, but tuned and applied to the special domain of *external and/or artificial cognitive aids*—the domain, as I shall say, of *wideware or cognitive technology.*

It helps, at this point, to abandon all pretence at unbiased discussion. For the interest in the relations between mind and cognitive technology lies squarely at the heart of my own current research program, taking its cue from Dennett (1995, 1996), Hutchins (1995), Kirsh and Maglio (1994), and others.

The central idea is that mindfulness, or rather the special *kind* of mindfulness associated with the distinctive, top-level achievements of the human species, arises at the *productive collision points* of multiple factors and forces—some bodily, some neural, some technological, and some social and cultural. As a result, the project of understanding what is distinctive about human thought and reason may depend on a much broader focus than that to which cognitive science has become most accustomed, one that includes not just body, brain, and the natural world, but the props and aids (pens, papers, PCs, institutions) in which our biological brains learn, mature, and operate.

A short anecdote helps set the stage. Consider the expert bartender. Faced with multiple drink orders in a noisy and crowded environment, the expert mixes and dispenses drinks with amazing skill and accuracy. But what is the basis of this expert performance? Does it all stem from finely tuned memory and motor skills? By no means. In controlled psychological experiments comparing novice and expert bartenders (Beach, 1988, cited in Kirlik, 1998, p. 707), it becomes clear that expert skill involves a delicate interplay between internal and environmental factors. The experts select and array *distinctively shaped glasses* at the time of ordering. They then use these persistent cues so as to help recall and sequence the specific orders. Expert performance thus plummets in tests involving uniform glassware, whereas novice performances are unaffected by any such manipulations. The expert has learned to sculpt and exploit the working environment in ways that transform and simplify the task that confronts the biological brain.

Portions of the external world thus often function as a kind of extraneural memory store. We may deliberately leave a film on our desk to remind us to take it for developing. Or we may write a note "develop film" on paper and leave that on our desk instead. As users of words and texts, we command an especially cheap and potent means of off-loading data and ideas from the biological brain onto a variety of external media. This trick, I think, is not to be underestimated. For it affects not just the quantity of data at our command, but also the kinds of operation we can bring to bear on it. Words, texts, symbols, and diagrams often figure *intimately* in the problem-solving routines developed by biological brains nurtured in language-rich environmental settings. Human brains, trained in a sea of words and text, will surely develop computational strategies that directly "factor-in" the reliable presence of a wide variety of such external props and aids.

Take, for example, the process of writing an academic paper. You work long and hard and at days end you are happy. Being a good physicalist, you assume that all the credit for the final intellectual product belongs to your brain: the seat of human reason. But you are too generous by far. For what really happened was (perhaps) more like this. The brain supported some rereading of old texts, materials, and notes. While rereading these, it responded by generating a few fragmentary ideas and criticisms. These ideas and criticisms were then stored as more marks on paper, in margins, on computer discs, etc. The brain then played a role in reorganizing these data on clean sheets, adding new on-line reactions and ideas. The cycle of reading, responding, and external reorganization is repeated, again and again. Finally, there is a product. A story, argument, or theory. But this intellectual product owes a lot to those repeated loops out into the environment. Credit belongs to the embodied, embedded agent in the world. The naked biological brain is just a part (albeit a crucial and special part) of a spatially and temporally extended process, involving lots of extraneural operations, whose joint action creates the intellectual product. There is thus a real sense (or so I would argue) in which the notion of the "problem-solving engine" is really the notion of the *whole caboodle* (see Box 8.1): the brain and body operating within an environmental setting.

One way to understand the cognitive role of many of our self-created cognitive technologies is as affording *complementary* operations to those that come naturally to biological brains. Thus recall the connectionist image of biological brains as pattern-completing engines (Chapter 4). Such devices are adept at linking patterns of current sensory input with associated information: you hear the first bars of the song and recall the rest, you see the rat's tail and conjure the image of the rat. Computational engines of that broad class prove extremely good at tasks such as sensorimotor coordination, face recognition, voice recognition, etc. But they are not well suited to deductive logic, planning, and the typical tasks of sequential reason (see Chapters 1 and 2). They are, roughly speaking, "Good at Frisbee, Bad at Logic"—a cognitive profile that is at once familiar and alien: familiar, because human intelligence clearly has something of that flavor; alien, because we repeatedly transcend these limits, planning vacations, solving complex sequential problems, etc.

One powerful hypothesis, which I first encountered in McClelland, Rumelhart, Smolensky, and Hinton (1986), is that we transcend these limits, in large part, by combining the internal operation of a connectionist, pattern-completing device with a variety of external operations and tools that serve to reduce the complex, sequential problems to an ordered set of simpler pattern-completing operations of the kind our brains are most comfortable with. Thus, to take a classic illustration, we may tackle the problem of long multiplication by using pen, paper, and numerical symbols. We then engage in a process of external symbol manipulations and storage so as to reduce the complex problem to a sequence of simple pattern-completing steps that we already command, first multiplying 9 by 7 and storing the result on paper, then 9 by 6, and so on.

Box 8.1

THE TALENTED TUNA

Consider, by way of analogy, the idea of a swimming machine. In particular, consider the bluefin tuna. The tuna is paradoxically talented. Physical examination suggests it should not be able to achieve the aquatic feats of which it is demonstrably capable. It is physically too weak (by about a factor of 7) to swim as fast as it does, to turn as compactly as it does, to move off with the acceleration it does, etc. The explanation (according to the fluid dynamicists M. and G. Triantafyllou) is that these fish actively create and exploit additional sources of propulsion and control in their watery environments. For example, the tuna use naturally occurring eddies and vortices to gain speed, and they flap their tails so as to actively create additional vortices and pressure gradients, which they then exploit for quick take-offs, etc. The real swimming machine, I suggest, is thus the fish *in its proper context*: the fish plus the surrounding structures and vortices that it actively creates and then maximally exploits. The *cognitive machine*, in the human case, looks similarly extended (see also Dennett, 1995, Chapters 12 and 13). We humans actively create and exploit multiple external media, yielding a variety of encoding and manipulative opportunities whose reliable presence is then factored deep into our problem-solving strategies. [The tuna story is detailed in Triantafyllou and Triantafyllou (1995) and further discussed in Clark (1997)].

The value of the use of pen, paper, and number symbols is thus that—in the words of Ed Hutchins, a cognitive anthropologist—

[such tools] permit the [users] to do the tasks that need to be done while doing the kinds of things people are good at: recognizing patterns, modeling simple dynamics of the world, and manipulating objects in the environment. (Hutchins, 1995, p. 155)

A moments reflection will reveal that this description nicely captures what is best about *good* examples of cognitive technology: recent word-processing packages, web browsers, mouse and icon systems, etc. It also suggests, of course, what is wrong with many of our first attempts at creating such tools—the skills needed to use those environments (early VCR's, word-processors, etc.) were *precisely* those that biological brains find hardest to support, such as the recall and execution of long, essentially arbitrary, sequences of operations. See Norman (1999) for discussion.

It is similarly fruitful, I believe, to think of the practice of using words and linguistic labels as *itself* a kind of original "cognitive technology"—a potent add-on to our biological brain that literally transformed the space of human reason. We noted earlier the obvious (but still powerful and important) role of written inscriptions as both a form of external memory and an arena for new kinds of manipulative activity. But the very presence of words as *objects* has, I believe, some further, and generally neglected (though see Dennett, 1994, 1996), consequences. A word, then, on this further dimension.

Words can act as potent filters on the search space for a biological learning device. The idea, to a first approximation, is that learning to associate concepts with discrete arbitrary labels (words) makes it easier to use those concepts to constrain future search and hence enables the acquisition of a progressive cascade of more complex and increasingly abstract ideas. The claim (see also Clark and Thornton, 1997) is, otherwise put, that associating a perceptually simple, stable, external item (such as a word) with an idea, concept, or piece of knowledge effectively freezes the concept into a sort of cognitive building block—an item that can then be treated as a simple baseline feature for future episodes of thought, learning, and search.

This broad conjecture (whose statistical and computational foundations are explored in Clark and Thornton, 1997) seems to be supported by some recent work on chimp cognition. Thompson, Oden, and Boyson (in press) studied problem solving in chimps (*pan troglodytes*). What Thompson et al. show is that chimps trained to use an arbitrary plastic marker (a yellow triangle, say) to designate pairs of identical objects (such as two identical cups), and to use a different marker (a red circle, say) to designate pairs of different objects (such as a shoe and a cup), are then able to learn to solve a new class of abstract problems. This is the class of problems—intractable to chimps not provided with the symbolic training—involving recognition of *higher order* relations of sameness and difference. Thus presented with two (different) pairs of identical items (two shoes and two cups, say) the higher order task is to judge the pairs as exhibiting the *same* relation, i.e., to judge that you have two instances of *sameness*. Examples of such higher order judgments (which even human subjects can find hard to master at first) are shown in Table 8.1.

TABLE 8.1 Higher Order Sameness and Difference

Cup/Cup	Shoe/Shoe
=	two instances of first-order sameness
=	an instance of higher order sameness
Cup/Shoe	**Cup/Shoe**
=	two instances of first-order difference
=	an instance of higher order sameness
Cup/Shoe	**Cup/Cup**
=	one instance of first-order difference and one of first-order sameness
=	an instance of higher order difference

The token-trained chimps' success at this difficult task, it is conjectured, is explained by their experience with external tokens. For such experience may enable the chimp, on confronting, e.g., the pair of identical cups, to retrieve a mental representation of the *sameness* token (as it happens, a yellow triangle). Exposure to the two identical shoes will likewise cause retrieval of that token. At that point, the higher order task is effectively reduced to the simple, lower order task of identifying the two yellow plastic *tokens* as "the same."

Experience with external tags and labels thus enables the brain itself—by *representing* those tags and labels—to solve problems whose level of complexity and abstraction would otherwise leave us baffled—an intuitive result whose widespread applicability to human reason is increasingly evident (see Box 8.2). Learning a set of tags and labels (which we all do when we learn a language) is, we may thus speculate, rather closely akin to acquiring a new perceptual modality. For like a perceptual modality, it renders certain features of our world concrete and salient, and allows us to target our thoughts (and learning algorithms) on a new domain of basic objects. This new domain compresses what were previously complex and unruly sensory patterns into simple objects. These simple objects can then be attended to in ways that quickly reveal further (otherwise hidden) patterns, as in the case of relations between relations. And of course the whole process is deeply iterative— we coin new words and labels to concretize regularities that we could only originally conceptualize as a result of a backdrop of other words and labels. The most powerful and familiar incarnation of this iterative strategy is, perhaps, the edifice of human science itself.

The augmentation of biological brains with linguaform resources may also shed light on another powerful and characteristic aspect of human thought, an aspect mentioned briefly in the introduction but then abandoned throughout the subsequent discussion. I have in mind our ability to engage in second-order discourse, to think about (and evaluate) our own thoughts. Thus consider a cluster of powerful capacities involving self-evaluation, self-criticism, and finely honed remedial responses.[1] Examples would include recognizing a flaw in our own plan or argument and dedicating further cognitive efforts to fixing it; reflecting on the unreliability of our own initial judgments in certain types of situations and proceeding with special caution as a result; coming to see why we reached a particular conclusion by appreciating the logical transitions in our own thought; thinking about the conditions under which we think best and trying to bring them about. The list could be continued, but the pattern should be clear. In all these cases, we are ef-

---

[1]Two powerful treatments that emphasize these themes have been brought to my attention. Jean-Pierre Changeux (a neuroscientist and molecular biologist) and Alain Connes (a mathematician) suggest that self-evaluation is the mark of true intelligence—see Changeux and Connes (1995). Derek Bickerton (a linguist) celebrates "off-line thinking" and notes that no other species seems to isolate problems in their own performance and take pointed action to rectify them—see Bickerton (1995).

Box 8.2

NUMERICAL COMPETENCE

Stanislas Dehaene and colleagues adduce a powerful body of evidence for a similar claim in the mathematical domain. Biological brains, they suggest, display an innate, but fuzzy and low-level numerical competence: a capacity to represent simple numerocity (1-ness, 2-ness, 3-ness), an appreciation of "more," "less," and of change in quantity. But human mathematical thought, they argue, depends on a delicate interplay between this innate system for low-grade, approximate arithmetic and the new cultural tools provided by the development of language-based representations of numbers. The development of such new tools began, they argue, with the use of body parts as stand-ins for the basic numerical quantities, and was progressively extended so as to provide a means of "pinning down" quantities for which we have no precise innate representation.

More concretely, Dehaene, Sperke, Pinel, Stanescu, and Triskin (1999) depict mature human arithmetical competence as dependent on the combined (and interlocking) contributions of two distinct cognitive resources. One is an innate, parietal lobe-based tool for approximate numerical reasoning. The other is an acquired, left frontal lobe-based tool for the use of language-specific numerical representations in exact arithmetic. In support of this hypothesis, the authors present evidence from studies of arithmetical reasoning in bilinguals, from studies of patients with differential damage to each of the two neural subsystems, and from neuroimaging studies of normal subjects engaged in exact and approximate numerical tasks. In this latter case, subjects performing the exact tasks show significant activity in the speech-related areas of the left frontal lobe, whereas the approximate tasks recruit bilateral areas of the parietal lobes implicated in visuospatial reasoning. These results are together presented as a demonstration "that exact calculation is language dependent, whereas approximation relies on nonverbal visuo-spatial cerebral networks" (Dehaene et al., 1999, p. 970) and that "even within the small domain of elementary arithmetic, multiple mental representations are used for different tasks" (Dehaene et al., 1999, p. 973). What is interesting about this case is that here the additional props and scaffolding (the number names available in a specific natural language) are rerepresented internally, so the process recruits images of the external items for later use. This is similar to the story about the chimps judgments about higher order relations, but quite unlike the case of artistic sketching that I consider later in the chapter.

fectively thinking about either our own cognitive profiles or about specific thoughts. This "thinking about thinking" is a good candidate for a distinctively human capacity—one not evidently shared by the other non-language-using animals who share our planet. As such, it is natural to wonder whether this might be an entire species of thought, in which language plays the generative role, that is not just reflected in, or extended by, our use of words but is directly dependent on language for its very existence.

It is easy to see, in broad outline, how this might come about. For as soon as we formulate a thought in words (or on paper), it becomes an object for both ourselves and for others. As an object, it is the kind of thing we can have thoughts about. In creating the object, we need have no thoughts about thoughts—but once it is there, the opportunity immediately exists to attend to it as an object in its own right. The process of linguistic formulation thus creates the stable structure to which subsequent thinkings attach. Just such a twist on the potential role of the inner rehearsal of sentences has been presented by Jackendoff (1996), who suggests that the mental rehearsal of sentences may be the primary means by which our own thoughts are able to become objects of further attention and reflection. The emergence of such second-order cognitive dynamics is plausibly seen as one root of the veritable explosion of varieties of external technological scaffolding in human cultural evolution. It is because we can think about our own thinking that we can actively structure our world in ways designed to promote, support, and extend our own cognitive achievements. This process also feeds itself, as when the arrival of written text and notation allowed us to begin to fix ever more complex and extended sequences of thought and reason as objects for further scrutiny and attention.

As a final example of cognitive technology (wideware) in action, let us turn away from the case of words and text and symbol-manipulating tools (PCs, etc.) and consider the role of sketching in certain processes of artistic creation. van Leeuwen, Verstijnen, and Hekkert (1999, p. 180) offer a careful account of the creation of abstract art, depicting it as heavily dependent on "an interactive process of imagining, sketching and evaluating [then resketching, reevaluating, etc.]." The question the authors pursue is, why the need to sketch? Why not simply imagine the final artwork "in the mind's eye" and then execute it directly on the canvas? The answer they develop, in great detail and using multiple real case studies, is that human thought is constrained, in mental imagery, in some very specific ways in which it is *not* constrained during on-line perception. In particular, our mental images seem to be more interpretively fixed: less enabling of the discovery of novel forms and components. Suggestive evidence for such constraints includes the intriguing demonstration [Chambers and Reisberg (1985)—see Box 8.3] that it is much harder to discover the second interpretation of an ambiguous figure in recall and imagination than when confronted with a real drawing. It is quite easy, by contrast, to compose imagined elements into novel wholes—for example, to imag-

Box 8.3

Imaginative versus Perceptual "Flipping" of Ambiguous Images

Chambers and Reisberg (1985) asked subjects (with good imagistic capacities) to observe and recall a drawing. The drawing would be "flippable"—able to be seen as either one of two different things, though not as both at once. Famous examples include the duck/rabbit (shown below), the old lady/young lady image, the faces/vase image, and many others.

The experimenters chose a group of subjects ranged across a scale of "image vividness" as measured by Slee's Visual Elaboration scale (Slee, 1980). The subjects, who did not already know the duck/rabbit picture, were trained on related cases (Necker cubes, face/vase pictures) to ensure that they were familiar with the phenomenon in question. They were briefly shown the duck/rabbit and told to form a mental picture so that they could draw it later. They were then asked to attend to their mental image and to seek an alternative interpretation for it. Hints were given that they should try to shift their visual fixation from, e.g., lower left to upper right. Finally, they were asked to draw their image and to seek an alternative interpretation of their drawing. The results were surprising.

> Despite the inclusion of several "high vividness" imagers, none of the 15 subjects tested was able to reconstrue the imaged stimulus. . . . In sharp contrast, all 15 of the subjects were able to find the alternate construal in their own drawings. This makes clear that the subjects did have an adequate memory of the duck/rabbit figure and that they understood our reconstrual task. (Chambers and Reisberg, 1985, p. 321)

The moral, for our purposes, is that the subject's problem-solving capacities are significantly extended by the simple device of externalizing information (*drawing* the image from memory) and then confronting the external trace using on-line visual perception. This "loop into the world" allows the subject to find new interpretations, an activity that (see text) is plausibly central to certain forms of artistic creation. Artistic intelligence, it seems, is not "all in the head."

Figure 8.1

inatively combine the letters D and J to form an umbrella ⊤ (see Finke, Pinker, and Farah, 1989).

To accommodate both these sets of results, van Leeuwen et al. suggest that our imaginative (intrinsic) capacities do indeed support "synthetic transformations" in which components retain their shapes but are recombined into new wholes (as in the J + D = umbrella case), but lack the "analytic" capacity to decompose an imagined shape into wholly new components (as in the hourglasses-into-overlapping parallelograms case shown in Figure 8.2). This is because (they speculate) the latter type of case (but not the former) requires us to first undo an existing shape interpretation.

Certain forms of abstract art, it is then argued, depend heavily on the deliberate creation of "multilayered meanings"—cases in which a visual form, on continued inspection, supports multiple different structural interpretations (see Figure 8.3). Given the postulated constraints on mental imagery, it is likely that the discovery of such multiply interpretable forms will depend heavily on the kind of trial-and-error process in which we first sketch and then perceptually (not imaginatively) reencounter the forms, which we can then tweak and resketch so as to create an increasingly multilayered set of structural interpretations.

Thus understood, the use of the sketchpad is not just a convenience for the artist, nor simply a kind of external memory, or durable medium for the storage of particular ideas. Instead, the iterated process of externalizing and reperceiving is integral to the process of artistic cognition itself. A realistic computer simulation of the way human brains support this kind of artistic creativity would need likewise to avail itself of one (imaginative) resource supporting synthetic transformations and another, environmentally looping resource, to allow its on-line perceptual systems to search the space of "analytic" transformations.

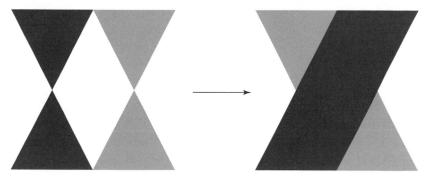

Figure 8.2 Novel decomposition as a form of analytic transformation that is hard to perform in imagery. The leftmost figure, initially synthesized from two hourglasses, requires a novel decomposition to be seen as two overlapping parallelograms. [Reproduced from van Leeuwen et al. (1999) by kind permission of the authors and the publisher, University Press of America.]

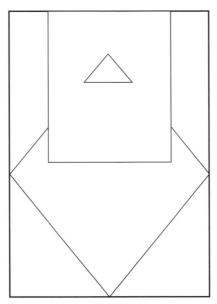

Figure 8.3 A simple example of the kind of multilayered structure found in certain types of abstract art. [Reproduced from van Leeuwen et al. (1999) by kind permission of the authors and the publisher, University Press of America.]

The conjecture, then, is that one large jump or discontinuity in human cognitive evolution involves the distinctive way human brains repeatedly create and exploit wideware—various species of cognitive technology able to expand and reshape the space of human reason. We, more than any other creature on the planet, deploy nonbiological wideware (instruments, media, notations) to *complement* our basic biological modes of processing, creating extended cognitive systems whose computational and problem-solving profiles are quire different from those of the naked brain.

8.2 Discussion

A. THE PARADOX OF ACTIVE STUPIDITY (AND A BOOTSTRAPPING SOLUTION)

The most obvious problem, for any attempt to explain our distinctive smartness by appeal to a kind of symbiosis of brain and technology, lies in the threat of circularity. Surely, the worry goes, only intrinsically *smart* brains could have the knowledge and wherewithal to create such cognitive technologies in the first place. All that wideware cannot come from nowhere. This is what I shall call the "paradox of active stupidity."

There is surely something to the worry. If humans are (as I have claimed) the only animal species to makes such widespread and interactive use of cognitive technologies, it seems likely that the explanation of this capacity turns, in some way, on distinctive features of the human brain (or perhaps the human brain and body; recall the once-popular stories about tool use and the opposable thumb). Let us be clear, then, that the conjecture scouted in the present chapter is not meant as a denial of the existence of certain crucial neural and/or bodily differences. Rather, my goal is to depict any such differences as the *seed*, rather than the full explanation, of our cognitive capabilities. The idea is that some relatively *small* neural (or neural/bodily) difference was the spark that lit a kind of intellectual forest fire. The brain is, let us assume, wholly responsible (courtesy, perhaps of some quite small tweak of the engineering) for the fulfillment of some precondition of cultural and technological evolution. Thus Deacon (1997) argues that human brains, courtesy of a disproportionate enlargement of our prefrontal lobes relative to the rest of our brains, are uniquely able to learn rich and flexible schemes associating arbitrary symbols with meanings. This, then, is one contender for the neural difference that makes human language acquisition possible, and language (of that type) is, quite plausibly, the fundamental "cognitive technology" (the UR-technology) that got the whole ball rolling. There are many alternative explanations [an especially interesting one, I think, is to be found in Fodor (1994)].[2] But the point is that once the process of cultural and technological evolution is under way, the explanation of our contemporary human achievements lies largely in a kind of iterated bootstrapping in which brains and (first-generation) cognitive technologies cooperate so as to design and create the new, enriched technological environments in which (new) brains and (second-generation) cognitive technologies again conspire, producing the third-generation environment for another set of brains to learn in, and so on.

This idea of a potent succession of cognitive technologies is especially suggestive, I believe, when combined with the (still speculative) neuroscientific perspective known as neural contructivism. The neural contructivist (see Box 8.4) stresses the role of developmental plasticity in allowing the human cortex to actively build and structure itself in response to environmental inputs. One possible result of such a process is to magnify an effect I call "cognitive dovetailing." In cognitive dovetailing, neural resources become structured so as to factor reliable *external* resources and operations into the very heart of their problem-solving routines. In this way, the inner and outer resources come to complement each other's operations, so that the two fit together as tightly as the sides of a precisely dovetailed joint. Thus think, for example, of the way the skilled bartender (see text) combined biological recall and the physical arrangement of differing shaped glasses to solve the cocktail bar problem, or the way the tuna (Box 8.1) swims by creating aquatic

---

[2]Fodor (1994) locates the principal difference in the capacity (which he thinks is unique to humans) to become aware of the contents of our own thoughts: to not just think that it is raining, but to know that "it is raining" is the content of our thought. This difference could, Fodor argues, help explain our unique ability to actively structure our world so as to be reliably caused to have true thoughts—the central trick of scientific experimentation.

Box 8.4

NEURAL CONSTRUCTIVISM

The neural constructivist depicts neural (especially cortical) growth as experience—dependent, and as involving the actual construction of new neural circuitry (synapses, axons, dendrites) rather than just the fine-tuning of circuitry whose basic shape and form are already determined. The result is that the learning device *itself* changes as a result of organism–environmental interactions—learning does not just alter the knowledge base, it alters the computational architecture itself. Evidence for the neural constructivist view comes primarily from recent neuroscientific studies (especially work in developmental cognitive neuroscience). Key studies include work involving cortical transplants, in which chunks of visual cortex were grafted into other cortical locations (such as somatosensory or auditory cortex) and proved plastic enough to develop the response characteristics appropriate to the new location (see Schlagger and O'Leary, 1991; Roe et al., 1990). There is also work showing the deep dependence of specific cortical response characteristics on developmental interactions between parts of cortex and specific kinds of input signal (Chenn et al., 1997) and a growing body of constructivist work in artificial neural networks: connectionist networks in which the architecture (number of units and layers, etc.) itself alters as learning progresses—see, e.g., Quartz and Sejnowski (1997). The take home message is that immature cortex is surprisingly homogeneous, and that it "requires afferent input, both intrinsically generated and environmentally determined, for its regional specialization" (Quartz, 1999, p. 49). It is this kind of profound plasticity that best underscores the very strongest version of the dovetailing claim made in the text.

vortices that it then exploits. Now picture the young brain, learning to solve problems in an environment packed with pen, paper, PC, etc. That brain may develop problem-solving strategies that factor in these props just as the bartender's brain factors in the availability of differently shaped glasses to reduce memory load. What this suggests, in the rather special context of the neural constructivist's (see Box 8.4) developmental schema, is that young brains may even develop a kind of cortical *architecture* especially suited to promoting a symbiotic problem-solving regime, in which neural subsystems, pen, paper, and PC-based operations are equal partners, performing complementary and delicately orchestrated operations.

The neural constructivist vision thus supports an especially powerful version of the story about cognitive technological bootstrapping. If neural constructivism is true, it is not just that basic biological brains can achieve more and more as the technological surround evolves. It is that the biological brain literally grows a cortical cognitive architecture suited to the specific technological environment in which it learns and matures. This symbiosis of brain and cognitive technology, repeated again and again, but with new technologies sculpting new brains in different ways, may be the origin of a golden loop, a virtuous spiral of brain/culture influence that allows human minds to go where no animal minds have gone before.

B. CASH VALUE

Some will argue that there is nothing new or surprising in the simple observation that brains plus technology can achieve more than "naked brains." And even the radical "dovetailing" image, in which brains plus reliable props come to act as integrated problem-solving ensembles may seem to have few practical implications for the cognitive scientific project. What, then, is the cash value of treating the human mind as a complex system whose bounds are not those of skin and skull?

One practical, but wholly negative, implication is that there can be no single "cognitive level" (recall Chapter 2) at which to pitch all our investigations, nor any uniquely bounded system (such as the brain) to which we can restrict our interest (*qua* cognitive scientists seeking the natural roots of thought and intelligence). To understand the bartender's skills, for example, we cannot restrict our attention to the bartender's brain; instead we must attend to the problem-solving contributions of active environmental structuring. Nonetheless, it is unrealistic to attempt—in general—to take everything (brain, body, environment, action) into account all at once. Science works by simplifying and focusing, often isolating the contributions of the different elements. One genuine methodological possibility, however, is to use alternate means of focusing and simplifying. Instead of simplifying by dividing the problem space (unrealistically, I have argued) into brain–science, body–science, and culture–science, we should focus (where possible) on the interactions. To keep it tractable we can focus on the interactions in small, idealized cases in which the various elements begin to come together. Work in simple real-world robotics (such as the robot cricket discussed in Chapter 6) provides one window onto such interactive dynamics. Another useful tool is the canny use of multiscale simulations: representative studies here include work that combines artificial evolution with individual lifetime learning in interacting populations (Ackley and Littman, 1992; Nolfi and Parisi, 1991), work that investigates the properties of very large collections of simple agents (Resnick, 1994), and work that targets the relations between successful problem solving and the gradual accumulation of useful environmental props and artifacts (Hutchins, 1995; Hutchins and Hazelhurst, 1991).

The cash value of the emphasis on extended systems (comprising multiple heterogeneous elements) is thus that it forces us to attend to the interactions themselves: to see that much of what matters about human-level intelligence is hidden not in the brain, nor in the technology, but in the complex and interated interactions and collaborations between the two. (The account of sketching and artistic creation is a nice example of the kind of thing I have in mind: but the same level of interactive complexity characterizes almost all forms of advanced human cognitive endeavor.) The study of these interaction spaces is not easy, and depends both on new multidisciplinary alliances and new forms of modeling and analysis. The pay-off, however, could be spectacular: nothing less than a new kind of cognitive scientific collaboration involving neuroscience, physiology, and social, cultural, and technological studies in about equal measure.

C. THE BOUNDS OF SELF

One rather problematic area, for those of us attracted to the kind of extended systems picture presented above, concerns the notions of self and agency. Can it be literally true that the physical system whose whirrings and grindings constitute *my* mind is a system that includes (at times) elements and operations that loop outside my physical (biological) body? Put dramatically, am I a dumb agent existing in a very smart and supportive world, or a smart agent whose bounds are simply not those of skin and skull? This is a topic that I have addressed elsewhere (see Clark and Chalmers, 1998), so I shall restrict myself to just a few points here.

We can begin by asking a simple question. Why is it that when we use (for example) a crane to lift a heavy weight, we (properly) do not count the crane as increasing our individual muscle power, whereas when we sit down to fine-tune an argument, using, paper, pen, and diagrams, we are less prone to later "factor out" the contributions of the props and tools and tend to see the intellectual product as purely the results of *our* efforts? My own view, as suggested in the text, is that one difference lies in the way neural problem-solving processes are *themselves* adapted to make deep and repeated use of the cognitive wideware. Another lies, perhaps, in the looping and interactive nature of the interactions themselves. The crane driver and the crane each makes a relatively *independent* contribution to lifting the girders, whereas the patterns of influence linking the artist and the sketches seems significantly more complex, interactive, and reciprocal. It is perhaps no accident that it is in those cases in which the patterns of reciprocal influence uniting the user and tool are most mutually and continuously modulatory (the racing driver and car, windsurfer and rig, etc.) that we are most tempted, in everyday discourse, to speak of a kind of agent–machine unity.

The main point to notice, in any case, is just that the issues here are by no means simple. Consider another obvious worry, that the "extended system" picture, *if* it is meant to suggest (which it need not) a correlative *mental* extension, leads rapidly to an absurd inflation of the individual mind. The worry (discussed in length in Clark and Chalmers, 1998) is thus that allowing (to take the case from

Box 8.5

CYBORGS AND SOFTWARE AGENTS

Two kinds of technological advance seem ready to extend human mindfulness in radically new kinds of ways.

The first, already familiar but rapidly gaining in ubiquity and sophistication, is exemplified by so-called software agents. A simple example of a software agent would be a program that monitors your on-line reading habits, which newsgroups you frequently access, etc., or your on-line CD buying habits, and then searches out new items that fit your apparent interests. More sophisticated software agents might monitor on-line auctions, bidding and selling on your behalf, or buy and sell your stocks and shares.

Reflect on the possibilities. Imagine that you begin using the web at age 4. Dedicated software agents track and adapt to your emerging interests and random explorations. They then help direct your attention to new ideas, web pages, and products. Over the next 70 years you and your software agents are locked in a complex dance of coevolutionary change and learning, each influencing, and being influenced by, the other. In such a case, in a very real sense, the software entities look less like part of your problem-solving environment than part of you. The intelligent system that now confronts the wider world is biological-you-plus-the-software-agents. These external bundles of code are contributing rather like the various subpersonal cognitive functions active in your own brain. They are constantly at work, contributing to your emerging psychological profile. Perhaps you finally count as "using" the software agents only in the same attenuated and ultimately paradoxical way that you count as "using" your hippocampus or frontal lobes?

Whereas dedicated, coevolving software resources are extending individual cognitive systems outside the local bounds of skin and skull, various forms of bioelectronic implant seem ready to transform the computational architecture from within the biological skin-bag itself. Perceptual input systems are already the beneficiaries of restorative technologies involving the direct linkage of implanted electronics to biological nerves and neurons. Cochlear implants, some of which now bypass the auditory nerve and jack directly into the brain stem (see LeVay, 2000), already help the deaf, and experimental retinal implants are now ready to offset certain causes of adult blindness, such as age-related macular degeneration. The next step in our cyborg future must be to link such implanted electronics evermore directly to the neural systems involved in reason, recall, and imagination. Such a step is already being taken, albeit in a crude and avowedly exploratory way, by pioneers such as Kevin Warwick, a Reading University professor of Cybernetics. Warwick is experimenting with implants interfacing nerve bundles in his body to a digital computer able to record, replay, and share (via similar implants in others) the signals (see Warwick, 2000). We might imagine, indeed, that the artist's sketchpad, displayed (see text) as a critical external loop in certain processes of artistic creation may one day be replaced, or complemented, by implanted technologies enabling us to deploy our normal perceptual abilities on a kind of secondary visual display, opening the door to an even more powerful symbiosis between biological capacities and the artifactual (but now internalized) support.

In short, human mindfulness is set fast on an explosive trajectory, annexing more and more external and artifactual structures as integral parts of the cognitive machine, while simultaneously reinventing itself from within, augmenting on-board biological systems with delicately interfaced electronics. Just *who* we are, *what* are we, and *where* we are must count among the prime cultural, scientific, and moral puzzles facing the next generations of human (?) life.

the text) the sketchpad operations to count as part of the artist's own mental processes leads inevitably to, e.g., counting the database of the *Encyclopedia Britannica*, which I keep in my garage, as part of my general knowledge. Such intuitively pernicious extension ("cognitive bloat") is not, however, inevitable. It is quite proper to restrict the props and aids that can count as part of *my* mental machinery to those that are, at the very least, reliably available when needed and used (accessed) as automatically as biological processing and memory. Such simple criteria may again allow the incorporation of the artist's sketchpad and the blind-person's cane while blocking the dusty encyclopedia left in the garage. And they positively invite mind-extending depictions of possible future technologies: the cyberpunk neural implant that allows speed-of-thought access to the *Encyclopedia Britannica* database, not to mention the cochlear and retinal implants that already exist and are paving the way for future, more cognitively oriented, kinds of biotechnological explorations (see Box 8.5).

The cyberpunk cases can be misleading, however, for they may seem to support the idea that once equipment lies *inside* the bounds of skin and skull, it can count as part of the physical basis of individual mind, *but not a moment before.* This seems unprincipled. If a functional copy of the implant was strapped to my belt, or carried in my hand, why should *that* make the difference? Easy availability and automatic deployment seem to be what really matter here. Being part of the biological brain pretty well ensures these key features. But it is at most a sufficient, and not a necessary, condition.

Box 8.6

COGNITIVE REHABILITATION

Consider, as a kind of coda, a case brought to my attention by Carolyn Baum, head of Occupational Therapy at the Washington University School of Medicine. Baum had been puzzled by the capacity of certain Alzheimer's sufferers to live alone in the community, maintaining a level of independent functioning quite out of step with their scores on standard tests designed to measure their capacity to live independently. The puzzle was resolved when Baum and her coworkers (see, e.g., Baum, 1996) observed these patients in their home environments. The environments turned out to be chock full of props and scaffolding able to partially offset the neural deficiency: rooms might be labeled, important objects (bank books, etc.) left in full view so as to be easily found when needed, "memory books" of faces, names, and relations kept available, and specific routines (e.g., bus to Denny's at 11 A.M. for lunch) religiously adhered to. Such cognitive scaffolding might be the work of the patients themselves, put gradually in place as the biological degeneration worsened, and/or set up by family and friends.

Now, when first confronted with such extreme reliance on external scaffolding, it is tempting to see it as underscoring a biocentric view of the individual agent, as deeply psychologically compromised. I submit, however, that this temptation is rooted not in any deep facts about the internal/external boundary, but in a mixture of unfamiliarity (these are not the external props that most of us use) and insufficiency (the external props are currently able to offset only a few of the debilitating effects of the Alzheimer's).

Thus consider, once again, the artist and the sketchpad. In this case we do not find ourselves lamenting the artist's lack of "real" creativity just because the creative process involves repeated and essential episodes of sketching and reperceiving. Nor do we reduce our admiration for the poet, just because the poetry emerges only courtesy of much exploratory activity with pen and paper. To see what I am getting at here, imagine next that *normal* human brains displayed the typical characteristics of the Alzheimer's brains. And imagine that we had slowly evolved a society in which the kinds of props and scaffolding deployed by Baum's Alzheimer's patients were the norm. Finally, reflect that that is exactly (in a sense) what we have done: our PCs, sketchpads, and notebooks complement our basic biological cognitive profile in much the same kind of way. Perhaps seeing the normal deep cognitive symbiosis between human brains and external technologies will prompt us to rethink some ideas about what it *is* to have a cognitive deficit, and to pursue, with increased energy, a vision of full and genuine cognitive rehabilitation using various forms of cognitive scaffolding.

There is also a real danger of erring to the opposite extreme. Once mind is located firmly *inside* the skull, one is tempted to ask whether even finer grained localization might be indicated. Thus consider a view expressed by Herbert Simon. Simon saw, very clearly, that portions of the external world often functioned as a nonbiological kind of memory. But instead of counting those portions (subject to the provisos just rehearsed) as proper parts of the knowing system, Simon chose to go the other way. Regarding biological, on-board memory, Simon invites us to "view this information-packed memory as less a part of the organism than of the environment to which it adapts" (Simon, 1982, p. 65). Part of the problem here no doubt originates from Simon's overly passive (mere storage) view of biological memory—we now know that the old data/process distinction offers precious little leverage when confronting biological computational systems. But the deeper issue, I suspect, concerns the underlying image of something like a "core agent" surrounded by (internal and external) support systems (memories, etc.). This image is incompatible with the emerging body of results from connectionism, neuroscience, and artificial life that we have been reviewing in the past several chapters. Instead of identifying intelligence with any kind of special core process, these recent investigations depict intelligence as arising from the operation of multiple, often quite special-purpose routines, some of which criss-cross neural bodily and environmental boundaries, and which often operate within the benefits of any kind of stable, unique, centralized control. Simon's view makes best sense against the backdrop of a passive view of memory and a commitment to some kind of centralized engine of "real" cognition. To whatever extent we are willing to abandon these commitments, we should be willing to embrace the possibility of genuine systemic extensions in which external processes and operations come to count as integral aspects of individual human intelligence (see Box 8.6 for some further considerations).

8.3 Suggested Readings

For further ideas about *the use of environmental structure* to augment biological cognition, see especially E. Hutchins, *Cognition in the Wild* (Cambridge, MA: MIT Press, 1995), a fantastically rich and detailed account of how multiple external factors contribute to the process of ship navigation (it's a good idea, oddly, to read Chapter 9 of Hutchins' book first). Daniel Dennett has done pioneering conceptual work hereabouts; see especially D. Dennett, *Darwin's Dangerous Idea* (New York: Simon and Schuster, 1995, Chapters 12 and 13) and D. Dennett, "Making Things to Think With," Chapter 5 of his excellent *Kinds of Minds* (New York: Basic Books, 1996). For my own attempts at bringing similar ideas into focus, see A. Clark, *Being There* (Cambridge, MA: MIT Press, 1997, Chapters 9 and 10).

For another (broadly Vygotskian) perspective on *socially and instrumentally mediated action*, see J. Wertsch, *Mind as Action* (New York: Oxford University Press, 1998).

Somewhat more *computationally oriented accounts of the role of environmental structure* include D. Kirsh and P. Maglio, "On Distinguishing Epistemic from Pragmatic Action," *Cognitive Science*, 18, 513–549, 1996, and various papers in P. Agre and S. Rosenschein (eds.),

Computational Theories of Interaction and Agency (Cambridge, MA: MIT Press, 1995), especially the essays by Agre, Beer, Hammond et al., and Kirsh.

For much more *on the possible relations between language and thought,* see the collection by P. Carruthers and J. Boucher (eds.), *Language and Thought* (Cambridge, England: Cambridge University Press, 1998), especially the essays by Carruthers and by Dennett. My paper, A. Clark, "Magic Words: How Language Augments Human Computation," appears there also. For more on the *language/thought/culture connection,* see J. Bruner, *Acts of Meaning* (Cambridge, MA: Harvard University Press, 1990).

For *the interplay between neural differences and the cascade of technological innovation,* see D. Dennett, *Kinds of Minds* (New York: Basic Books, 1996, Chapters 4–6), M. Donald, *Origins of the Modern Mind* (Cambridge, MA: Harvard University Press, 1991, Chapters 6–8), T. Deacon's difficult, but rewarding *The Symbolic Species* (New York: Norton, 1997), and S. Mithen, *The Prehistory of the Mind* (London: Thames and Hudson, 1996, especially Chapters 9–11).

For the specific idea of *language as enabling our own thoughts to become objects of further thought and attention,* see R. Jackendoff, "How language helps us think," published with replies in *Pragmatics and Cognition,* 4(1), 1–34, 1996. See especially the replies by Barnden, Clark, and Ellis.

For a *different, difficult, but very worthwhile* take on such issues, see C. Taylor, "Heidegger, language and ecology." In C. Taylor (ed.), *Philosophical Arguments* (Cambridge, MA: Harvard University Press, 1995).

On the topic *"where does the mind stop and the rest of the world begin?"* try A. Clark and D. Chalmers, "The extended mind." *Analysis,* 58, 7–19, 1998. Also J. Haugeland, "Mind embodied and embedded." In J. Haugeland (ed.), *Having Thought* (Cambridge, MA: Harvard University Press, 1998). For a careful, critical (and negative) appraisal of the "extended mind" idea, see K. Butler, *Internal Affairs* (Dordrecht, The Netherlands: Kluwer, 1998, Chapter 6).

Finally, for a fairly concrete *connectionist proposal about the role of external symbols,* see the chapter "Schemata and sequential thought processes in PDP models" in J. McClelland, D. Rumelhart, and the PDP Research Group, *Parallel Distributed Processing,* Vol. 2 (Cambridge, MA: MIT Press, 1986, pp. 7–58).

(NOT REALLY A) CONCLUSION

Firm conclusions are out of place in what was meant simply as a somewhat challenging, discursive little text. But there is one modestly reliable moral to be drawn from our rapid-fire tour. It is that the human mind, understood as whatever it is that supports and explains our patterns of flexible, appropriate, and (sometimes) reason-sensitive response, is a *constitutively leaky system*. It is a system that resists any single *approach* such as that of classical A.I. or connectionism, that resists any single *level of analysis*, such as the level of computation, or of physical dynamics, and that resists any single *disciplinary perspective*, such as that of philosophy, neuroscience, cultural and technological studies, artificial intelligence, or cognitive psychology. Moreover, it is not just a complex, multifaceted system, but a genuinely *leaky* one—"leaky" in the sense that many crucial features and properties depend precisely on the *interactions* between events and processes occurring at different levels of organization and on different time scales.

Human mindfulness thus inhabits a little-visited corner of the design space for intelligent systems. It inhabits a corner of design space that is profoundly *boundary blind*, marked by strategies and solutions that criss-cross the intuitive divides between mind and body, between person and environment, and between the thinker and her tools for thought.

This boundary blindness has some clear advantages. Unimpressed by the intuitive divide between the inner and the outer, processes of cultural and biological adaptation can search a wonderfully—but dauntingly—rich space of ploys and stratagems, often uncovering robust, cheap, surprising, boundary-busting routes to success and survival. Examples are manifold and manifest in the preceding chapters. To somewhat arbitrarily recall but three, we have seen how neural motor control is simplified and transformed by the in-built synergies of spring-like muscle and tendon systems, how biological vision repeatedly exploits bodily motion and environmental information storage, and how more advanced cognitive capacities (such as the creation of abstract art) depend on the complex interplay of neural operations, bodily actions, and the use of multiple aids, props, and artifacts.

What we think of as the "mindfulness" that makes intelligent behavior possible may thus be best understood as a product of immense and multifaceted leakage. As an intrinsically boundary-crossing phenomenon, mind presents an especially difficult object of study—a moving target, whose best descriptions and explanations simply cannot, in principle, be constructed by the use of a single tool, perspective, or analytic mode. The scientific study of mind thus demands interdisciplinary effort and multidisciplinary cooperation on a whole new scale, probing adaptive response at multiple organizational levels including those incorporating bodily, cultural, and environmental scaffolding. "Mindware as software"? That was a good slogan once. But it has served its purpose, and it is time to move on.

Some Backdrop
Dualism, Behaviorism, Functionalism, and Beyond

The present text begins quite close to where most philosophical treatments end: with recent attempts to understand mindfulness using the tools of neuroscience, cognitive psychology, and artificial intelligence. In these brief notes[1] I offer some rough-and-ready background, in the form of a few cameos of a few historically important positions.

1. Dualism

When we introspect, or reflect on our own thoughts, feelings, and beliefs, we do not find anything much like physical objects. Beliefs may be important or trivial, feelings strong or weak, but not literally big, or colored, or heavy, and so on. On the evidence of introspection alone, then, we might be inclined to conclude that the mind is something quite separate from, and deeply distinct from, the physical world. This perfectly natural viewpoint is known as *dualism.*

Considered as a philosophical theory of the nature of mind, Dualism is somewhat uninformative. It tells us what the mind is *not*; it is not a normal physical item like a body, brain, table, or chair. But it is embarrassingly silent about what it might actually *be.* But still, knowing that the moon is not made of green cheese is quite handy, even if you do not know what it is actually made of instead. So let us begin by giving the dualists' claim—that the mind is not a physical item—the benefit of the doubt. The question then arises: What is the relationship between this nonphysical item and the physical body that accompanies it around the world?

---

[1] These notes are based on some of my longstanding classroom teaching materials, and in one or two places I wonder whether something might have been unwittingly borrowed from some other source. My best efforts at checking this reveal no such unacknowledged borrowings. But should something have slipped the net of appropriate citation, I hereby apologize: and do let me know!

When dualism was in its heyday, around the time of the seventeenth century, there were three major contenders as an account of this relation:

1. Parallelism

2. Epiphenomenalism

3. Interactionism

1. According to the parallelist, the mind and the body are distinct and causally isolated. Neither is capable of affecting the other. How, then, are we to account for the *appearance* of causal linkage; the impression we have of wishes causing action and blows to the head causing hallucinatory experiences? Synchronization was to be the key. God, or some other force or agency, had arranged matters so that the two causal orders—the mental and the physical—would run along in harmony, like two ideally accurate clocks set to the same initial time and left to run for eternity; neither sustaining or consulting the other, but the two in perfect accord nonetheless.

The trouble with parallelism is who set the clocks? And why, if it was God, did God resort to such a clumsy piece of trickery?

2. *Epiphenomenalism* is like parallelism in asserting the causal isolation of the physical from the mental. But it relaxes the requirement in the other direction. The epiphenomenalist allows that the physical can cause the mental, but denies that the mental can affect the physical. The mind, on this account, is somewhat (though only somewhat) like the exhaust fumes from a car. The fumes accompany and are caused by the activity of the engine. But they do not (typically) power the car. Just so, the epiphenomenalist holds that beliefs and thought and other mental experiences accompany and are caused by brain activity. But they do not actually cause the body to act. They are just the icing on the cognitive cake. This is a counterintuitive prospect indeed; it certainly *feels* as if it is my desire for a Pete's Wicked Ale that prompts the trek to the local hostelry. Insofar as the whole impetus for accounts that reserve a special place for mental phenomena comes from a desire to respect the introspective evidence, this seems an odd conclusion to have to accept.

3. *Interactionism* is the most immediately appealing of the dualist positions. It treats the mental and the physical as distinct but causally integrated items, thus avoiding some of the metaphysical excesses and introspective implausibility of parallelism and epiphenomenalism. The most famous form of interactionism is Cartesian dualism. On Descartes' famous model, the mind is a totally nonphysical substance that acts on the body by influencing the pineal gland at the base of the neck. The body, by the same route, influences the mind.

The problem most commonly urged against Cartesian dualism is: How do two such distinct items—the body and the mind—manage to be parts of a single causal network? We understand, we think, how the physical can affect the physical; but how can the nonphysical do so?

The argument has some force. Cartesian dualism would certainly gain in plausibility if we had some such account. Still, we allow that many things that are not at all *like* physical objects may still act on them. Witness (to take a classic case) the iron filings acted on by a magnetic field. So it is not obviously the case that Cartesian interactionism is *conceptually* impossible.

So why give up dualism?

Dualist doctrines of the kind outlined above have been largely abandoned by science and philosophy. The mind is now taken to be grounded in the physical body in such a way that the problem of interaction need not arise. Many factors have contributed to dualism's downfall. Probably the most important of these are the following.

1. The obvious *dependence* of the mental on the physical. Drugs (such as Prozac, or ecstasy), which affect the physical constitution of the brain in moderately well understood ways, systematically affect our moods and emotions. Brain damage—for example, an iron spike through the prefrontal cortex—is likewise disruptive. The evolution of intelligent creatures is correlated with changes in brain structure. All this suggests (as presented in Churchland, 1984) that we must *at least* look for a systematic correlation of brain activity and mental activity. Why, then, assume that there are two *items* here, in need of correlation, instead of one item exhibiting a variety of properties? Materialism—the thesis that we are dealing with just one kind of *item* or substance, viz. physical matter—seems to win out on grounds of simplicity.

2. The *positive* arguments in favor of dualism are unconvincing. These are (a) the "how could . . . ?" argument, and (b) the argument from introspection.

a. The "how could . . . ?" argument relies on finding properties of human beings and asking "Now how could any mere *physical* system do *that*?" Descartes suggested that *reasoning* and *calculation* were beyond any mere physical system. But today, with our intuitions molded by shops full of Palm Pilots, G4s and even modest pocket calculators, we are unlikely to choose calculation to fill in the blank. Now people are more likely to choose some ability like "falling in love," "appreciating a symphony," or "being creative." But work in neuroscience and artificial intelligence is steadfastly eroding our faith that there are some things that no mere physical system could ever do. As such, the fact that *we* do *X*, *Y*, or *Z* no longer cuts much ice as an argument to the effect that we *cannot possibly* be "mere" physical systems.

b. The argument from introspection is a harder nut to crack. The idea is that we *just know* that a belief is not a state of brain or body. We can tell just by looking "inside ourselves" and seeing what a feeling is *like*. The trouble here is that introspection is a weak kind of evidence. Granted, we know that our feelings do not *strike us* as being brain states. But so what? I may have a feeling in my stomach that does not strike me as being a mild case of salmonella. But it might still *be* a mild case of salmonella for all that. This oversimplifies the issue, but the general point is clear. Unless someone can show that what introspection reveals cannot be the *very same thing* as a bodily state, albeit under a different description, we need not accept introspection as decisive evidence in favor of dualism.

Dualism, then, lacks explanatory force and independent positive evidence in its favor. How else might we conceive the mind?

2. Behaviorism

Probably the first major philosophical reaction against Dualism came not as a result of the explanatory inadequacies just described, but instead grew out of a movement within philosophy that is sometimes referred to as the *linguistic turn.* The leading idea was that philosophical puzzles were at root puzzles about *language.* Gilbert Ryle, in *The Concept of Mind,* published in 1949, accuses dualism and the whole body–mind debate of a failure to understand the role of mental talk in our language. Philosophy of mind, according to Ryle, was captivated by *Descartes' myth.* And Descartes' myth was, in effect, the idea of mind as an inner sanctum known only by introspection. The myth inclined philosophers to seek some account of the relation of this inner sanctum to the public world of people, objects, and actions. But the task was thought to be misconceived. Philosophers, Ryle claimed, were failing to see the significance of mental talk, in much the same way as someone fails to see the significance of talk about a university who, on being shown the library and colleges and playing fields and accommodation, goes on to complain, "Yes. I see all that. But where is *the university?*" The answer is that the university is not something extra, beyond all the colleges, accommodation, and so on. It is just the organization of those very items. Just so, Ryle argued, the mind is not something beyond all its public behavioral manifestations—mindtalk is just a way of talking about the organization of the behavior itself. When we say that Mary loves teaching, we do not mean that inside Mary there is a ghostly loving that accompanies her professional acts. Rather we mean only that Mary's actual and potential behavior will follow a certain pattern. That pattern might be expressed as a very long conjunction of claims about what Mary would do in certain situations, e.g.,

if she is offered a new textbook she will take it;

if someone asks her if she likes teaching, she will say yes;

if she sees a good teacher in action, she will try to emulate them

and so on.

The idea, in short, is that mental talk picks out *behavioral dispositions.* It isolates what so and so is likely to do in such and such circumstances. It does not pick out a state of an inner mental sanctum. The classic analogy is with chemical dispositions such as solubility. To say that *X* is soluble is not to say that *X* contains some hidden spirit of solubility. It is just to say that if you put *X* in water, *X* would dissolve. Mental talk picks on more complex dispositions [what Paul Churchland (1984) calls "multi-tracked dispositions"]; but dispositions is still *all* they are.

Three worries afflict behaviorism in the form I have presented it.

1. The dispositional analysis looks either *infinite* or *circular*. It will be infinite if we have to list what a given belief will dispose an agent to do in *every possible situation* they could be in. And it will be circular if our list of dispositions makes irreducible reference to other mental states, e.g., Mary will try to teach well as long as she is happy and does not believe teaching is ruining her life.

2. The dispositional account seems to want to rule out the inner sanctum completely. But isn't there some truth in the idea? Don't we have inner feelings, pains, images, and the like?

3. It is *explanatorily shallow*. It tells us, at best, something about how we use mental concepts. But this need not be the end of the story of mind. Even if "soluble" just *means* "would dissolve in water," we can ask after the *grounds* of the disposition to dissolve. We can ask *how* it is possible for something to dissolve in water. So too we may ask how it is possible for someone to love teaching. And the explanation should appeal to a range of facts beyond the surface behavior of the teacher. Indeed, taken at face value, behaviorism seems to commit a kind of "method actors fallacy" (see Putnam, 1980), attributing genuine neural states (of, say, pain) to anyone exhibiting appropriate behavior, and denying pain to anyone able to suppress all the behavioral and verbal expressions of pain.

3. Identity Theory

In the mid to late 1950s philosophers began to realize—or rediscover—that there was more to philosophical life than the analysis of the concepts of ordinary language. Philosophy could, for example, contribute to the study of mind and mental mechanisms by examining the conceptual coherence of scientific theory *schemas*. By this I mean, not examining a particular, well worked out scientific theory in say, neurophysiology, but by considering the intelligibility and implications of general types of scientific account of the mind. One such account—the topic of this section—was the so-called Mind–Brain identity theory. The schema here in brief was mental states *are* brain processes.

This schema was advocated, discussed, and refined by philosophers such as U. T. Place, J. J. C. Smart, and D. Armstrong [see the collection edited by V. C. Chappell (1962) for some of the classic contributions]. The philosophical task, then, is not to decide *whether or not* mental states are brain processes. That is a job for ordinary science. Rather, it is to consider whether this general theory schema is one that is even *possibly* true. Does it even make sense to suppose that thoughts, beliefs, and sensations could be identical with brain processes?

Reasons to doubt that it does include

1. Leibniz' law problems

2. species-chauvinism objections.

Leibniz' law states that if two descriptions pick out the same object, then whatever is true of the object under one description must be true of it under the other. Thus, if Spiderman really is Peter Parker, then whatever is true of Spiderman must be true of Peter Parker, and vice versa. If Aunt May is Peter Parker's ailing relative, then she must be Spiderman's ailing relative also. If Spiderman clings to ceilings, then Peter Parker must cling to ceilings also. Formally,

$$(X)\,(Y)\,[(X = Y) \to (F)\,(FX \leftrightarrow FY)]$$

Whatever their opinion about Spiderman, many philosophers were unable to see how the mind–brain identity thesis could live up to the Leibniz' law requirement. For consider

- [Spatial location] A brain state may be located in space, say 10 cm behind my eyeball. But it surely won't be true of any mental state—say, my belief that Mark McGuire plays for the Cardinals—that it is 10 cm behind my eyeball.
- [Truth value] A belief may be true or false. But how can a brain state be true or false?
- [Sensational content] A pain may be sharp or tingly. But could a brain state be sharp or tingly?
- [Authority] I seem to have some authority over my mental states. If I sincerely believe I am in agony, it looks as if I must be right. But I do not seem to have any authority over my brain states; a neurophysiologist could surely correct me with regard to those.

One way of responding to these objections is simply to grasp the nettle we are offered and say, "It may not *seem* as if brain states can be true or false, or mental states located in space, but they *are*." It does not seem as if a flash of lightning is an electrical discharge, but it is. And if you have some authority when it comes to spotting flashes of lightning, then you have it when it comes to spotting some kinds of electrical discharge whether you know it or not. The idea behind this kind of response is that Leibniz' law is unreliable in contexts that involve people's *beliefs* about properties of objects, rather than just the *actual* properties of the objects. To once again adapt a strategy used by Paul Churchland (1984), we can display the problem by constructing the following clearly fallacious argument:

1. Mary Jane Watson believes that Spiderman is a hero.

2. Mary Jane Watson does not believe that Peter Parker is a hero.

so,

3. By Leibniz' law—Peter Parker is not identical with Spiderman.

Identity theory thus survives the Leibniz' law crisis. Historically, it succumbed (although sophisticated revivals are increasingly popular today) to a very different kind of objection [first raised by Hilary Putnam (1960) in a series of papers beginning with "Minds and machines"]. The objection is one of *species-chauvinism*. On a *strong* reading of the identity theorists' claims it looks as if *types* of mental state (e.g., being happy, angry, seeing blue, believing that Reagan is dangerous) are now being identified with types of brain state (e.g., the firing of a certain group of neurons, or C-fibers, or whatever). But this claim, on closer examination, looks distinctly implausible. For consider one example.

Suppose we type-identify, say, being in pain with having C-fibers 1–9 firing. Then it follows that *no being without C-fibers can be in pain*. But this seems a very rash, even imperialistic, claim. Might we not encounter extraterrestrial beings who look clearly capable of feeling pain (they wince and groan and so on) yet *lack* C-fibers? Maybe many animals to which we happily ascribe psychological properties such as feeling hungry or angry lack C-fibers, too. Maybe we will soon build intelligent computer systems that have neuromorphic VSLI chips instead of neurons. Must we simply *rule out* the possibility that all these different kinds of physical systems may share some of our psychological states? Surely not. Suppose we discovered that various human beings had different kinds of brain structure, such that when Fred felt pain C-fibers 1–9 fired, but when Andy felt pain D-fibers 1–7 fired. Psychological ascriptions seem almost *designed* to class together different brain states in virtue of their common role in determining types of behavior. Strong type–type identity theory does no justice to this capacity for generalization, and can seem species-chauvinistic as a result.

One way out is for the identity theorist to claim that each individual occurrence of a mental state is identical with some brain state. This is the "token" version of identity theory, so named because it associates *tokens* (individual occurrences) of mental events with brain events, without making claims about the identity of types of mental event with types of brain event. One trouble with this as it stands is that it is explanatorily weak; it leaves us unenlightened as to *why* any particular physical state should be identical with the particular mental event with which it is. One way to remedy this is to build on the idea that psychological ascriptions are in part designed to group together physically disparate brain states in virtue of their common *role* in determining behavior, but to build on it in such a way as to avoid the behaviorist's mistake of *identifying* the psychological state with the outward behavior. This is exactly what Putnam did and the result was another philosophical schema for a scientific theory of mind, viz. *functionalism*.

4. Machine Functionalism

The first wave identity theorist faced a hopeless task, akin, as Daniel Dennett has pointed out, to finding a purely physical account of what all clocks, say, have in common. We would find no useful description, in the language of physics, of the commonality in virtue of which a sundial, a clockwork alarm, and a quartz digital alarm are all said to be *clocks*. What unites these disparate physical objects is the purpose, function, or use that we assign to them. Just so, it seems, there need be no useful physical description that captures what my anger, the dog's anger, the Martian's anger, and the robot's anger all have in common. In some sense it looked to be the functionality of the different physical states that realize our several angers that unites the states *as* angers. Hence, *functionalism* is a schema for a scientific theory of mind.

One way of understanding the functionalist approach is by analogy with computer programs. A program is just a recipe for getting a job done, and can be specified, at a very abstract level, as a set of operations to be performed on an input and yielding a certain output—maybe a number or sentence. Defined at such an abstract level the same program can be written in different high-level languages (BASIC, PASCAL, LISP, JAVA, or whatever) and run on machines with very different kinds of hardware. The abstract idea of a program (its input-inner operations–output profile) is captured in its specification as a *Turing machine* (see Chapter 1), which is, in effect, just a description of a fixed set of operations to be performed on whatever strings of symbols it is given as input. The point is that this abstract notion of a program is not "hardware-chauvinist"; the same program, so defined, may run on lots of different physical machines. The functionalist claim, in effect, is that the mind is to the body/brain as the program is to the physical machine.

The analogy is so satisfying, indeed, that the original functionalists went further and claimed not just

C1 The mind is to the brain as the program is to the machine, but

C2 The mind *is* a program, run (in humans) with the brain as its supporting hardware.

C2 is often called *machine functionalism*. Since much of the present text is concerned with versions of machine functionalism, I shall not pursue this position any further here.

4. Eliminativism

The task so far has been to see what general kind of schema for a scientific theory could make sense of the relation between our talk of the mind and some kind of description (functional, behavioral, or whatever) of the physical world. The question was thus:

> What *kind* of scientific theory could possibly count as a theory of the mind?

Some would regard this as a mistaken goal. For it seems to assume that our commonsense ideas about mental phenomena, which together make up our commonsense idea of *mind*, are (at least largely) correct. It assumes, in effect, that there really are such things as hopes, desires, fears, beliefs, and so on, and that the job of science is to *explain* them. But, after all, people once thought that there were ghosts and vampires and that apparently empty space was filled by mysterious ether and much else that science has shown to be misguided. Imagine, then, a discipline devoted to investigating what *kind* of scientific theory could possibly account for the existence of the ether. What a waste of time! What science shows is that there is no ether and so the task of accounting for its existence never arises. Could the commonsense notion of mind meet a similar fate? Those who think so call themselves *eliminative materialists* (e.g., Churchland, 1981). The task of philosophy, as they see it, is not to prejudge the issue by simply setting out to discover what scientific schema explains the commonsense view of mind, but also to critically examine scientific accounts to see whether the commonsense view is *sound*. Once again, this is a topic treated in the main text and I shall not pursue it far here. Notice, however, that eliminative materialism need not be an all or nothing doctrine. Dennett (1987), for example, allows that some of our common sense ideas about the mental may find a home in some future scientific theory. He just denies that we should *demand* that any good theory capture all our pretheoretical intuitions.

The most radical versions of eliminative materialism predict that virtually nothing of the commonsense framework will be preserved. Beliefs, desires, hopes, and fears will all be abandoned in some future science of the mind. It is, I suspect, extremely hard to even make sense of this claim *in advance* of the science being developed and offering us alternative concepts to use when we formulate it. From here, it is hard to see how such a future science could *be* a science of the mind at all. But that, of course, may just be predictable conceptual myopia. On the other hand, it does seem as if there is a whole cluster of related concepts involving actions, beliefs, and desires that just *constitute* the idea of mind. We could certainly give some up and revise others. But could we really drop them all? And to what extent does the legitimacy of those concepts depend on their finding a place in some scientific theory anyway? It is a virtue of eliminative materialism that it is radical enough to bring these issues to the fore.

Suggested Readings

Several recent textbooks offer superb introductions to the topics covered in this appendix. I especially recommend J. Kim, *Philosophy of Mind* (Boulder, CO: Westview, 1996) and D. Braddon-Mitchell and F. Jackson's *Philosophy of Mind and Cognition* (Oxford, England: Blackwell, 1996). Other useful treatments include G. Graham, *Philosophy of Mind: An Introduction* (Oxford, England: Blackwell, 1993) and P. Churchland's classic, *Matter and Consciousness* (Cambridge, MA: MIT Press, 1984, and many subsequent and expanded editions). W. Lycan (ed.), *Mind and Cognition: A Reader* (Oxford, England: Blackwell, 1990) offers a fine collection of papers covering functionalism, identity theory, eliminativism, and much else besides.

Consciousness and the Meta-Hard Problem

Readers of some early versions of this text suggested that it paid too little attention to the hot topics of consciousness and subjective experience. This was no accident. But it is undeniably the case that a complete and satisfying scientific account of the nature of mindware cannot remain forever silent concerning what is, arguably, the single most puzzling fact about mind! It is with some trepidation, then, that I offer a sketch of the issues (as they appear to me) and a few critical and constructive remarks.

Consciousness has certainly come out of the closet. After a long period during which the word was hardly mentioned in scientific circles, consciousness is now the star of a major growth industry. There are books, meetings, and journals. There are Internet discussion groups and web sites. There is hope, interest, and excitement. But is there a theory—or even a promising sketch for a story? It is, strangely, rather hard to say. It is hard to say because first, the word "consciousness" does not seem to aim at a single, steady target. We need to distinguish various possible targets and assess the state of the art relative to each one. And second, it is unclear (especially with respect to some of the more recondite targets) exactly what would *count* as a theory, sketch, story, or explanation, anyway.

Some possible targets for a theory of consciousness include simple awakeness, self-awareness, availability for verbal report, availability for the control of intentional action, and, of course, the star of the show—raw feels or qualia, the distinct feels and sensations that make life worth living or (sometimes) worth leaving.

Simple awakeness may be roughly defined as the state in which we are quite sensitive to our surroundings, able to process incoming information and respond appropriately. Self-awareness involves the capacity to represent ourselves and to be aware of ourselves as distinct agents. Availability for verbal report involves both a capacity to somehow access our own inner states and to describe what we find using words (or sign language, etc.). Availability for the control of intentional action suggests a certain kind of "informational poise," such that some of our knowledge or ideas become capable of guiding an open-ended range of projects and activities—the kind of informational poise that is missing in, e.g., a blindsight patient's limited capacity to use visual information coming from a "blind" region (more on this below). And qualia, raw feels? It is depressingly hard to say much more about exactly what these are. We resort to the well-worn hints and phrases: the very *redness* of the apple, the taste of the peach, the precise and unutterable piercingness of the grief, and so on. As Jaegwon Kim recently put it: "If this doesn't help, perhaps nothing will" (Kim, 1996, p. 180).

There is something striking about even this partial list of possible targets for a theory of consciousness. What is striking is that it is only the final target ("qualia") that threatens to present any *special* kind of problem for our standard modes of cognitive scientific explanation and understanding. All the rest have to do either with *what* it is we are informed about (what, to beg a few questions, is internally represented) or with the way that information is poised for the control of action or for sharing with other cognitive subsystems. Theories about informational content and informational poise thus have the resources to explain a large portion of what is often meant by "conscious awareness." The question is, can they go all the way?

To get some sense of just how far they *can* go, consider three bodies of research in cognitive neuroscience: work on blindsight, work on binding, and Milner and Goodale's (1995) recent work on dorsal versus ventral processing.

"Blindsight" names an intriguing phenomenon that has become one of the staples of cognitive scientific conjecture concerning consciousness. Blindsight patients have damage to the visual cortex, resulting in the presence of a scotoma or blind spot. Such patients claim to see nothing in this region, but can, if forced to guess, perform way above chance (Weiskrantz, 1986). For example, the patients can successfully guess whether a light has flashed in the blind region, and can even orient hand and wrist in response to the shape of presented objects (Marcel, 1988, p. 136). But when asked if they actually have visual experience on which to base these successful responses, they either insist there is no experience at all, or report something faint, inconclusive, and not really visual in nature. The standard account of the condition has been that the successful responses are rooted in primitive, mid-brain processing and that full-fledged phenomenal consciousness (the experiential quality, raw feel, etc.) thus depends on the more evolutionarily recent overlay of higher cortical activity. A competing account, however, explains blindsight as the preservation *within* the so-called blind region of small areas of preserved vision—visual "hot spots" that offer a cortical route to the successful responses (see Gazzaniga, 1998, pp. 80–83). Either way, what remains intriguing is the patient's denial of actual visual experience in these cases. The kind of visually guided action that we ordinarily take to be indicative of visual experience is here produced without the accompanying experience. The tempting—though clearly simplistic—thought is: find the key neural differences between the two cases and you have found the physiological seat of those ever-elusive qualia.

Another famous neuroscientific contribution to the debate is Crick and Koch's (1997) work on consciousness and 40-Hz oscillations. The focus of the work is on the neural mechanisms that achieve binding, where binding involves establishing a certain relation between neural populations carrying different types and items of information, e.g., binding MT motion detectors to V4 hue detectors as part of the process of representing a certain face in the act of speaking (see Crick and Koch, 1997, p. 284). Such binding, Crick and Koch claim, is achieved by frequency-locked oscillations in the various neural populations, with the locking perhaps mediated by circuitry linking the cortex to the highly connected thalamus—the so-called thalamocortical loop. Spike synchronizations in the 40-Hz range (actually, anywhere between 35 and 70 Hz) are then depicted as joining the various neurally represented features into a coherent whole, which is then placed in working memory, which in turn renders the coherent percept poised for the widespread control of action and report (Crick and Koch, 1997, p. 288).

As a final excursion into neuroscientific conjecture, consider Milner and Goodale's (1995) account of the different functional roles of two anatomically distinct streams (of connected neural regions) identified in visual processing. The two streams (the dorsal and the ventral) were long classed as "what" and "where" streams, with the ventral stream thought to be most responsible for identification and recognition of objects, and the dorsal stream responsible for spatial localization (see Ungerleider and Mishkin, 1982). The Milner and Goodale hypothesis, by contrast, is that the dorsal stream supports the guidance of fine motor action and the ventral stream supports the kind of perception involved in visual awareness. Thus, for example, we may be visually aware of an object in virtue of ventral stream activity, whereas our capacity to reach for and grasp an object depends on the goings-on in the dorsal stream, which is said to act "in large part alone" (Milner and Goodale, 1998, Section 3). Such a theory helps explain why some lesioned monkeys and human patients (e.g., D.F.) can perform visually guided action without visual awareness. In such cases, the ventral stream is impaired whereas the dorsal stream is unaffected. Similarly, dorsal stream impairment combined with intact ventral processing seems to yield reach-and-grasp deficits alongside normal object identification, and normal orientation and spatial location judgments (see Jeannerod, 1986). The relatively independent activity of the two streams also shows up in normal performance. Certain visual illusions (see Chapter 7, Box 7.2) involve the conscious experience of an object as larger than it is. Yet despite the illusion, our motor and action routines yield correct preparatory grasping: the finger-thumb placement is keyed to the object's actual size, not to the consciously perceived illusion (see Haffendale and Goodale, 1998).

The most important aspect of the Milner and Goodale model, for our purposes, is thus the identification of conscious visual awareness with ventral stream activity, and the claim that "the processing accomplished by the ventral stream [involves forms of coding that] coincide with those that render the representations accessible to our awareness" (Milner and Goodale, 1998, Section 3).

Our exemplar neuroscientific excursions are at an end. But the vexing problem remains: What can this kind of evidence, theory, and conjecture tell us about the phenomenon of consciousness itself? The answer, naturally, depends on the precise spin we give to the weasel-word "consciousness," and on how we conceive the relation between the various phenomena of access, poise, reportability, and qualitative feel.

One influential move, at about this point, is to firmly distinguish two notions. One is what Ned Block (1997, p. 382) calls access-consciousness. The other is what Block (1997, p. 380) calls phenomenal-consciousness. Access-consciousness is all about informational poise: "A state is A-conscious if it is poised for direct control of thought and action" (Block, 1997, p. 382). When information (e.g., about a visually present object) is able to guide intentional action and verbal report, it counts as A-conscious. Phenomenal-consciousness, on the other hand, is something we cannot define but can only "point to" (Block, 1997, p. 380). It is about the felt quality of tastes, smells, and colors, about "what it is like" to taste a fresh Margarita while feeling the hot, Mexican sun on your back and enjoying (or not) the relentless beat of a mariachi band. *That's* P-consciousness.

Suppose now that someone offers to explain blindsight by invoking the idea of an intact, low-level processing mechanism, capable of guiding forced responses, combined with an impairment of some other device whose role is to make information available for verbal report and the control of intentional action? Or suppose we discover that the blindsight patient has a disruption of the 40-Hz oscillations that Crick and Koch implicate in binding and the passage of information to working memory? Such explanations seem, indeed, well within the reach of current neuroscience. Would such stories finally explain the phenomenon of P-consciousness itself?

Block responds with a resounding "no." All that these stories can currently do, Block maintains, is illuminate the vastly less mysterious realm of A-consciousness. And the great mistake in scientific and philosophical thinking about consciousness (still according to Block) is to confuse the two; to offer a nice, well-motivated story about access and informational poise, and then to claim to have said something illuminating about its reclusive cousin, P-consciousness, the "what-it's-likeness" that infuses the computational shell with, well, what-it's-likeness.

To see the difference, consider this. I could (let us suppose) build a robot that has a silicon-based equivalent to Milner and Goodale's ventral and dorsal streams. One computational cascade thus supports verbal response and object recognition, etc., whereas another uses visual input to guide reaching and grasping and so on. But it is surely possible (isn't it?) that such a robot will lack P-consciousness altogether. It will be a dual stream zombie, acting like us but lacking all felt experience. We could even understand why, for example, certain kinds of silicon-rot disable its capabilities of object recognition and report, while leaving intact its capacity to reach and grasp. But we would not be one whit closer to understanding what it is about us that causes the phenomenal *experience* that, in us, accompanies ventral stream processing (or 40-Hz oscillation, or whatever).

The idea that current scientific speculations illuminate access-consciousness while leaving the phenomenal aspects unexplained is also manifest in David Chalmer's distinction between "easy" and "hard" problems concerning conscious awareness. The easy problems, as Chalmers (1996, 1997a) has it, concern functional capacities and are characterized by questions such as "How can the brain recognize objects?" "How can it integrate object-features into a single whole?" "How can it distinguish vegemite and marmite?" etc. In describing these questions as "easy," Chalmers means only to *contrast* them with what he sees as the deeper mysteries: Why does the act of distinguishing marmite and vegemite by taste involve any "what-it's-likeness" at all? And why is the "what-it's-likeness" of marmite the particular way it is? Chalmers' claim is that the standard moves in cognitive scientific explanation cannot resolve such "hard" problems. For all standard stories describe functional capacities (to say such-and-such, to discriminate so-and-so, to use this information for this or that purpose, etc.). But (so it is argued) it is always conceivable (logically possible) that a being might display the functional profile yet have no qualitative experience ("zombies") or have very different qualitative experiences ("inversion"). So whatever explains the functional profiles cannot itself explain the most puzzling facts about phenomenal experience—the presence of real feels, with determinate qualitative contents. There thus threatens what Levine (1983) calls an "explanatory gap." For even supposing we got a perfect grip on the neural *correlates* of consciousness in human beings, and were able to identify patterns of neural activity that always yield, e.g., the experience of tasting marmite or whatever, still, "the question of *why* [the pattern] gives rise to consciousness remains unanswered" (Chalmers, 1996, p. 47). In short, then, if some specific kind of informational poise turned out to be both necessary and sufficient for phenomenal consciousness, there could still be something left unexplained—P-consciousness, "what-it's-likeness," the taste of that Margarita.

But would there *really* be something missing? There are several ways to doubt it, but I shall sketch just two: representationalism and (what I shall call, a little clumsily) narrationism.

Representationalists claim that the mental (including all aspects of so-called phenomenal awareness) is exhausted by the representational. As Bill Lycan has it "the mind has no special properties that are not exhausted by its representational properties" (Lycan, 1997, p. 755). The simplest way to be a representationalist is to claim that the feeling of pain, for example, is nothing but the internal representation of (something like) "tissue damage at location X." Thus Dretske (1997, p. 786) argues that what makes certain states conscious is "the way they make us conscious of something else—the world we live in and . . . the condition of our own bodies." It is an open question among representationalists just how to unpack the relevant notion of internal representation. Michael Tye, for example, holds that we need not overintellectualize the idea: it is not that the agent has to develop *concepts* such as "tissue damage." Rather, the pain may consist of a *"sensory* representation" whose content fixes the phenomenal character (Tye, 1997, p. 333). (A possibly related proposal, with an experimental/neuroscientific spin, is considered in Box AII.1.)

Representationalism also comes in two distinct grades: simple, or first-order, representationalism (as above) and what has become known as *higher order thought theory*. This latter is the idea that a neural state is phenomenally conscious when it is *itself* the object of a thought. Roughly, to feel a stabbing pain is not (just) to represent a certain kind of tissue damage. It is, rather, to have a thought *about* the representation of tissue damage. As Rosenthal (1997, p. 741) has it, "a neural state will be conscious if it is accompanied by a thought about the state."

Why be a representationalist? The attraction is both practical and theoretical. On the theory side, it can be argued that all phenomenally conscious states must involve some kind of representational content. Even the much-cited orgasm can, if one is sufficiently hard-nosed, be claimed to be *about* certain bodily events and processes. It is less clear, however, why we should hold that such contents *exhaust* the phenomenal feel, such that accounting for the content simply *is* accounting for the full experience. Higher order versions, especially, have something to say here—but I postpone further discussion of this until later. The *practical* attraction is, of course, undeniable. We have a much better grasp of the notion of content-carrying inner states (representations) than we have of qualia, raw feels, and their ilk. (For myself, I see nothing wrong with looking where the light is brightest.) Finally (a kind of methodological point), if a difference in representational content can, indeed, always be found alongside every difference in phenomenal feel, what possible grounds could we have for insisting that there is something more to explain?

A second gap-denying response, related to (but not identical with) the first, is what I am calling "narrationism." This is a clumsy term, but it captures the position better than its rivals ["qualia nihilism" (Kim, 1996), "eliminativism," etc.]. The originator and prime mover of narrationism is Daniel Dennett, and it is his (complex but rewarding) version that I shall, with some trepidation, now try to sketch.

Dennett's seminal treatment of these issues comes in the long (1991a) study *Consciousness Explained*—a book I think might have been better titled *Consciousness Achieved*. For it is the essence of Dennett's view that consciousness is, in a sense, constructed rather than given. It is constructed by the use (the operation within us) of a variety of "mind-tools" (Dennett, 1996, Chapter 5) made available by our immersion in culture and language. I cannot hope to do justice to the full story here. But a not-too-misleading sketch might go like this.

Box AII.1

BODY AND FEELING

Damasio (1994) suggests that bodily feedback and persisting bodily imagery contribute a crucial element to human thought. The central claim is as follows:

> Were it not for the possibility of sensing body states that are inherently ordained to be painful or pleasurable, there would be no suffering or bliss, no longing or mercy, no tragedy or glory in the human condition. (Damasio, 1994, p. XV)

In absolute microcosm, the story goes something like this. Detection of success or failure—based, in the first instance, on innate goals and biological systems of "reward and punishment"—sets up an array of what Damasio calls "somatic markers." A somatic marker is a state that ties the image/trace of an event to a gut reaction (aversion, if we failed; attraction, if we succeeded). This marker system operates automatically (in normal subjects) in future similar encounters, influencing both on-the-spot responses and the array of options that we generate for considered, reflective action. The root and foundation of this whole system are our capacity to sense our own bodily states and our (initially) innate proclivity to take some such states as good (pleasurable) and others as bad (painful). Of special importance here are our capacities to detect and represent inner biochemical states, states of the viscera, and skin, and of the musculoskeletal system. Human conscious awareness is thus said to be constantly informed by a "qualifying body state": an apprehension—not always consciously felt—of a positive or negative body state. Even when we are thinking of nonbodily matters (recalling a mathematical theorem, say) we are said to be activating a bodyscape recollection that has become associated with the item, person or event. It is the continuous presence of this associated body state "image," with its positive or negative spin, that gives our experience its emotional tone: that makes the pain hurt, the memory pleasant, or the sight thrilling. Finally, what makes the feeling *ours*, according to Damasio, is some process by which the body representation becomes correlated with—or perhaps participates in the construction of—a neural representation of the self (which is not to be understood as an inner homunculus, but simply as a mental construct based on present and past body representations, autobiographical memory, semantic knowledge, and current perception).[1]

---

[1] I here condense, I hope without undue distortion, the long and careful story developed by Damasio (1994). See especially Chapter 8 and comments on pages 226–227, 236–244, and 266.

Damasio's account is, I should admit, not focused directly on phenomenological ("what-it's-like") consciousness. The primary targets are, instead, emotion, feeling, and reason, and the deep links between the three. It is clear, nonetheless, that this is also a story about at least some varieties of full-blown phenomenological awareness.[2] Feeling an emotion is, after all, one of the paradigm cases of phenomenological consciousness, and Damasio's claim is clear: "the essence of feeling an emotion is the experience of such changes [changes in body-state representations] in juxtaposition to the mental images that initiated the cycle" (1994, p. 145).

Such a coarse sketch can make it seem as if the account—considered as a story about phenomenological consciousness—is question begging. Surely we cannot explain phenomenal consciousness by appeal to *phenomenal* states of pain, or pleasure, or "positive and negative" spins. But in fact, the story is much deeper. The claim, as I read it, is not that phenomenological consciousness depends on gross or subtle ("background") emotional shading. Rather, it is that phenomenological shading, in these cases, just *is* the juxtaposition of body image (including visceral input, acquired positive and negative associations, and so on) with perceptual or imaginative processing.

First move: The Intentional Stance. The idea here—examined in detail in Chapter 3 of the text—is that a system has a belief just in case its behavior is well predicted by treating it as a believer. This is, as Dennett (1998, p. 331) notes, a "maximally permissive understanding," which makes no specific claims about inner structure or organization.

Second move: Multiple Drafts. Based on a variety of neuroscientific and cognitive psychological findings, Dennett (see also Dennett and Kinsbourne, 1992) depicts the biological brain as the locus of multiple, quasiindependent processing streams. There is no single, ultimate judgment issued by the brain in response to an input—no decisive moment in space or time where the system settles on a unique definitive content fixing the conscious state. Contrast this with a traditional model in which "central processing" names an area in which, in Dennett's recurrent phrase, "it all comes together," and a judgment is made whose content fixes how things seem to the conscious subject.

Third Move: The Narrative Twist. So whence the conscious experience of seeing such-and-such *as* so-and-so, of feeling the pain *as* a sharp stabbing in the arm, etc.? This kind of content-fixation, Dennett suggests, is probably a peculiar achievement of *human* biological brains—made possible not by the presence of some spe-

---

[2]Thus Damasio writes of "feeling your emotion states, which is to say being conscious of emotions" (1994, p. 133).

cial biologically-evolved circuitry so much as by the cultural imprinting of a kind of "user-illusion." "*Our* kind of consciousness," as Dennett (1998, p. 346) puts it "is not anything we are born with, not part of our innate hard-writing, but in surprisingly large measure, an artifact of our immersion in human culture." Our extraordinary immersion in a sea of culture and language (itself, to be sure, made possible by *some* small difference in innate hardware) creates, in the human brain, a new kind of cognitive organization—a new "virtual machine"—that allows us to make cognitive objects of our own thought processes and to weave a kind of on-going narrative (about who we are, and what we are doing, and why we are doing it) that artificially "fixes" the cognitive contents. The content is, of course, not *really* fixed, because underneath the personal-level narrative stream the more fundamental multiple processing streams are still going like the clappers. But there is, courtesy of the new top-level virtual organization, a striking difference: we now *report* the presence of a specific stream of experiences, a stream, if you will, of *judgings* or *macrotakings*, in which there seems to be a clear fact of the matter concerning the nature of our current subjective state. It is the presence of this serial stream of apparently fixed contents that explains, on Dennett's account, our tendency to believe in *qualia*. But what these qualia really are now turns out to be nothing but the string of judgments made by the top-level, linguistically infected, narrative-spinning virtual machine, installed not by nature, but by the almost-incalculable effects, on reasonably plastic human brains, of our early immersion in a sea of words and culture, or more generally (and for more on this, see Chapter 8) by our immersion in a sea of external symbolic items and self-reflective cultural practices.

The result is that *believing* is pervasive and fundamental. But human-style conscious awareness requires an extra layer of judgment rooted in a culturally inculcated capacity to spin a privileged report or narrative: "the story you or I will tell if asked (to put a complicated matter crudely)" (Dennett, 1998, p. 348). Consciousness *achieved*, not given.

There are many other positions on consciousness that really should be considered, but these must, for now, remain casualties of (too little) time and space. There is, for example, the view (McGinn, 1989; Pinker, 1997) that full-blooded qualitative awareness has a perfectly good physicalistic explanation, but one that minds (brains?) like ours are congenitally ill equipped to comprehend. We will revisit *this* gloomy prognosis shortly. But for now, let us close the stable doors. We have already let loose a puzzling assortment of beasts, and it is time to take stock of the menagerie.

Recall Ned Block's caution against confusing accounts of access-consciousness with accounts of phenomenal-consciousness. Access-consciousness is said to be much less puzzling (an "easy problem," to use Chalmers' phrase). We explain access-consciousness by explaining variations in "informational poise"—whether an item of knowledge or stored data can control many or few reactions and judg-

ments, whether it is available for verbal report, etc. And we can see, in broad outline, how specific neuroscientific or computational conjectures might explain such
patterns of control. Failures of binding, à la Crick and Koch, will result in failures
of integration and availability for control. Selective damage to the ventral stream,
à la Milner and Goodale, will result in failures of verbal report while preserving
availability for certain kinds of motor control, and so on.

At this point, Block and Chalmers insist that no amount of *this kind* of understanding (understanding of patterns of information flow and availability for
control) can discharge the mystery of *phenomenal* consciousness. For suppose
something like informational poise (availability for widespread control, including
control of verbal report or symbolic judgment) turns out to be a *perfect* correlate
for phenomenal experience. Suppose, that is, that a certain kind of informational
poise is always and only present just in case the subject is having a phenomenal
experience. Still, the worry goes, we will not have explained *why* the two go together, nor why the phenomenal experiences have the specific character they (at
least seem to) have. The problem, to put it bluntly, is that, *correlation is not explanation.* But—and this, I suppose, is Chalmers' main point—it is hard to see how
current scientific approaches can take us any further.

It would be wise, at this point, to stop and wonder. If we explain *all* the facts
about access-consciousness, is there really something left over? Or is the apparent
shortfall merely apparent: just some "imaginary dazzle in the eye of a Cartesian
homunculus" (Dennett, 1995, p. 34). Thus, Dennett (1997, p. 417) suggests that
where Block and others see a difference in kind, there is really only a difference in
degree along two key dimensions—"richness of content and degree of influence."
The blindsight cases, on this analysis, are cases of thin content and restricted influence. The full phenomenological Monty, by contrast, involves rich, detailed content and widespread influence. But the difference lies not in the presence, in the
latter case, of some ghostly extra ("real qualitative awareness"). It is just more of
the same.

I find myself increasingly tempted by some variant of a Dennett-style deflationary approach. In its favor is a kind of innocent verificationism, and a principle of explanatory economy. The verificationist thread is the observation that the
right pattern of informational poise, access, etc. will fix the behavior of a being in
a way that makes it scientifically indistinguishable from a seat of real phenomenological consciousness. But once all *that* is fixed, why believe in some additional
extra? The economy is obvious. If access-consciousness (or some close variant) is
perfectly correlated with the observable manifestations of phenomenal-consciousness, why not pronounce the two identical?

Against such a line it may simply be urged that the first-person perspective
cannot be so deftly ignored. As Kim recently argued, if you are inclined to doubt
the existence of the qualitative "extra," there may be nothing, scientific or philosophical, anyone can do to convince you. Here, Kim—following Block—quotes
Louis Armstrong on the appeal of Jazz: "If you got to ask, you ain't never gonna

know" (Kim, 1996, p. 180 citing Block, 1980). Such a response should, however, give us pause. In no other scientific or philosophical debate would such a move be acceptable. Why here?

There is, moreover, a clear sense in which a story such as Dennett's does *not* ignore the first-person perspective. For it is, we saw, of the essence of Dennett's larger story that "our [human] kind of consciousness" is created by the effects of culture and linguistic experience, which conspire to instill habits of thought that support a "user-illusion"—the illusion of a unified consciousness whose decisions and judgments form the narrative chain that makes us who we are. The distinctive feel of our first-person perspective is thus explained. But, in a certain sense, it is *personhood* that now emerges as the primary, culture-driven achievement; it is the sense of personhood that gives human experience its special character.

Yet there seems to be a tension in Dennett's position here. For, on the one hand, Dennett wants to claim that the fans of mysterious qualia are "inflating differences in degree [of richness, control, etc.] into imaginary differences in kind" (Dennett, 1997, p. 419). But he *also* wants to claim that humans really are *different*, courtesy of the culture-dependent user-illusion.

> In order to be conscious—in order to be the sort of thing it is like something to be—it is necessary to have a certain sort of informational organization . . . [one] that is swiftly achieved in one species, ours, and in no other. . . . My claim is not that other species lack our kind of *self*-consciousness. . . . I am claiming that what must be added to mere responsivity, mere discrimination, to count as consciousness *at all* is an organization that is not ubiquitous among sentient organisms. (Dennett, 1998, p. 347)

I find it hard to reconcile this notion of an organizational dividing line among species with Dennett's equally firm insistence that *within* the human species the various phenomena of response and discrimination are different only in degree. For pretty clearly, *some* of those phenomena, such as the motor responses mediated largely by dorsal stream activity, are rooted in phylogenetically old pathways that we share with many other animals. A cleaner, and still Dennettian, story might, for example, have intentional states (beliefs, etc.) as ubiquitous, and differing only in richness of content and poise for control between us and other animals, while accepting that "our kind of consciousness" (which now seems to be the only kind of real consciousness—see the above quote) is a special achievement, with distinctive organizational roots.

Consider next the very idea of the Zombie. The Zombie is

> Molecule for molecule identical to me, and identical in all the low-level properties postulated by a completed physics, but he lacks conscious [phenomenal] experience entirely . . . he is embedded in an identical environment . . . he will be processing the same sort of information, reacting in a similar way to inputs . . . he will be awake, able to report the contents of his internal states, able to focus attention in various places and so on. It is just that none of this functioning will be accompanied by any real conscious experience. There will be no phenomenal feel. There is nothing it is like to be a Zombie. (Chalmers, 1996, p. 95)

The Zombie, in short, is response identical, and inner processing identical, to you and me, but is (tragically? comically? impossibly?) bereft of real phenomenological consciousness. The Zombie *says* the bruises hurt and the chocolate tastes good, but there is no experience present.

There are (as far as we know) no Zombies. Indeed, we would never have cause to even suspect someone of being a Zombie, since their responses and inner structure are, by definition, the same as those of a non-Zombie. So who cares? Why tell the story? The story matters to those (like Chalmers) who seek to sever any *noncontingent* connection between physical facts and facts about phenomenal content. A contingent connection is one that just happens to hold, but that could have been otherwise. In Chalmers' view, no amount of physical, functional, or information-processing-based story-telling can explain why we have experiences, or why they have the specific felt characters they do. And one argument, or consideration, in support of this is the logical possibility of Zombies. For if you *could*—in principle—satisfy the physical story yet lack phenomenal consciousness, then the physical story cannot determine, fix, or explain the phenomenal dimension.

Are Zombies logically possible? It doubtless depends on the logic! There is, as Chalmers rightly insists, no obvious contradiction in the very idea. But I am not convinced that that fact alone makes the possibility genuinely conceivable. My own view, which I will not pursue here, is that the actual facts about the particular "possible world" we inhabit set limits to the set of worlds of which we can genuinely conceive: limits much narrower than those set by the simple, almost grammatical, facts of noncontradiction.

But let us leave the technicalia aside. The deep problem with Zombies is surely two-fold. First, they are by definition unrecognizable by any means short of "inside knowledge," and this offends against the (to my mind) innocent verificationism that insists that real differences should be in principle *detectable* by communally agreed means. Second, even Chalmers admits that "it is unlikely that Zombies are naturally possible. In the real world, it is likely that any replica of me would be conscious" (Chalmers, 1996, p. 96). But if, in the actual world, the links between the physical and the phenomenological facts can be this watertight, it is unclear why a full appreciation of the nature and origin of those links would *not* amount to a full understanding (for our actual-world purposes) of phenomenological consciousness itself. Of course, the mere uncovering of a few isolated neural correlates of conscious experience cannot give us that warm glow of deep explanatory understanding. But what if we uncover a whole system, traceable some way down the phylogenetic tree? What if we begin to see how certain tweaks and damage will systematically repair or cause certain experiential distortions? Such a body of knowledge, once it became familiar and widely tested in use, would surely come to *seem like* a deep explanatory understanding of the physical/phenomenological nexus. If Chalmers then says "Ah well, you've cracked it for the actual world, but your theory is incomplete because it fails to account for all logically possible worlds," then scientists will be (properly) puzzled. In any world that the scientist can richly conceive, the same links will hold. The other worlds will seem thin, "grammatical fictions," whose genuine conceivability is now open to serious doubt.

These are complicated issues, and I cannot go much further here. [For additional discussion, see Dennett (1994, pp. 518–519, 537–541); for a defense, see Levine (1994).] But I am convinced of this much: whatever the conceptual niceties, the questions about phenomenal-consciousness are too important to be tied to insecure and ill-regulated intuitions concerning what is and is not "conceivable." There just *has* to be a better way to proceed.

Chalmers' own response to the puzzle is to treat phenomenal experience as fundamental. That is to say, to accept that it cannot ultimately be explained and to work instead on understanding the shape of the web of correlations that links physical facts to experiential ones. Just as "nothing in physics tells us why there is matter in the first place" (Chalmers, 1997a, p. 20), so nothing will tell us why there is consciousness in the physical world. But that does not stop us seeking correlations of the kind mentioned earlier in the chapter. More radically, Chalmers suggests that we might need to recognize a kind of fundamental "double aspect" to physical states that carry information, with the result that where there is information there is always some degree of phenomenal content (Chalmers, 1997a, pp. 26–28).

Such a proposal, however, strikes me as premature. For, as Chalmers admits, to treat phenomenal content as fundamental is to give up on the search for a genuine reductive explanation. Yet the prima facie distribution of phenomenal experience in the universe strongly suggests that it is a feature caused by fairly complex organizational properties, and found only in restricted pockets of highly ordered matter, rather than a fundamental and hence more "evenly spread" (Chalmers, 1997a, p. 27) property. If the Zombie argument fails, we have no special reason to think that such an organization-based story is impossible. Hence (again, *if* the Zombie argument fails) it is premature pessimism to depict experience as simply a brute fact.

A different (but equally premature) kind of pessimism is suggested by the philosopher Colin McGinn (1989) and the cognitive scientist Steven Pinker (1997), who think that human brains may be congenitally unable to penetrate (may be cognitively closed with respect to) the mystery of phenomenal consciousness. Given the kinds of relationships and causal chains that human brains evolved to comprehend, they argue, we may have no more chance of understanding consciousness than a hamster has of understanding quantum mechanics.

Might we thus be permanently blinkered? I don't see why we should think so just yet. Human brains, unlike the brains of rodents, reap the incalculable benefits of language, culture, and technology (see Chapter 8). We distribute subtasks, across time and space, preserve intermediate results, and create all manner of tools, props, and scaffolding to help us along the way. It is not obvious *what* ultimately limits the cognitive horizons of such inveterate mind-expanders, nor why the problem of consciousness should lie on one side of any such (putative) divide rather than the other.

Finally, what about representationalism: the thesis that the phenomenal facts are exhausted by the representational facts? This story appeals strongly to the philosophical community. The reason, I think, is that issues concerning content are a philosophical staple, and it is reassuring to think that something as apparently exotic as phenomenal consciousness might be reduced to facts about familiar kinds of content. It is reassuring, but is it true? Clearly, it is too soon to say. But there are certainly grounds for doubt.

The most basic worry concerns cases in which it is far from obvious what the representational content could *be*. Maybe a pain in the foot is, in a sense, *about* current or impending tissue damage (Dretske, 1995; Tye, 1997). But a feeling of generalized unease? An endogenous depression? An orgasm? In all these cases, we seem to have feelings without any clear representational content or role. [One countermove here is to depict such contents as "nonconceptual," hence only imperfectly pointed to via linguistic expressions (see Tye, 1997, p. 333).]

Another worry concerns the apparent *insufficiency* of representational content. If we allow (as we surely should) that *some* representational states have no phenomenological dimension, then why suppose it is the representational content and not the missing "extra ingredient" that is making the other states phenomenologically conscious? Even if representational content is part of the story, it does not look like the whole thing.

Second-order representationalism (also known as "higher order thought theory") may look like a better bet here. For the idea here is to identify the "missing ingredient" as an extra *layer* of thought. Phenomenally conscious contents, on this account, occur when we represent our own representings: when we represent ourselves to ourselves *as* having a thought about the sunset, or about the taste of the cocktail. The immediate worry about the higher order approach is that it seems to tie phenomenal consciousness to the presence of rather advanced meta-cognitive capacities. Thinking about your thoughts is, on the face of it at least, something that most animals and young infants are probably unable to do. So the fans of higher order thought theory must make a hard call. Either bite the bullet, and suggest that therefore "almost all species of animal will lack conscious experiences" (Carruthers, 1996, p. 222), or find some way of understanding the notion of higher order thought that makes it a more plausibly widespread phenomena. Dennett (whose 1991 story about the "user-illusion" commits him, I think, to a rather sophisticated form of higher order thought theory) bites the bullet and deems it unlikely that other animals enjoy states that count as phenomenally conscious at all (see, e.g., Dennett, 1998, p. 347), whereas theorists such as Lycan (1997) and Armstrong (1997) try to sweeten the pill by making the higher order states less rationalistic, and more like an inner *perception* of ongoing mental activity (this distinction, however, may be less clear than it seems (see Güzeldere, 1997)).

At the end of the day, the real mystery, it seems to me, is this: Is there a "hard problem" of consciousness or isn't there? Is there something special about phenomenal consciousness that places it outside the reach of current scientific approaches (as Chalmers and others believe), or is it just a matter of explaining a pattern of responsiveness and report (as Dennett and others suggest)? The *meta-hard* problem, then, is how to decide between these options. The reason this is difficult is, essentially, because (as we saw) the zombie thought experiment—the crucial point in Chalmers' argument—is itself every bit as problematic as the topic on which it is meant to cast light!

Given the impasse, I think we need to explore some alternative ways of thinking. One approach, which has much to recommend it, is to investigate what Price (1997) calls the "psychology of the hard problem." The idea is to accept that there seems to be a special problem about explaining phenomenal awareness, but to try to explain this appearance as a result not of logical, ontological, or metaphysical differences, but as a kind of epistemic illusion rooted in our psychological make-up. This is to appeal, in essence, to the same kinds of facts (concerning our basic experiences of successful explanation, etc.) as do the proponents of "cognitive closure." But whereas they believe that the psychological dimension blocks our capacity to find the right explanation, Price argues that the effect is to make us unsatisfied with perfectly good explanations even when they are staring us in the face. Such a story would "psychologize" the hard problem and explain why we are so strongly tempted (despite the efforts of Dennett and others) to see an intractable divide where there is really (so this story goes) just one more scientific question, like any other.

Price begins by asking why we don't find "explanatory gaps" and "hard problems" all around. What is it that sometimes "allows us to walk away from a problem . . . with a smile on our face and a warm glow in our hearts feeling 'Yes, I understand that now'" (Price, 1997, p. 84).

This feeling of understanding is, when you look at things closely, rather a surprise. For as Hume (1740) and others have argued, all we ever seem to find is robust conjunction (x reliably follows y) and not some kind of intrinsic, transparent connection. Even allowing (see Mackie, 1974) that we need to find counterfactually robust conjunctions, so as to avoid mistaking accidental regularities for causes, there remains a sense in which causation itself seems always elusive. Perhaps all we *ever* understand is that certain types of events are reliably (robustly, counterfactually) correlated (see also Popper, 1980).

But if (deep, robust, counterfactually sound, systematically structured) correlation is all we *ever* find, why does the "explanatory gap" look so daunting in the case of explaining phenomenal consciousness? If there is *always* a gap, bridged only by deep, robust, counterfactually sound, systematically structured correlation, then we should expect to explain consciousness exactly as we explain anything else, by (in this case) unearthing a system of neural or organizational correlates for different aspects of phenomenal awareness.

The difference, Price suggests (and here he follows Rosch, 1994) is merely psychological. The "warm glow of explanatory understanding" is the result of a piece of self-deception in which we hallucinate an outcome as "already contained in [its] grounds" (Price, 1997, p. 87). (Think of those old embryological stories—quite false, of course—in which the adult form was stored in miniature in the fertilized egg.) The problem, in the case of phenomenal consciousness, is that our usual tricks for "seeing" the outcome in the cause do not work here. But this is just a psychological hurdle (not a logical, ontological, or metaphysical one).

Following Rosch, Price lists four ways in which we can fool ourselves into seeing effects as transparently contained in their causes. First, by "seeing" the transfer of a property from ground to outcome, as when we see one billiard ball hit another and "impart" its motion. Second, from within, by seeing our actions as effects of our intentions. Third, by seeing the outcome as an "acceptable" transformation of its cause (the kitten turns into a cat). Lastly, by seeing the outcome as generic to the category of the cause (acids cause burning). Perhaps we use other tricks, too; these four need not be exhaustive. The point is, it is hard to see the relation between phenomenal consciousness and its physical grounds in any of these ways. It is, in a sense, a sui generis case—one "unlike anything else in our experience" (Price, 1997, p. 91).

The psychological tricks are, however, just that: tricks. The fact that a cause–effect relation is similar to one we are already comfortable with, or the fact that we can *hallucinate* the effect as already present in the cause, goes no way at all toward making the actual relation ontologically, metaphysically, or even (genuinely) logically transparent. The moral is that, when we first encounter or try to explain new *kinds* of things, we should not *expect* any warm glow of explanatory understanding—not even if we are getting the (robust, counterfactual, etc.) correlations just right.

Price thus argues that phenomenal consciousness may present a case like modern physics, where it takes *time and familiarity* for accounts initially seen as technically adept but explanatorily unsatisfying to become accepted as genuine explanations. Our intuitive sense of understanding, he concludes, is a poor guide to our real progress.

In reply to Price, Chalmers (1997b, pp. 394–395) concedes that explanatory gaps *always* lurk at the bottom of causal stories, but claims that this is exactly his point: that the gap, in all cases, is "due to some contingency in the connecting principles, because of underlying brutally contingent fundamental laws, which is of course just what I suggest. We have here an inter-level relationship that *could have been otherwise*" (Chalmers, 1997b, 395). Such gaps do not intervene, he argues, in all cases. For sometimes (he cites the relation between statistical mechanics and thermodynamics) high-level facts are *necessitated* by the low-level ones. It is when necessitation fails, that gaps arise. Chalmers' reply, in short, is that Price's story actually *supports* Chalmers' own view rather than undermining it.

I remain, however, unconvinced. If, as Chalmers allows (1997b, p. 394) we can give a physically based story about phenomenal consciousness that is *exactly as adequate*, ultimately, as our account of why pressing the remote control causes the TV to come on, then surely the "hard problem" is indeed a kind of cognitive illusion. In both cases, as Chalmers admits, the trouble comes at the very end, when we unpack all the higher level regularities and ask why the most fundamental underlying principles hold. Here, to be briefly Wittgensteinian, our explanatory excavations end and the spade is turned. But so what? We don't let fear of "remote control zombies" (devices just like our TV remotes but that fail to cause the channels to change in alternative, logically possible universes) shake our faith in the electromagnetic framework as fully explanatory of the operation of the actual, real-world device. Instead, we understand the device when we understand how such-and-such an *organization* (in a world subject to the fundamental laws of physics) yields the pattern of effects we seek to explain. I am not yet persuaded that explaining phenomenal consciousness presents any fundamentally different *kind* of problem. So *is* there really a hard problem of phenomenal consciousness? This meta-hard problem may yet prove the hardest and most important of them all.

Suggested Readings

For a *thorough and argumentative overview of nearly all the terrain*, see D. Chalmers, *The Conscious Mind* (New York: Oxford University Press, 1996).

For a *selection of essays discussing the "hard problem,"* see J. Shear (ed.), *Explaining Consciousness: The Hard Problem* (Cambridge, MA: MIT Press, 1995). The essays include philosophical, phenomenological, and neuroscientific perspectives, and highlights include the pieces by D. Dennett, P. S. Churchland, M. Price, C. McGinn, F. Crick and C. Koch, B. Baars, and F. Varda. For a powerful deflationary treatment, see P. M. Churchland, "The rediscovery of light." *Journal of Philosophy*, 93(5), 211–228, 1996.

A *useful and philosophically rich collection* of papers can be found in M. Davies and G. Humphries (eds.), *Consciousness: Psychological and Philosophical Essays* (Oxford, England: Blackwell, 1993). A more recent, very comprehensive, and wide-ranging collection is N. Block, O. Flanagan, and G. Güzeldere (eds.), *The Nature of Consciousness: Philosophical Debates* (Cambridge, MA: MIT Press, 1997). This covers all the territory scouted in the present chapter and includes a classic selection from William James as well as seminal contributions from McGinn, Dennett and Kinsbourne, Crick and Koch, Block, Searle, Flanagan, and others. I especially recommend the (hard, but rewarding) section "Consciousness and content," with contributions from Colin McGinn, Martin Davies, Michael Tye, and Christopher Peacocke. For a nicely provocative development of these themes, see M. Tye, "The problem of simple minds: Is there anything it is like to be a honey bee?" *Philosophical Studies*, 88, 289–317, 1997.

A good, though now slightly dated, *collection with an empirical focus* is A. Marcel and E. Bisiach, *Consciousness in Contemporary Science*, (Oxford, England: Oxford University Press, 1988). For a recent review of the literature on blindsight see L. Weiskrantz, "Blindsight revisited." In L. Squire and S. Kosslyn (eds.), *Findings and Current Opinion in Cognitive Neuroscience* (Cambridge, MA: MIT Press, 1998). The papers by Farah ("Perception and awareness after brain damage") and by Koch and Braun ("Towards the newer correlate of visual awareness") are also recommended, and appear in the same volume.

For issues concerning *language and consciousness,* see P. Carruthers and J. Boucher (eds.), *Language and Thought: Interdisciplinary Themes* (Cambridge, England: Cambridge University Press, 1998).

Dennett's story about the human construction of conciousness is detailed at length in his long, hard, but entertaining *Consciousness Explained* (New York: Little Brown, 1991). But a wonderfully clear and compressed version of some of the main themes is to be found in Chapters 5 and 6 of his small popular treatment: D. Dennett, *Kinds of Minds: Towards an Understanding of Consciousness* (New York: Basic Books, 1996). Several good critiques appear, along with a reply by Dennett, in *Philosophical Topics,* 22(1 and 2), 1994. A useful treatment is K. Akins, "Lost the plot? Reconstructing Dennett's multiple drafts theory of consciousness." *Mind and Language,* 11(1), 1–43, 1996.

Finally for a powerful and *neuroscientifically based account linking consciousness, bodily feedback, and emotional tone,* see A. Damasio, *Descartes' Error: Emotion, Reason and the Human Brain* (New York: Grosset/Putman, 1994).

REFERENCES

Abraham, R., and Shaw, C. (1992). *Dynamics—The Geometry of Behavior*. Redwood, CA: Addison-Wesley.

Ackley, D., and Littman, D. (1992). Interactions between learning and evolution. In C. Langston (ed.), *Artificial Life II*. Reading, MA: Addison-Wesley, 487–509.

Aglioti, S., Goodale, M., and Desouza, J. (1995). Size contrast illusions deceive the eye but not the hand. *Current Biology*, 5, 679–685.

Agre, P. (1995). Computational research on interaction and agency. In P. Agre and S. Rosenschein (eds.), *Computational Theories of Interaction and Agency*. Cambridge, MA: MIT Press, 1–52.

Amis, M. (1973). *The Rachel Papers*. London: Penguin.

Antony, L., and Levine, J. (1991). The nomic and the robust. In B. Loewer and G. Rey (eds.), *Meaning in Mind: Fodor and His Critics*. Oxford, England: Blackwell, 1–16.

Arbib, M. (1994). Review of A. Newell *Unified Theories of Cognition*. In W. Clancey, S. Smoliar, and M. Stefik (eds.), *Contemplating Minds*. Cambridge, MA: MIT Press, 21–39.

Armstrong, D. (1997). What is consciousness? In N. Block, O. Flanagan, and G. Güzeldere (eds.), *The Nature of Consciousness*. Cambridge, MA: MIT Press, 721–728.

Ashby, R. (1952). *Design for a Brain*. London: Chapman and Hall.

Ashby, R. (1956). *Introduction to Cybernetics*. New York: Wiley.

Ballard, D. (1991). Animate vision. *Artificial Intelligence*, 48, 57–86.

Ballard, D., Hayhoe, M., Pook, P., and Rao, R. (1997). Deictic codes for the embodiment of cognition. *Behavioral and Brain Sciences*, 20, 4.

Baum, C. (1996). Supporting the family: Strategies for managing neurological deficits in alzheimer's and related disorders. MS, Washington University School of Medicine.

Beach, K. (1988). The role of external mnemonic symbols in acquiring an occupation. In M. M. Gruneberg and R. N. Sykes (eds.), *Practical Aspects of Memory*. New York: Wiley, 1, 342–346.

Bechtel, W. (1993) Currents in connectionism. *Minds and Machines*, 3, 125–153.

Beckers, R., Holland, O., and Denenbourg, J. (1994). From local actions to global tasks: Stigmergy and collective robotics. In R. Brooks and P. Maes (eds.), *Artificial Life*, IV. Cambridge, MA: MIT Press.

Bedau, M. (1996). The nature of life. In M. Boden (ed.), *The Philosophy of Artificial Life.* Oxford, England: Oxford University Press, 332–360.

Beer, R. (1995). A dynamical systems perspective on agent-environment interaction. *Artificial Intelligence,* 72, 173–215.

Beer, R., and Gallagher, J. C. (1992). Evolving dynamical neural networks for adaptive behavior. *Adaptive Behavior,* 1, 91–122.

Bickerton, D. (1995). *Language and Human Behavior.* Seattle, WA: University of Washington Press.

Bisson, T. (1991, April). Alien/nation. *Omni.*

Block, N. (1980). Troubles with functionalism. In N. Block (ed.), *Readings in Philosophy of Psychology.* London: Methuen, 1, 268–305.

Block, N. (1997). On a confusion about a function of consciousness. In N. Block, O. Flanagan, and G. Güzeldere (eds.), *The Nature of Consciousness.* Cambridge, MA: MIT Press, 375–416. Originally appeared in *Behavioral and Brain Sciences,* 18, 227–247, 1995.

Boden, M. (1977). *Artificial Intelligence and Natural Man.* New York: Basic Books.

Boden, M. (1999). Is metabolism necessary? *British Journal of the Philosophy of Science,* 50, 231–248.

Braddon-Mitchell, D., and Jackson, F. (1996). *Philosophy of Mind and Cognition.* Oxford, England: Blackwell.

Brooks, R. (1991). Intelligence without representation. *Artificial Intelligence,* 47, 139–159.

Brooks, R. (1994). Coherent behavior from many adaptive processes. In D. Cliff, P. Husbands, J. A. Meyer, and S. Wilson (eds.), *From Animals to Animats 3.* Cambridge, MA: MIT Press.

Bruner, J. (1990). *Acts of Meaning.* Cambridge, MA: Harvard University Press.

Butler, K. (1998). *Internal Affairs: A Critique of Externalism in the Philosophy of Mind.* Dordrecht, The Netherlands: Kluwer.

Carruthers, P. (1996). *Language, Thought and Consciousness: An Essay in Philosophical Psychology.* Cambridge, England: Cambridge University Press.

Chalmers, D. (1990). Syntactic transformations on distributed representations. *Connection Science,* 2, 53–62.

Chalmers, D. (1996). *The Conscious Mind.* New York: Oxford University Press.

Chalmers, D. (1997a). Facing up to the problem of consciousness. In J. Shear (ed.), *Explaining Consciousness: The Hard Problem.* Cambridge, MA: MIT Press.

Chalmers, D. (1997b). Moving forward on the problem of consciousness. In J. Shear (ed.), *Explaining Consciousness: The Hard Problem.* Cambridge, MA: MIT Press, 379–422.

Chambers, D., and Reisberg, D., (1985). Can mental images be Ambiguous? *Journal of Experimental Psychology: Human Perception and Performance,* II(3), 317–328.

Changeux, J., and A. Connes (trans. 1995). *Conversations on Mind, Matter and Mathematics.* Princeton, NJ: Princeton University Press.

Chappell, V. C. (ed.) (1962). *The Philosophy of Mind.* Englewood Cliffs, NJ: Prentice-Hall.

Chenn, A. (1997). Development of the cerebral cortex. In W. Cowan, T. Jessel, and S. Ziputsky (eds.), *Molecular and Cellular Approaches to Neural Development.* Oxford, England: Oxford University Press, 440–473.

Chiel, H., and Beer, R. (1997). The brain has a body: Adaptive behavior emerges from interactions of nervous system, body and environment. *Trends in Neurosciences,* 20(12), 553–557.

Churchland, P. M. (1981). Eliminative materialism and the propositional attitudes. *Journal of Philosophy*, 78(2), 67–90.

Churchland, P. M. (1984). *Matter and Consciousness*. Cambridge, MA: MIT Press.

Churchland, P. M. (1989). *The Neurocomputational Perspective*. Cambridge, MA: MIT/Bradford Books.

Churchland, P. M. (1993). Fodor and Lepore: State-space semantics and meaning holism. *Philosophy and Phenomenological Research*, 53, 679–682.

Churchland, P. M. (1995). *The Engine of Reason, the Seat of the Soul*. Cambridge, MA: MIT Press.

Churchland, P. M., and Churchland, P. S. (1990). Could a machine think? *Scientific American* 1990, 26–31. Reprinted in E. Dietrich (ed.), *Thinking Computers and Virtual Persons*, San Diego, CA: Academic Press, 157–171.

Churchland, P. M., and Churchland, P. S. (1998). *On the Contrary: Critical Essays 1987–1997*. Cambridge, MA: MIT Press.

Churchland, P. S., and Sejnowski, T. (1990). Neural representation and neural computation. In W. Lycan (ed.), *Mind and Cognition: A Reader*. Oxford, England: Blackwell, 224–251.

Churchland, P. S., and Sejnowski, T. (1992). *The Computational Brain*. Cambridge, MA: MIT Press.

Churchland, P.S., Ramachandran, V., and Sejnowski, T. (1994). A critique of pure vision. In C. Koch and J. Davis (eds.), *Large-Scale Neuronal Theories of the Brain*. Cambridge, MA: MIT Press.

Clark, A. (1987). From folk psychology to naive psychology. *Cognitive Science*, 11(2), 139–154.

Clark, A. (1989). *Microcognition: Philosophy, Cognitive Science and Parallel Distributed Processing*. Cambridge, MA: MIT Press.

Clark, A. (1990). Connectionist minds. *Proceedings of the Aristotelian Society*, XC, 83–102.

Clark, A. (1993). *Associative Engines: Connectionism, Concepts and Representational Change*. Cambridge, MA: MIT Press.

Clark, A. (1995). Moving minds: Re-thinking representation in the heat of situated action. In J. Tomberlin (ed.), *Philosophical Perspectives 9: AI Connectionism and Philosophical Psychology*. Atascadero, CA: Ridgeview.

Clark, A. (1996). Connectionism, moral cognition and collaborative problem solving. In L. May, M. Friedman, and A. Clark (eds.), *Minds and Morals*. Cambridge, MA: MIT Press, 109–128.

Clark, A. (1997). *Being There: Putting Brain, Body and World Together Again*. Cambridge, MA: MIT Press.

Clark, A. (1998a). Magic words: How language augments human computation. In S. Boucher and P. Carruthers (eds.), *Thought and Language*. Cambridge, England: Cambridge University Press.

Clark, A. (1998b). Where brain, body and world collide. *Daedalus*, 127(2), 257–280.

Clark, A. (1998c). Time and mind. *Journal of Philosophy*, 95(7), 354–376.

Clark, A. (1999a). Visual awareness and visuomotor action. *Journal of Consciousness Studies*, 6(11–12), 1–18.

Clark, A. (1999b). An embodied cognitive science? *Trends in Cognitive Sciences*, 3(9), 345–351

Clark, A., and Chalmers, D. (1998). The Extended mind. *Analysis*, 58, 7–19.

Clark, A., and Grush, R. (1999). Towards a cognitive robotics, *Adaptive Behavior* 7(1), 5–16.

Clark, A., and Thornton, C. (1997). Trading spaces: Connectionism and the limits of uninformed learning. *Behavioral and Brain Sciences*, 20(1), 57–67.

Clark, A. and Toribio, J. (1994). Doing without representing? *Synthese*, 101, 401–431.

Colby, K. M. (1975). *Artificial Paranoia*. New York: Pergamon.

Connell, J. (1989). *A Colony Architecture for an Artificial Creature*. Cambridge: MIT AI Laboratory.

Crick, F. (1981). *Life Itself: Its Origin and Nature*. New York: Simon & Schuster.

Crick, F., and Koch, C. (1997). Towards a neurobiological theory of consciousness. In N. Block, O. Flanagan, and G. Guzeldere (eds.), *The Nature of Consciousness*. Cambridge, MA: MIT Press, 277–292.

Crutchfield, J., and Mitchell, M. (1995). The evolution of emergent computation. *Proceedings of the National Academy of Sciences U.S.A.*, 92, 10742–10746.

Cummins, R. (1996). *Representations, Targets, and Attitudes*. Cambridge, MA: MIT Press.

Damasio, A. (1994). *Descartes' Error*. New York: Grosset/Putnam.

Damasio, A. (1999). *The Feeling of What Happens*. New York: Harcourt, Brace and Co.

Damasio, A., and Damasio, H. (1994). Cortical systems for retrieval of concrete knowledge: The convergence zone framework. In C. Koch and J. Davis (eds.), *Large-Scale Neuronal Theories of the Brain*. Cambridge, MA: MIT Press.

Dawkins, R. (1982). *The Extended Phenotype*. Oxford, England: Oxford University Press.

Dawkins, R. (1986). *The Blind Watchmaker*. New York: Norton.

Deacon, T. (1997). *The Symbolic Species*. New York: Norton.

Decety, J., and Grezes, J. (1999). Neural mechanisms subserving the perception of human actions. *Trends in Cognitive Sciences*, 3(5), 172–178.

Dehaene, S. (1997). *The Number Sense*. Oxford, England: Oxford University Press.

Dehaene, S., Sperke, E., Pinel, P., Stanescu, R., and Tviskin, S. (1999). Sources of mathematical thinking: Behavioral and brain imaging evidence. *Science*, 284, 970–974.

Dennett, D. (1981). *Brainstorms*. Sussex, England: Harvester Press.

Dennett, D, (1984). *Elbow Room: The Varieties of Free Will Worth Wanting*. Oxford, England: Oxford University Press.

Dennett, D. (1987). *The Intentional Stance*. Cambridge, MA: MIT Press.

Dennett, D. (1991b). Mother Nature versus the Walking Encyclopedia. In W. Ramsey, S. Stich, and D. Rumelhart (eds.), *Philosophy and Connectionist Theory*. Hillsdale, NJ: Erlbaum, 21–30.

Dennett, D. (1991a). *Consciousness Explained*. New York: Little Brown.

Dennett, D. (1994). Learning and labeling: Commentary on A. Clark & A. Karmiloff-Smith. *Mind & Language*, 8, 540–548.

Dennett, D. (1995). *Darwin's Dangerous Idea*. New York: Simon & Schuster.

Dennett, D. (1996). *Kinds of Minds*. New York: Basic Books.

Dennett, D. (1997). The path not taken. In N. Block, O. Flanagan, and G. Güzeldere (eds.), *The Nature of Consciousness*. Cambridge, MA: MIT Press, 417–420.

Dennett, D. (1998). *Brainchildren: Essays on Designing Minds*. Cambridge, MA: MIT Press.

Dennett, D. *How to Do Other Things with Words*. Unpublished manuscript.

Dennett, D., and Kinsbourne, M. (1992). Time and the observer: The where and when of consciousness in the brain. *Behavioral and Brain Sciences*, 15, 183–247.

Di Pelligrino, J., Klatzky, R., and McCloskey, B. (1992). Time course of preshaping for functional responses to objects. *Journal of Motor Behavior*, 21, 307–316.

Donald, M. (1991). *Origins of the Modern Mind.* Cambridge, MA: Harvard University Press.

Dretske, F. (1988). *Explaining Behavior.* Cambridge, MA: MIT Press.

Dretske, F. (1995). *Naturalizing the Mind.* Cambridge, MA: MIT Press.

Dretske, F. (1997). Conscious experience. In N. Block, O. Flanagan, and G. Güzeldere (eds.), *The Nature of Consciousness.* Cambridge, MA: MIT Press, 773–788.

Dreyfus, H. (1972). *What Computers Can't Do.* New York: Harper & Row.

Dreyfus, H. (1997). From micro-worlds to knowledge representation: AI at an impasse. In J. Haugeland (ed.), *Mind Design II.* Cambridge, MA: MIT Press, 161–205.

Dreyfus, H. (1992). *What Computers Still Can't Do.* Cambridge, MA: MIT Press.

Dreyfus, H., and Dreyfus, S. (1986). *Mind over Machine.* New York: Free Press.

Dreyfus, H., and Dreyfus, S. (1990). Making a mind versus modeling the brain: Artificial intelligence at a branch point. In M. Boden (ed.), *The Philosophy of Artificial Intelligence*, Oxford, England: Oxford University Press, 309–333.

Elman, J. (1991a). *Incremental learning or the importance of starting small* (Technical Report 9101). Center for Research in Language, University of California, San Diego.

Elman, J. (1991b). Representation and structure in connectionist models. In G. Altman (ed.), *Cognitive Models of Speech Processing.* Cambridge, MA: MIT Press.

Felleman, D., and Van Essen, D. (1991). Distributed hierarchial processing in primate visual cortex. *Cerebral Cortex*, 1, 1–47.

Finke, R., Pinker, S., and Farah, M., (1989). Reinterpreting visual patterns in mental imagery. *Cognitive Science*, 13, 51–78,

Fodor, J. (1986). Why paramecia don't have mental representations. *Midwest Studies in Philosophy*, 10, 3–23.

Fodor, J. (1987). *Psychosemantics: The Problem of Meaning in the Philosophy of Mind.* Cambridge, MA: MIT Press.

Fodor, J. (1991). Replies. In B. Loewer and G. Rey (eds.), *Meaning in Mind: Fodor and His Critics.* Oxford, England: Blackwell.

Fodor, J. (1994). *The Elm and the Expert.* Cambridge, MA: MIT Press.

Fodor, J. (1998). *In Critical Condition: Polemical Essays on Cognitive Science and the Philosophy of Mind.* Cambridge, MA: MIT Press.

Fodor, J.. and LePore, E. (1993). Reply to Churchland. *Philosophy and Phenomenological Research*, 53, 679–682.

Fodor, J., and Pylyshyn, Z. (1988). Connectionism and cognitive architecture: A critical analysis. *Cognition*, 28, 3–71.

Franklin, S. (1995). *Artificial Minds.* Cambridge, MA: MIT Press.

French, R. (1992). Using semi-distributed representations to overcome catastrophic forgetting in connectionist networks. *Connection Science*, 4(314), 365–378.

French, R. (1999). Catastrophic forgetting in connectionist networks. *Trends in Cognitive Sciences*, 3(4), 128–135.

Gazzaniga, M. (1998). *The Mind's Past.* Berkeley, CA: University of California Press.

Gibson, J. J. (1979). *The Ecological Approach to Visual Perception.* Boston, MA: Houghton-Mifflin.

Gleick, J. (1987). *Chaos.* New York: Viking.

Gleick, J. (1995). Really remote control. *New York Times Magazine*, December 3, 1995, 42–44.

Glymour, C., Ford, K., and Hayes, P. (1995). The pre-history of android epistemology. In K. Ford, C. Glymour, and P. Hayes, (eds.), *Android Epistemology*. Cambridge, MA: MIT Press: 3–21.

Godfrey-Smith, P. (1996a). Spencer and Dewey on life and mind. In M. Boden (ed.), *The Philosophy of Artificial Life*. Oxford, England: Oxford University Press, 314–331.

Godfrey-Smith, P. (1996b). *Complexity and the Function of Mind in Nature*. Cambridge, England: Cambridge University Press.

Goodwin, B. (1995). *How the Leopard Changed Its Spots*. London: Phoenix.

Grasse, P. P. (1959). La reconstruction du nid et les coordinations inter-individuelles chez *Bellicositermes Natalensis et Cubitermes* sp. La theorie de la stigmergie: Essai d'interpretation des termites constructeurs. *Insect Societies*, 6, 41–83.

Grush, R. (1995). *Emulation and Cognition*. Ph.D. Dissertation, University of California.

Güzeldere, G. (1997). Is consciousness the perception of what passes in one's own mind? In N. Block, O. Flanagan, and G. Güzeldere (eds.), *The Nature of Consciousness*. Cambridge, MA: MIT Press, 789–806.

Haffendale, A., and Goodale, M. (1998). The effect of pictorial illusion on prehension and perception. *Journal of Cognitive Neuroscience*, 10, 122–136.

Haken, H., Kelso, J. A. S., and Bunz, H. (1985). A theoretical model of phase transitions in human hand movements. *Biological Cybernetics*, 51, 347–356.

Hallam, J. and Malcolmn, C. (1994). Behavior, perception, action and intelligence—The view from situated robotics. *Proceedings of the Royal Society of London, Series A*, 349, 29–42.

Harnad, S. (1994). What is computation? *Minds and Machines*, 4(4), 377–488.

Haugeland, J. (1981a). Semantic engines: An introduction to mind design. In J. Haugeland, (ed.), *Mind Design*. Cambridge, MA: MIT Press.

Haugeland, J. (1981b). The nature and plausibility of cognitivism. In J. Haugeland (ed.), *Mind Design*. Cambridge, MA: MIT Press, 243–281.

Haugeland, J. (1985). *Artificial Intelligence: The Very Idea*. Cambridge, MA: MIT Press.

Haugeland, J. (1997). What is mind design? In J. Haugeland (ed.), *Mind Design II*. Cambridge, MA: MIT Press.

Hayes, P. (1979). The naive physics manifesto. In D. Michie (ed.), *Expert Systems in the Micro-Electronic Age*. Edinburgh, Scotland: Edinburgh University Press.

Hayes, P. (1985). The second naive physics manifesto. In J. Hobbs and R. Moore (eds.), *Formal Theories of the Commonsense World*. Norwood, NJ: Ablex, 1–36.

Hayes-Roth, B. (1994). On building integrated cognitive agents: A review of Allen Newell's Unified Theories of Cognition. In W. Clancey, S. Smoliar, and M. Stefile (eds.), *Contemplating Minds*. Cambridge, MA: MIT Press.

Heidegger, M. (1961). *Being and Time* (J. Macquarrie E. Robinson, Trans.). (First published in 1927 ed.). New York: Harper & Row.

Hinton, G., and Shallice, T. (1989). Lesioning a connectionist network. University of Toronto Technical Report, CRG-TR-89-3.

Hodges, A. (1983). *Alan Turing: The Enigma*. New York: Simon & Schuster.

Holland, J. (1975). *Adaptation in Natural and Artificial Systems*. Ann Arbor, MI: University of Michigan Press.

Holland, J. (1992). Genetic algorithms. *Scientific American*, June, 66–72.

Hume, D., (ed.) (1740). *A Treatise on Human Nature*. Oxford, England: Clarendon Press.

Husbands, P., Smith, T., Jakobi, N. and O'Shea, M. (1998). Better living through chemistry: Evolving gas nets for robot control. *Connection Science*, 10(314), 185–210.

Hutchins, E. (1995). *Cognition in the Wild*. Cambridge, MA: MIT Press.

Hutchins, E., and Hazelhurst, B. (1991). Learning in the cultural process. In C. Langton (ed.), *Artificial Life II*. Reading, MA: Addison-Wesley.

Jackendoff, R. (1996). How language helps us think. *Pragmatics and Cognition*, 4(1), 1–34.

Jackson, F. (1982). Epiphenomenal qualia. *Philosophical Quarterly*, 32, 127–136.

Jackson, F. (1996). Mental causation: The state of the art. *Mind*, 105(419), 377–413.

Jackson, F., and Pettit, P. (1988). Functionalism and broad content. *Mind*, 97(387), 381–400.

Jacob, F. (1977). Evolution and tinkering. *Science*, 196(4295), 1161–1166.

Jacobs, R., Jordan, M., and Barto, A. (1991a). Task decomposition through competition in a modular connectionist architecture: The what and where visual tasks. *Cognitive Science*, 15, 219–250.

Jacobs, R., Jordan, M., Nowlan, S., and Hinton, G. (1991). Adaptive mixtures of local experts. *Neural Computation*, 3, 79–87.

Jeannerod, M. (1986). The formation of finger grip during prehension: A cortically mediated visuomotor pattern. *Behavioral Brain Research*, 19, 99–116.

Jeannerod, M. (1997). *The Cognitive Neuroscience of Action*. Oxford, England: Blackwell.

Jordan, M. (1986). *Serial Order: A Parallel Distributed Processing Approach* (Report 8604). Institute for Cognitive Science, University of California, San Diego.

Jordan, M., Flash, T., and Arnon, Y. (1994). A model of the learning of arm trajectories from spatial deviations. *Journal of Cognitive Neuroscience*, 6(4), 359–376.

Karmiloff-Smith, A. (1992). *Beyond Modularity: A Developmental Perspective on Cognitive Science*. Cambridge, MA: MIT Press/Bradford Books.

Kauffman, S. (1995). *At Home in the Universe*. London: Viking Press.

Keijzer, F. (1998). Doing without representations which specify what to do. *Philosophical Psychology*, 11(3), 269–302.

Keijzer, F., and Bem, S. (1996). Behavioral systems interpreted as autonomous agents and as coupled dynamical systems: A criticism. *Philosophical Psychology*, 9(3), 323–346.

Kelso, J.A.S. (1981). On the oscillatory basis of movement. *Bulletin of Psychonomic Society*, 18, 63.

Kelso, J.A.S. (1995). *Dynamic Patterns*. Cambridge, MA: MIT Press.

Kim, J. (1996). *Philosophy of Mind*. Boulder, CO: Westview Press.

Kirlik, A. (1998). Everyday life environments. In W. Bechtel and G. Graham (eds.), *A Companion to Cognitive Science*. Oxford, England: Blackwell, 702–712.

Kirsh, D., and Maglio, P. (1994). On distinguishing epistemic from pragmatic action. *Cognitive Science*, 18, 513–549.

Knierim, J., and Van Essen, D. (1992). Visual cortex: Cartography, connectivity and concurrent processing. *Current Opinion in Neurobiology*, 2, 150–155.

Kripke, S. (1980). *Naming and Necessity*. Oxford, England: Blackwell.

Laakso, A. and Cottrell, G. (In Press). Qualia and cluster analysis: Assessing representational similarity between neural systems. *Philosophical Psychology*.

Landi, V. (1982). *The Great American Countryside*. London: Collier Macmillan.

Langton, C. (1989). Artificial life. In C. Langton (ed.), *Artificial Life. Santa Fe Institute Studies in the Sciences of Complexity* (6). Reading, MA: Addison-Wesley.

Lenat, D., and Feigenbaum, E. (1992). On the thresholds of knowledge. In D. Kirsh (ed.), *Foundations of Artificial Intelligence*. Cambridge, MA and Amsterdam, The Netherlands: MIT Press and Elsevier Science Publishers, 195–250.

LeVay, S. (2000). Brain invaders. *Scientific American*, 282(3), 27.

Levine, J. (1983). Materialism and qualia: The explanatory gap. *Pacific Philosophical Quarterly*, 64, 354–361.

Levine, J. (1994). Out of the closet: A qualophile confronts qualophobia. *Philosophical Topics*, 22(1), 1994.

Lund, H., Webb, B., and Hallam, J. (1997). A robot attracted to the cricket species *Gryllus bimaculatus*. In P. Husbands and I. Harvey (eds.), *4th European Conference on Artificial Life*. Cambridge, MA: MIT Press, 246–255.

Lycan, W. (1991). Homuncular functionalism meets PDP. In W. Ramsey, S. Stich, and D. Rumelhart (eds.), *Philosophy and Connectionist Theory*. Hillsdale, NJ: Erlbaum, 259–286.

Lycan, W. (1997). Consciousness as internal monitoring. In N. Block, O. Flanagan, and G. Güzeldere (eds.), *The Nature of Consciousness*. Cambridge, MA: MIT Press, 755–771.

MacDonald, C., and MacDonald, G. (1995). *Connectionism: Debates on Psychological Explanation*. Oxford, England: Blackwell.

Mackie, J. L. (1974). *The Cement of the Universe*. Oxford, England: Oxford University Press.

Marcel, A. (1988). Phenomenal experience and funtionalism. In A. Marcel and E. Bisiach (eds.), *Consciousness in Contemporary Science*. Oxford, England: Clarendon Press, 121–158.

Marr, D. (1969). A theory of cerebellar cortex. *Journal of Physiology*, 202, 437–470.

Marr, D. (1982). *Vision*. San Francisco: W.H. Freeman.

Mataric, M. (1991). Navigating with a rat brain: A neurobiologically inspired model for robot spatial representation. In J. A. Meyer and S. Wilson (eds.), *From Animals to Animats I*. Cambridge, MA: MIT Press.

Maturana, H., and Varela, F. (1980). *Autopoiesis and Cognition*. Dordrecht, The Netherlands: Reidel.

McCauley, R. N. (ed.) (1996). *The Churchlands and Their Critics*. Oxford, England: Blackwell.

McClelland, J. L. (1989). Parallel distributed processing—Implications for cognition and development. In R. Morris (ed.), *Parallel Distributed Processing—Implications for Psychology and Neurobiology*. Oxford, England: Clarendon Press.

McClelland, J., and Kawamoto, A. (1986). Mechanisms of sentence processing. In J. McClelland, D. Rumelhart, and P. R. Group (eds.), *Parallel Distributed Processing: Explorations in the Microstructure of Cognition*. Cambridge, MA: MIT Press/Bradford Books, II, **272–326.**

McClelland, J., Rumelhart, D., et al. (1986). The appeal of parallel distributed processing. In J. McClelland, D. Rumelhart, and PDr Research Group (eds.), *Parallel Distributed Processing: Explorations in the Microstructure of Cognition*. Cambridge, MA: MIT Press/Bradford Books, II, 3–44.

McClelland, J., McNaughton, B., and O'Reilly, R. (1995). Why there are complementary learning systems in the hippocampus and neocortex: Insights from the successes and failures of connectionist models of learning and memory. *Psychological Review*, 102, 419–457.

McConkie, G. W. (1990). *Where Vision and Cognition Meet*. Paper presented at the H.F.S.P. Workshop on Object and Scene Perception, Leuven, Belgium.

McGinn, C. (1989). Can we solve the mind-body problem? In N. Block, O. Flanagan, and G. Güzeldere (eds.), *The Nature of Consciousness*. Cambridge, MA: MIT Press, 529–542.

McNaughton, B., and Nadel, L. (1990). Hebb-Marr networks and the neurobiological representation of action in space. In M. Gluck and D. Rumelhart (eds.), *Neuroscience and Connectionist Theory*. Hillside, NJ: Erlbaum.

Mead, C. (1989). *Analog VLSI and Neural Systems*. Reading, MA: Addison-Wesley.

Michie, D., and Johnson, R. (1984). *The Creative Computer*. New York: Penguin.

Millikan, R. (1984). *Language, Thought and Other Biological Categories*. Cambridge, MA: MIT Press.

Millikan, R. (1996). Pushmi-Pullyu representations. In L. May, M. Friedman, and A. Clark (eds.), *Minds and Morals*. Cambridge, MA: MIT Press, 145–162.

Milner, A., and Goodale, M. (1995). *The Visual Brain in Action*. Oxford, England: Oxford University Press.

Milner, D., and Goodale, M. (1998). The visual brain in action. *Psyche*, 4(12).

Minsky, M. (1994). Society of mind: A response to four reviews. In W. Clancey, S. Smoliar, and M. Stefik (eds.), *Contemplating Minds*. Cambridge, MA: MIT Press, 308–334.

Mitchell, M. (1995). Genetic algorithms: An overview. *Complexity*, 1(1), 31–39.

Mitchell, M. (1999). Can evolution explain how the mind works? *Complexity*, 4(3), 17–24.

Mitchell, M., Crutchfield, J., and Hraber, P. (1994). Evolving cellular automata to perform computations. *Physica D*, 75, 361–391.

Mithen, S. (1996). *The Prehistory of the Mind*. London: Thames and Hudson.

Nagel, T. (1974). What is it like to be a bat? *Philosophical Review*, 83, 435–450.

Newell, A. (1990). *Unified Theories of Cognition*. Cambridge, MA: Harvard University Press.

Newell, A., and Simon, H. (1958). Heuristic problem-solving: The next advance in operations research. *Operations Research*, 6, 6.

Newell, A., and Simon, H. (1976). Computer science as empirical inquiry: Symbols and search. *Communications of the Association for Computing Machinery*, 19, 113–126. Reprinted in J. Haugeland (ed.), (1997). *Mind Design II*. Cambridge, MA: MIT Press, 81–110.

Newell, A., Shaw, J., and Simon, H. (1959). *Report on a General Problem-Solving Program*. Paper presented at the Proceedings of the International Conference of Information Processing.

Nolfi and Parisi, (1991). *Auto-Teaching: Networks that develop their own teaching input*. (Technical Report PCIA91-03). Rome: CNR Institutes of Psychology.

Norman, D. (1992). Approaches to the study of intelligence. In D. Kirsh (ed.), *Foundations of Artificial Intelligence*. Cambridge, MA: MIT Press, 327–346. (First appeared in (1991) *Artificial Intelligence*, 47, 327–346.)

Norman, D. (1999). *The Invisible Computer*. Cambridge, MA: MIT Press.

Patterson, K., Seidenberg, M., and McClelland, J. (1989). Connections and disconnections. In R. Morris (ed.), *Parallel Distributed Processing: Implications for Psychology and Neurobiology*. Oxford, England: Oxford University Press.

Pinker, S. (1997). *How the Mind Works*. New York: Norton.

Plunkett, K., and Sinha, C. (1992). Connectionism and developmental theory. *British Journal of Developmental Psychology*, 10, 209–254.

Pollack, J. (1988). *Recursive Auto-Associative Memory*. Proceedings of the 10th Annual Conference of the Cognitive Science Society, Computing Research Lab, New Mexico State University.

Pollack, J. (1994). On wings of knowledge: A review of Allen Newell's Unified Theories of Cognition. In W. Clancey, S. Smoliar and M. Stefik (eds.), *Contemplating Minds*. Cambridge, MA: MIT Press, 109–123.

Popper, K. (1980). *The Logic of Scientific Discovery.* New York: Routledge.

Port, R., and van Gelder, T. (eds.) (1995). *Mind as Motion: Dynamics, Behavior, and Cognition.* Cambridge, MA: MIT Press.

Port, R., Cummins, F., and McCauley, J. (1995). Naive time, temporal patterns and human audition. In R. Port and T. van Gelder (eds.), *Mind as Motion.* Cambridge, MA: MIT Press.

Premack, D. and Premack, A. (1983). *The Mind of an Ape.* New York: Norton.

Price, M. (1997). Should we expect to feel as if we understand consciousness? In J. Shear (ed.), *Explaining Consciousness: The Hard Problem.* Cambridge, MA: MIT Press, 83–96.

Putnam, H. (1960). Minds and machines. In S. Hook (ed.), *Dimensions of Mind.* New York: New York University Press.

Putnam, H. (1967). Psychological predicates. In W. Capitan and D. Merrill (eds.), *Art, Mind, and Religion.* Pittsburgh, PA: University of Pittsburgh Press, 37–48.

Putnam, H. (1975). Philosophy and our mental life. In H. Putnam (ed.), *Mind, Language and Reality.* Cambridge, England: Cambridge University Press, 291–303.

Putnam, H. (1980). Brains and behavior. In N. Block (ed.), *Readings in the Philosophy of Psychology,* Vol. 1. Cambridge, England: Cambridge University Press.

Pylyshyn, Z. (1986). *Computation and Cognition.* Cambridge, MA: MIT Press.

Quartz, S. (1999). The constructivist brain. *Trends in Cognitive Sciences,* 3(2), 48–57.

Quartz, S., and Sejnowski, T. (1997). The neural basis of cognitive development: A constructivist manifesto. *Behavioral and Brain Sciences,* 20, 537–596.

Quine, W. V. O. (1969). Natural kinds. In W. V. O. Quine (ed.), *Ontological Relativity and Other Essays.* New York: Columbia University Press, 114–138.

Ramsey, W., Stich, S., and Rumelhart, D. (eds.) (1991a). *Philosophy and Connectionist Theory.* Hillsdale, NJ: Erlbaum.

Ramsey, W., Stich, S., and Garon, J. (1991b). Connectionism, eliminativism, and the future of folk psychology. In W. Ramsey, S. Stich, and D. Rumelhart (eds.), *Philosophy and Connectionist Theory.* Hillsdale, NJ: Erlbaum, 199–228.

Ray, T. (1991). An approach to the synthesis of life. In C. Langton, C. Taylor, J. Farmer, and S. Rasmussen (eds.), *Artificial Life II.* Redwood City, CA: Addison-Wesley, 371–408.

Ray, T. (1994). An evolutionary approach to synthetic biology: Zen and the art of creating life. *Artificial Life,* 1, 179–210.

Reeke, G., and Edelman, G. (1988). Real brains and artificial intelligence. *Daedalus,* Winter, 143–173.

Resnick, M. (1994). *Turtles, Termites and Traffic Jams: Explorations in Massively Parallel Microworlds.* Cambridge, MA: MIT Press.

Reynolds, C. (1987). Flocks, herds and schools: A distributed behavioral model. *Computer Graphics,* 21, July.

Rizzolatti, G., Fadiga, L., and Fogassi, L. (1996). Premotor cortex and the recognition of motor actions. *Cognitive Brain Research,* 3, 131–141.

Roe, A., Pallas, S., Hahn, J., and Sur, M. (1990). A map of visual space induced in auditory cortex. *Science,* 250, 818–820.

Rosch, E. (1994). Is causality circular? *Journal of Consciousness Studies,* 1(1), 50–65.

Rosenbloom, P., and Laird, J. (1993). On unified theories of cognition: A response to the reviews. *Artificial Intelligence,* 59, 389–413.

Rosenbloom, P., Laird, J., Newell, A., and McCarl, R. (1992). A preliminary analysis of the SOAR architecture as a basis for general intelligence. In D. Kirsh (ed.), *Foundations of Artificial Intelligence.* Cambridge, MA: MIT Press, 289–326.

Rosenthal, D. (1997). A theory of consciousness. In N. Block, O. Flanagan, and G. Güzeldere (eds.), *The Nature of Consciousnes.* Cambridge, MA: MIT Press, 729–754.

Ruben, D. (1994). A counterfactual theory of causal explanation. *Noûs*, 28, 465–481.

Rudder-Baker, L. (1994). Instrumental intentionality. In S. Stich and T. Warfield (eds.), *Mental Representation: A Reader.* Oxford, England: Blackwell, 332–344. (First appeared in *Philosophy of Science*, 56, 1989.)

Rumelhart, D., and McClelland, J. (1986). On learning the past tenses of English verbs. In D. Rumelhart, J. McClelland, and the PDP Research Group (eds.), *Parallel Distributed Processing: Explorations in the Microstructure of Cognition.* Cambridge, MA: MIT Press, 2, 216–271.

Ryle, G. (1949). *The Concept of Mind.* London: Hutchinson.

Salzman, C., and Newsome, W. (1994). Neural mechanisms for forming a perceptual decision. *Science*, 264, 231–237.

Schank, R. (1975). Using knowledge to understand. *TINLAP*, 75.

Schank, R., and Abelson, R. (1977). *Scripts, Plans, Goals, and Understanding.* Hillsdale, NJ: Erlbaum.

Schieber, M. (1990). How might the motor cortex individuate movements? *Trends in Neuroscience*, 13(11), 440–444.

Schieber, M., and Hibbard, L. (1993). How somatotopic is the motor cortex hand area? *Science*, 261, 489–492.

Schlagger, B., and O'Leary D. (1991). Potential of visual cortex to develop an array of functional units unique to somatosensory cortex. *Science*, 252, 1556–1560.

Schöner, G. (1993). *What Can We Learn from Dynamic Models of Rhythmic Behavior in Animals and Humans?* Unpublished manuscript.

Schrödinger, E. (1969). *What is Life?* Cambridge, England: Cambridge University Press.

Searle, J. (1980). Minds, brains, and programs. *Behavioral and Brain Sciences*, 1, 417–424. Reprinted in J. Haugeland (ed.). (1997). *Mind Design II.* Cambridge, England: Cambridge University Press, 183–204.

Searle, J. (1992). *The Rediscovery of the Mind.* Cambridge, MA: MIT Press.

Sejnowski, T., and Rosenberg, C. (1986). *NETtalk: A Parallel Network That Learns to Read Aloud.* (Technical Report JHU/EEC-86/01.) Baltimore, MD: Johns Hopkins University.

Sejnowski, T., and Rosenberg, C. (1987). Parallel networks that learn to pronounce English text. *Complex Systems*, 1, 145–168.

Shoemaker, S. (1981). The inverted spectrum. *Journal of Philosophy*, 74(7), 357–381.

Simon, H. (1969). The architecture of complexity. In H. Simon (ed.), *The Sciences of the Artificial*, Cambridge, England: Cambridge University Press.

Simon, H. (1982). *Models of Bounded Rationality.* Cambridge, MA: MIT Press, Vols. I and II.

Simon, H. (1996). *The Sciences of the Artificial* (3rd ed.). Cambridge, MA: MIT Press.

Skarda, C., and Freeman, W. (1987). How brains make chaos in order to make sense of the world. *Behavioral and Brain Sciences*, 10, 161–195.

Slee, J. (1980). Individual differences in visual imagery ability and the retrieval of visual appearance. *Journal of Mental Imagery*, 4, 93–113.

Smart, J. (1959). Sensations and brain processes. *Philosophical Review*, 68, 141–156.

Smith, B. C. (1996). *On the Origin of Objects.* Cambridge, MA: MIT Press.

Smithers, T. (1994). Why better robots make it harder. In D. Cliff, P. Husbands, J. A. Meyer, and S. Wilson (eds.), *From Animals to Animats 3.* Cambridge, MA: MIT Press, 64–72.

Smolensky, P. (1988). On the proper treatment of connectionism. *Behavioral and Brain Sciences,* 11, 1–74.

Smolensky, P. (1991). Connectionism, constituency and the language of thought. In B. Loewer and G. Rey (eds.), *Meaning in Mind: Fodor and His Critics.* Oxford, England: Blackwell, 201–228.

Squire, L., and Zola-Morgan, S. (1988). Memory: Brain systems and behavior. *Trends in Neuroscience,* 11(4), 170–175.

Steels, L. (1994). The artificial life roots of artificial intelligence. *Artificial Life,* 1(1/2), 75–110.

Stein, L. (1994). Imagination and situated cognition. *Journal of Experimental Artificial Intelligence,* 6, 393–407.

Sterelny, K. (1995). Understanding life: Recent work in philosophy of biology. *British Journal for the Philosophy of Science,* 46(2), 155–183.

Stewart, I. (1989). *Does God Play Dice?* Oxford, England: Blackwell.

Stich, S. (1991). Causal holism and commonsense psychology: A reply to O'Brien. *Philosophical Psychology,* 4(2), 179–182.

Stich, S., and Warfield, T. (1995). Reply to Clark and Smolensky. In C. MacDonald and G. MacDonald (eds.), *Connectionism: Debates on a Psychological Explanation.* Oxford, England: Blackwell, 395–411.

Thach, W., Goodkin, H., and Keating, J. (1992). The cerebellum and the adaptive coordination of movement. *Annual Review of Neuroscience,* 15, 403–442.

Thelen, E. (1993). Self-organization in developmental processes. In M. Johnson (ed.), *Brain Development and Cognition: A Reader.* Oxford, England: Blackwell, 555–591.

Thelen, E., and Smith, L. (1994). *A Dynamic Systems Approach to the Development of Cognition and Action.* Cambridge, MA: MIT Press.

Thompson, A., Harvey, I. and Husbands, P. (1996). *Unconstrained Evolution and Hard Consequences* [Cognitive Sciences Research Report (CSRP) No 397] Sussex, England: University of Sussex.

Thompson, A. (1997). Temperature in natural and artificial systems. In P. Husbands and I. Harvey (eds.), *4th European Conference on Artificial Life.* Cambridge, MA: MIT Press, 388–397.

Thompson, R., and Oden, D. (1996). A profound disparity revisited: Perception and judgement of abstract identity relations by chimpanzees, human infants and monkeys. *Behavioral Processes,* 35, 149–161.

Thompson, R., Oden, D., and Boyson, S. (In press). Language-naive chimpanzees judge relations between relations in an abstract mapping task. *Journal of Experimental Psychology: Animal Behavior Processes.*

Tooby, J., and Cosmides, L. (1992). The psychological foundations of culture. In J. Barkow, L. Cosmides, and J. Tooby (eds.), *The Adapted Mind.* New York: Oxford University Press, 19–136.

Triantafyllou, M., and Triantafyllou, G. (1995). An efficient swimming machine. *Scientific American,* 272(3), 64–71.

Tulving, E. (1983). *Elements of Episodic Memory.* New York: Oxford University Press.

Tulving, E. (1989). Remembering and knowing the past. *American Scientist,* 77, 361–367.

Turing, A. (1936). On computable numbers, with an application to the entscheidungs problem. *Proceedings of the London Mathematical Society, Series* 2, 230–265.

Turing, A. (1950). Computing machinery and intelligence. *Mind*, LIX, 423–460. Reprinted in M. Boden (ed.), *The Philosophy of Artificial Intelligence*. Oxford, England: Oxford University Press, 40–66.

Tye, M. (1995). *Ten Problems of Consciousness*. Cambridge, MA: MIT Press.

Tye, M. (1997). A representational theory of pains and their phenomenal character. In N. Block, O. Flanagan, and G. Güzeldere (eds.), *The Nature of Consciousness*. Cambridge, MA: MIT Press, 329–340.

Ungerleider, L., and Mishkin, M. (1982). Two cortical visual systems. In D. Ingle, M. Goodale, and R. Mansfield (eds.), *Analysis of Visual Behavior*. Cambridge, MA: MIT Press, 549–586.

Vaina, L. (ed.) (1991). *From Retina to the Neocortex: Select papers of David Marr*. Boston, MA: Birkhauser.

Van Essen, D., and Anderson, C. (1990). Information processing strategies and pathways in the primate retina and visual cortex. In S. Zornetzer, J. Davis, and C. Lau (eds.), *An Introduction to Neural and Electronic Networks*. New York: Academic Press, 43–72.

Van Essen, D., and Gallant, J. (1994). Neural mechanisms of form and motion processing in the primate visual system. *Neuron*, 13, 1–10.

Van Essen, D., Anderson, C., and Olshausen, B. (1994). Dynamic routing strategies in sensory, motor, and cognitive processing. In C. Koch and J. Davis (eds.), *Large-Scale Neuronal Theories of the Brain*. Cambridge, MA: MIT Press, 271–300.

van Gelder, T. (1990). Compositionality: A connectionist variation on a classical theme. *Cognitive Science*, 14, 355–384.

van Gelder, T. (1995). What might cognition be, if not computation? *Journal of Philosophy*, XCII(7), 345–381.

van Gelder, T., and Port, R. (1993). Beyond symbolic: Prolegomena to a Kama-Sutra of compositionality. In V. Honovar and L. Uhr (eds.), *Symbol Processing and Connectionist Network Models in Artificial Intelligence and Cognitive Modeling: Steps Towards Principled Integration*. San Diego, CA: Academic Press, 107–125.

van Gelder, T., and Port, R. (1995). It's about time: An overview of the dynamical approach to cognition. In R. Port and T. van Gelder (eds.), *Mind as Motion: Explorations in the Dynamics of Cognition*. Cambridge, MA: MIT Press, 1–44.

van Leeuwen, C., Verstijnen, I., and Hekkert, P. (1999). Common unconscious dynamics underlie uncommon conscious effects: A case study in the interactive nature of perception and creation. In J. S. Jordan (ed.), *Modelling Consciousness across the Disciplines*. Lanhan, MD: University Press of America.

Varela, F., Maturana, H., and Uribe, R. (1974). Autopoiesis: The organization of living systems. *Biosystems*, 5, 187–196.

Varela, F., Thompson, E., and Rosch, E. (1991). *The Embodied Mind*. Cambridge, MA: MIT Press.

Vera, A., and Simon, H. (1993). Situated action: A symbolic interpretation. *Cognitive Science*, 17, 4–48.

Warwick, K. (2000). Cyborg 1.0. *Wired*, February 2000.

Webb, B. (1994). Robotic experiments in cricket phonotaxis. In D. Cliff, P. Husbands, J. A. Meyer, and S. Wilson (eds.), *From Animals to Animats 3*. Cambridge, MA: MIT Press, 45–54.

Webb, B. (1996). A cricket robot. *Scientific American*, 275, 62–67.

Weiskrantz, L. (1986). *Blindsight: A Case Study and Implications.* Oxford, England: Oxford University Press.

Welch, R. (1978). *Perceptual Modification: Adapting to Altered Sensory Environments.* New York: Academic Press.

Wertsch, J. (1998). *Mind as Action.* Oxford, England: Oxford University Press.

Wheeler, M. (1994). From activation to activity. *Artificial Intelligence and the Simulation of Behavior (AISB) Quarterly,* 87, 36–42.

Wheeler, M. (1997). Cognition's coming home: The reunion of life and mind. In P. Husbands and I. Harvey (eds.), *Proceeding of the 4th European Conference on Artificial Life.* Cambridge, MA: MIT Press, 10–19.

Wiener, N. (1948). *Cybernetics, or Control and Communication in the Animal and in the Machine.* New York: Wiley.

Wurz, R., and Mohler, C. (1976). Enhancement of visual response in monkey striate cortex and frontal eye fields. *Journal of Neurophysiology,* 39, 766–772.

Yarbus, A. (1967). *Eye movements and vision.* New York: Plenum Press.

INDEX